Beyond Naturalism

Beyond Naturalism

A New Realism in American Theatre

William W. Demastes

Contributions in Drama and Theatre Studies,
Number 27

GREENWOOD PRESS
New York • Westport, Connecticut • London

Library of Congress Cataloging-in-Publication Data

Demastes, William W.
  Beyond naturalism : a new realism in American theatre / William W.
  Demastes.
      p.   cm. — (Contributions in drama and theatre studies, ISSN
0163-3821 ; no. 27)
  Bibliography: p.
  Includes index.
  ISBN 0-313-26320-5 (lib. bdg. : alk. paper)
  1. American drama—20th century—History and criticism.
  2. Realism in literature. 3. Naturalism in literature. I. Title.
  II. Series.
  PS338.R42D46 1988
  812'.54'0912—dc10   88-17787

British Library Cataloguing in Publication Data is available.

Library of Congress Catalog Card Number: 88-17787
ISBN: 0-313-26320-5
ISSN: 0163-3821

First published in 1988

Greenwood Press, Inc.
88 Post Road West, Westport, Connecticut 06881

Printed in the United States of America

The paper used in this book complies with the
Permanent Paper Standard issued by the National
Information Standards Organization (Z39.48-1984).

10 9 8 7 6 5 4 3 2

Copyright Acknowledgments

The author and publisher gratefully acknowledge permission to reprint material from the following copyrighted sources.

Clive Barnes. "'Boom Boom Room' by Rabe at Lincoln Center." *New York Times* 9 November 1973. Copyright 1973 by The New York Times Company. Reprinted by permission.

Clive Barnes. "Streamers." *New York Times* 22 April 1976. Copyright 1976 by The New York Times Company. Reprinted by permission.

William Demastes. "Charles Fuller and *A Soldier's Play:* Attacking Prejudice, Challenging Form." *Studies in American Drama,* 1945-Present.

William Demastes. "Understanding Sam Shepard's Realism." *Comparative Drama* 21, no. 3.

Excerpts from *A Soldier's Play* by Charles Fuller. Copyright © 1981 by Charles Fuller. Reprinted by permission of Hill and Wang, a division of Farrar, Strauss and Giroux, Inc.

Walter Kerr. "David Rabe's 'House' Is Not a Home." *New York Times* 2 May 1972. Copyright 1972 by The New York Times Company. Reprinted by permission.

Walter Kerr. "When Does Gore Get Gratuitous." *New York Times* 22 February 1976. Copyright 1976 by The New York Times Company. Reprinted by permission.

David Mamet. *Glengarry Glen Ross.* New York: Grove Press, 1984. Reprinted by permission of Grove Press, Inc. Copyright © 1982, 1983 by David Mamet.

Marsha Norman. *'night, Mother.* New York: Hill and Wang, 1983. Reprinted by permission of the William Morris Agency.

David Rabe. *Hurlyburly.* New York: Grove Press, 1985. Reprinted by permission of Grove Press, Inc. Copyright © 1985 by Ralako Corp.

Sam Shepard. *Fool For Love.* San Francisco: City Lights, 1983. Copyright © 1983 by Sam Shepard. Reprinted by permission of City Lights Books.

Ross Wetzsteon. "David Mamet: Remember That Name." *Village Voice* 5 July 1976. Reprinted by permission of the author and the Village Voice © '76.

Contents

List of Illustrations

Acknowledgments

Though I am, of course, responsible for the final product, I am indebted to a great many mentors, colleagues, and friends. I wish to thank the various members of the English and Theatre departments of the University of Wisconsin-Madison who helped me formulate my ideas. In particular, I'd like to thank Michael Hinden, who helped me shape the basic ideas in this book and did much to solidify earlier drafts of this material; his general influence, however, goes well beyond that found in this book. Robert Skloot helped me to focus my often intuitive impressions and gave me insights into the theatrical aspects of the works discussed. John Lyons's pointed advice on both trends in the 20th century and on stylistic matters in general were also of great help. I have to thank Mike VandenHeuvel as well, with whom I spent many hours exchanging opinions, parrying criticism, and sharing a mutual enthusiasm for drama and theatre, often experiencing great hardships together trying to find the best (though sometimes suffering through the worst) examples of the art in some of the most obscure locations on two continents.

As concerns the book itself, I am inexpressibly indebted to Joseph Trahern and Edward Bratton of the University of Tennessee-Knoxville for their encouragement and to the John C. Hodges Fund of the University of Tennessee for its financial support.

Finally, to my parents and brother I must express a deepest gratitude for their continued enthusiasm and support. And to Jean, my biggest supporter, I can't begin to express my debt.

Arthur Miller's *Death of a Salesman*. Broadway revival
(1984). Pictured is Willy Loman (Dustin Hoffman).
Photo: Inge Morath/Magnum Photos.

Toward an Understanding of Realism in American Theatre

Drama, like all literary and artistic genres, is in a constant state of flux, forever working to reflect human actions in the cultural milieu of its particular origin, attempting to present perspectives on "truth" in such a way that its culture can digest that "truth." Consequently, dramatic form must maintain a dynamic posture, surging forward to present new perspectives that will stretch the imaginations of playwright and playgoer alike.

This century alone has seen the genre move from the styles of Chekhov and Ibsen to the German expressionists to the French absurdists and the experimental forms of the 60s, continually reaching new limits of presentation and interpretation. Despite this century's dynamic activity, however, there remains a sense of stylistic and formal tyranny stemming from what Eric Bentley in 1946 called "the triumph of realism"(2). It is a description that accurately describes contemporary theatre even today. Not only are realist dramas of the past regularly and enthusiastically revived, but the best of current dramatic talents has turned to the form as well. The result has been a critical concern that today's theatre is dying and that there is a need of a "new fix" to revolutionize and revitalize it. Many once thought that the events and "happenings" of the 60s provided an answer, and many, Robert Wilson and Richard Foreman to name the most notable, are following that path today. Others look for a "little theatre" uprising as occurred in the early part of the century, even though it failed to defeat the "tyranny" of realism then and even though conditions seem no more hopeful today for the success of such an uprising.

It seems, however, that the basis of such hope for a "new fix" is at least partially manifest in a misconception of the realist form itself. The term "realism" is one that many claim to understand but few have been able to define, a fact that has played into the critical hands of its opponents and often hurts its advocates. Mary McCarthy, for example, observes that opponents have argued that the label "real" identifies little more than a mere photographic or journalistic "re"-presentation of our world (115). Such reductive assessments of realism by its opponents is unfortunate and misleading. After all, as Martin Esslin notes,

> Reality itself, even the most mundane, everyday reality, has its own symbolic component. The postman who brings me the telegram which announces the death of a friend is also, in a sense, a messenger of death, an Angel of Death. Whether he is perceived in that symbolic sense is merely a matter of my own way of looking at him, my own awareness, my own mood . . . . What the stage gives us is an enhanced reality that itself becomes a sign, a metaphor, a dramatic symbol. ("The Stage" 9)

All objects and actions have the potential to be interpreted as meaningful symbols. And on the stage these objects clearly have the potential to be more than mere re-presentations; they are elements ready to be manipulated or orchestrated to convey something more than mere "pictures" of life.

There is, however, another misconception that is far more damaging to realism, partly because it is far more subtle. David Rabe, one of America's new playwrights who himself utilizes realism, illustrates this problem. In his "Afterword" to *Hurlyburly,* he describes the

> "realistic" or "well-made" play . . . that form which thinks that cause and effect are proportionate and clearly apparent, that people know what they are doing as they do it, and that others react accordingly, that one thing leads to another in a rational, mechanical way, a kind of Newtonian clock of a play, a kind of Darwinian assemblage of detail which would then determine the details that must follow, the substitution of the devices of logic for the powerful sweeps of pattern and energy that is our lives. (162)

In a 1985 interview, Rabe adds to this point the conclusion that realism "has truly run its course," arguing,

> I think the time has come when people will understand that the "well-made play" was developed out of other ideas, out of Darwin and Newton. I mean, the well-made play is an idea based on how Newton said the universe worked--like a big clock. It said theater was a pictorial, scientific, objective form, so it invented the fourth wall. And it invented realistic behavior. (Freedman 61-62)

Rabe is attacking what he calls realism while he himself uses "realistic behavior" in his own plays, *Hurlyburly* certainly included. Rabe's criticism follows a critical thread that has historically reviled realism as a form whose dominance in the late 19th and 20th centuries has limited theatre (and other literary fields as well) to restrictive and reductive presentations of complex thought and feeling. But this attitude is at least partially the result of claiming to understand realism and then proceeding to define it loosely or inaccurately. Such a misconception is evident in the discrepancy between Rabe's argument and his own practices. What Rabe is attacking above is a form of realism that does seem to be outdated, but it is only one of many forms that realism can take, a distinction that Rabe and many others have yet to make. That distinction is one to be made between "realism" and "naturalism," a distinction that critics have often helped confuse rather than clarify. For example, though he was aware of the distinction, John Gassner notes in *Form and Idea in Modern Theatre* (1956) that throughout his work he "employed the rather ambiguous term [naturalism] as though it were generally interchangeable with 'realism'" (66-67). He adds, "This has, indeed, been the case on the European continent, as Europeans will say 'Naturalismus' or 'naturalisme' when we would say 'realism'" (67). It seems that in many ways the future of realism depends on clarifying the meaning and intent of those forms, in all their permutations.

A major part of the reason for such a general confusion, of course, is the simple fact that "naturalism" and "realism" overlap in *apparent* meaning and are therefore very loosely applied. Apprehending this dilemma, Eric Bentley, for example, argues, "such terms [as realism] are useful enough to those who know their limitations. The rule here is to use them only where they clarify more than they mystify" (4). Creating what he calls a "rough definition," Bentley claims that realism is "the candid presentation of the natural world," explaining, "It is exact and detailed" (4). He continues:

> The attempt to be closer to the actual texture of daily living produces its own technique and manner . . . . In general there is a turning from all forms of elevated discourse to simple and colloquial discourse. When we have seen the leading intention of realism and its consequent need of special techniques, we may then choose to incorporate both within a larger historical or philosophical framework--which will be that of some form of modern scientific empiricism. (4)

Bentley and Rabe both see that the apparent essence of realism is an underlying scientific empiricism. However, this acknowledgement of a scientific and empirical base often leads to the assumption that realism, when most "pure," follows the tenets of the radical realism of naturalism. Bentley does distinguish, though, saying of naturalism that

> its intention is certainly a candid account of the world about us; it has a special technique--to present a slice of life instead of a carefully constructed plot--a technique, that is, which keeps us close to the raw flesh of life itself; and it adopts a particular form of empiricism--a philosophy of scientific determinism based on the "facts" of heredity and environment. (5)

In naturalism, empiricism in general is replaced by determinism in particular. C.D. Innes confirms Bentley's impressions of naturalism, noting that it has as its philosophical assumption Darwinian materialism, and adding the following:

> The primary criterion is physical accuracy and the comprehensive descriptions of stage properties, the three-dimensional illusionistic settings and attention to authenticating detail imply that personality is determined by environment. The protagonists are typically a single family . . . . Their past, progressively revealed, either shapes the action or is given such importance that its discovery is the action, and their future (if they survive) can only build on or repeat the present of the plot. All this implies that the essential fact about man is not his class nor his immortal soul but his individual psychology. (21)

The characters are unable to escape themselves, and present/future action is rationally consistent with expectations based on past actions, since such determinism is itself rationally or scientifically comprehensible.

Naturalism, then, is a tightly argued and constructed manifestation of more general realist designs. Finally, because the weight of critical attention has dogmatically identified naturalism's prescriptions as an integral element of the realist form, the term "naturalism" has become virtually interchangeable with the less restrictive "realism." But though realism assumes empirical inquiry, it is not necessarily Darwinian--nor even Newtonian or Freudian--in its bases. As Bentley argues, "The naturalism of the generation around 1880 [Zolaism] is a species of the genus we have been discussing. Realism embraces all writing in which the natural world is candidly presented" (3). Naturalism is one of many possible permutations of realism, and it is naturalism that Rabe--and, most likely, others--is attacking rather than realism, as he seems to believe. And other forms, of course, could be included in this general condemnation. For example, Bentley notes that the French well-made or thesis plays of Sardou are examples of another species, a form of realism that merely "weighted the scales in favor of the dull and prosaic"(5) while working under no specific determinist or naturalist assumptions whatsoever. Very likely, few if any would wish to resurrect this species, but condemning Sardou and even naturalism as outdated does not justify condemning realism altogether.

Realism is something more than either of these species, though it is something that does include both. J.L. Styan calls that "something more" a "realistic impulse, the desire to reproduce on the stage a piece of life faithfully"; it is an impulse that "has been persistent . . . even when realism as a technique has varied constantly in purpose and kind" (164). He adds, "In spite of all these variations, or perhaps because of them, the ability to depict a realistic scene seems to be an indispensable tool in the hands of the modern dramatist and his actors" (165). The ability, even the need, to integrate realist elements into, say, symbolist or expressionist drama is part of the reason Styan values realism. This ability to "mix" with other forms is important, of course, but perhaps even more significant is what Styan identifies as the "impulse" to be faithful to perceived existence. Martin Esslin similarly views the realistic "impulse" as the essential contribution of the form, noting that realism historically has actually *informed* other forms. Using the term "Naturalism" as a synonym for realism (as Gassner earlier did), Esslin notes that the essence of naturalism is not its efforts at scientific detail but a "spirit of free enquiry, totally unprejudiced, unburdened by preconceived ideas" ("Naturalism in Context" 70). Esslin notes of this spirit: "the Expressionism of the 1920's, Brecht's epic theatre of the Thirties and Forties, the Theatre of the Absurd of the Fifties and Sixties were still essentially both continuations of and reactions *against* Naturalism" (67). What Esslin is claiming is that the movements that followed early naturalism/ realism adopted the realist's spirit of enquiry, which he describes as "an experimental exploration of reality in its widest possible sense" (72). For him, Brecht, the Absurdists and others all benefitted from the groundbreaking efforts of the naturalists/realists.

Similarly, Bonnie Marranca admits the influence of naturalism/realism on recent avant-garde, non-traditional theatre: "The naturalism of nontraditional theatre is a curious phenomenon but one worth paying attention to because of its prevalence and diversity" (xiii). She notes of Richard Foreman, for example:

> He allows performers (untrained) a personal freedom of expression while at the same time making them appear highly stylized in slow-motion, speeded-up, noninflectional patterns of speech or movement. He also pays a great deal of attention to actual situation and detail and the factor of time. Foreman's work is stylized yet naturalistic. (xiii)

Marranca's use of "naturalistic" coincides in meaning with Styan's "realistic impulse" and Esslin's realistic "spirit of enquiry." And they all see realism's legacy as essential to modern theatre in general.

It seems, finally, that the differences between modern realism and the modern avant-garde does not entail a difference of type but rather a difference of degree. It does hold that if *appearances* are realistic, then the play is labelled realistic; and if *appearances* are altered, then the work is labelled symbolist, expressionist, or avant-garde. But, generally speaking, the informing impulses among realists often are the same as those experienced by non-traditionalists. And for many of today's realist playwrights, the impulses *are* the same. The realist playwrights discussed in this study can be seen not as a separate breed but as part of a continuum that includes the traditional as well as the non-traditional or avant-garde. Because these playwrights are not as stylized as those who are labelled avant-gardists, they are perhaps rightly called "realists." But being a realist is not necessarily reactionary. In fact, as noted above, an actual link between the traditionalist realist and the most radical avant-gardist does exist. As C.W.E. Bigsby notes, much of the avant-gardist's fear of the traditionalist is a fear which depends upon its [the avant-garde's] own unstated and unargued premises: that an "orthodox" solution is necessarily inadequate, unsophisticated and unselfconscious (the theatre of the 1960s, after all, had created its own orthodoxies, rigorously policed by the elaborators of performance theory); that frontal staging is inferior and incapable of subversion (Wilson and Foreman proved otherwise); . . . and that an an audience separated physically from performers is necessarily passive intellectually, imaginatively and emotionally (an assumption specifically attacked by Grotowski). (35)

Even current experimentalists raised on the agendas of the 60s must acknowledge that traditional theatre--realist theatre certainly included--can effect many of the same ends that the avant-garde is striving to realize. So it is a mistake to see these current realists necessarily as refashioned Millers or O'Neills, presenting dated and reactionary perspectives on existence. Rather it is possible to see them as manipulating the form into permutations that accurately present contemporary visions, provided the "impulse" itself remains fresh and contemporary. When freed from naturalist presumptions, the realist form can accommodate that freshness.

To varying degrees, the writers in this study have done exactly that: utilized the realist format to redirect perception to conform more completely to modern perspectives on existence. They have very consciously taken up the task of challenging old systems of thought from a base of new perspectives. Plainly stated, all six of the playwrights discussed in this study have moved beyond naturalism, beyond the assumptions and practices that are naturalism.

The direct challenges of Rabe, Mamet, and Shepard, and the more subtle challenges of Fuller, Henley, and Norman, are the result of contact with a growing tradition inherited from the experimental work of the absurdist theatre and experimentation of the 60s, among others. Because of this new infusion, realism itself has taken on a purpose different from that earlier realism in that it relates not to an earlier ethic but to one that grows out of a late 20th-century perspective on existence.

And if they are different from the early realists, these new realists are also different from the experimenters of the 60s and 70s in one essential point. Though the radical devices of the 60s and 70s succeeded at relaying a late 20th-century sense of fragmentation and isolation, they also succeeded at fragmenting and isolating a large portion of the American theatre-going public. These new realists, however, may succeed at winning back that lost audience, for realism, after all, is as close to a common language as we have, one with which the general American audience is comfortable, trained as it is in the form by television and other pervasive media. Realism can and does depict existence as it is commonly perceived. And it can use those readily comprehensible "signs" to concretely dramatize modern abstractions of despair conceptualized by other forms. Realism is still a viable form because it seems that the shifts in perception that our post-atomic world asks us to make in fact palpably benefit from a format that introduces a new perspective from a familiar point of demarcation.

So by taking realism and updating it, American theatre has at once made a serious move toward reclaiming its theatre public and has found an effective means of relaying the perspectives and attitudes that experimental forms had earlier delineated. Though perhaps not entirely satisfying from the experimentalist's perspective, it is a modification that promises to work well for America's general theatre community.

Drawing the distinction between the genus realism and its central species, naturalism, is therefore a central concern in this study. Chapter One studies, from an historical perspective, the growth of realism into the foremost aesthetic form in 20th-century Western theatre in general and American theatre in particular. Chapter Two through Chapter Five focuses on American playwrights, writing in the 70s and 80s, who have used realism to challenge outdated and essentially naturalist thought, thereby infusing realism with fresh and contemporary perspectives of the world around them. In essence, turning to modern perspectives on existence is the act that identifies this brand of realism as "new." These American playwrights have separately taken on the challenge to modify the form to fit contemporary visions of existence, breaking from old systems of thought and producing new, relevant realist drama in the process.

This study will additionally address the overall critical reception of these writers, which has suffered from the same realist/naturalist confusion demonstrated by the above-noted theoreticians and practitioners. Contemporary critics have invariably resisted the assault on old, naturalist authorities. Even though there has been a return to realism, a move that has won these new realists larger audiences and greater accessibility, the break from naturalist logic has nonetheless often confused American critics and audiences, leading them to conclude such works to be bad drama. Michael Kirby is one observer who sees the root of the problem. In "On Literary Theatre" (1974), Kirby discusses a continuum between what he calls literary theatre (where most naturalist theatre would lie) and non-literary theatre (toward which innovations in new realism are moving), noting, for example, that Broadway critic Walter Kerr utilizes a system of interpretation totally inappropriate to understanding anything but a thoroughly literary theatre (see 111). That which Kerr's training hasn't prepared him to "understand" is labelled, simply, bad theatre. Kirby's general assessment of traditional/literary critical response can be applied to the new realists' reception in particular. This resistance to the new in favor of the past is nearly institutionalized by such critics and leads to a confused "reading" of the nuances of the new realist, believing as these critics do that the shifts are simply unintelligible rather than that they require alternative means of interpretation. This problem is particularly obvious in the case of Shepard, but the other artists are subject to this mis-"reading" as well. The confusion, however, isn't insurmountable given the fact that these works are still utilizing a form essentially familiar to their spectators, which means a total "re-education" is less necessary than a need to understand various points of departure from the traditional norm. This seems less challenging a goal than trying completely to realign audiences to new forms whose staying power is questionable. (Consider the variety of forms instituted and then abandoned by the 60s revolution.) To uncover the various points of confusion, this study will not only analyze the above playwrights' unique contributions but will also utilize standard critical impressions of their productions--reviews, analyses, etc.--to assess the reactions of those among the theatre-going public raised on more traditionally naturalist assumptions who are now asked to adapt to the alterations that confront them. Such an approach will additionally aid in illustrating the evolution of both the new form and the audience's ability/willingness to adapt in order to understand the form. And viewing the works from these critics' perspectives on the deviations will help determine the degree to which "new" realism can legitimately be called a new form.

Works Cited

Bentley, Eric. *The Playwright as Thinker*. 1946. New York: Harcourt, Brace, and World, 1967.

Bigsby, C.W.E. *A Critical Introduction to Twentieth Century American Drama*, Vol. 3: *Beyond Broadway*. London: Cambridge UP, 1985.

Esslin, Martin. "Naturalism in Context." *The Drama Review* 13, ii (Winter 1968): 67-76.

--------. "The Stage: Reality, Symbol, Metaphor." *Themes in Drama*, Vol. IV. Ed. James Redmond. London: Cambridge UP, 1982: 1-12.

Freedman, Samuel G. and Michaela Williams. "The Craft of the Playwright: A Conversation Between Neil Simon and David Rabe." *New York Times Magazine* 26 May 1985: 37+.

Gassner, John. *Form and Idea in Modern Theatre*. New York: Dryden Press, 1956.

Innes, C.D. *Modern German Drama*. London: Cambridge UP, 1979.

Kirby, Michael. "On Literary Theatre." *The Drama Review* 18, ii (June 1974): 103-113.

Marranca, Bonnie, ed. *Theatre of Images*. New York: Drama Book Specialists, 1977.

McCarthy, Mary. "The American Realist Playwrights." *Discussions of Modern American Drama*. Ed. Walter Meserve. Boston: D.C. Heath, 1965. 114-27.

Rabe, David. Afterword. *Hurlyburly*. New York: Grove Press, 1985. 161-71.

Styan, J.L. *Modern Drama in Theory and Practice*, Vol. 1: *Realism and Naturalism*. London: Cambridge UP, 1981.

Broadway revival (1988) of Eugene O'Neill's *Long Day's Journey into Night*, directed by Jose Quintero. Pictured are James Tyrone (Jason Robards) and Mary Tyrone (Colleen Dewhurst).

Photo: Peter Cunningham.

Chapter One

Antecedents and Theoretical Roots of Dramatic Realism

To understand the recent trend in American realism, it is necessary first to trace the sources of discontent that led to the inception of a realist movement and then to follow the progress of realism through its various transformations, particularly into its current American manifestation.

Generally speaking, the rise to power of the actor-managers of the late 18th century resulted in the stagnation of dramatic literature of that period and of most of the 19th century. As Joseph Donohue has noted of the theatre of the romantic period, it "was emphatically not a playwright's theatre but an actor's theatre" (7). Rather than encouraging growth, the theatre was tied to the profit motive and star system that basically destroyed for playwriting the dynamic tension between the status quo and experimentation, opting rather for time-tested box office successes or sensational, sentimental, and melodramatic audience-grabbers. Often such productions evolved around presenting moral treatises on "right action" complete with a tidy sense of justice and decorum. Extremes of virtue and wickedness were illustrated--often exaggerated--presenting little of the troubling ambiguities of actual existence. Theatre had become a comfortable form of moralizing escapism. In fact, as Donohue notes of the decades surrounding the beginning of the 19th century, "[T]he autonomous artistic unity and vitality of individual Romantic plays cannot be the object of sustained pursuit" (7).

Romantic critics like William Hazlitt (1778-1830) and Charles Lamb (1775-1834) worked to help theatre return to more substantial pursuits, by way of "rediscovering" the "Old Drama" of the Elizabethan, Jacobean, and Restoration periods. Their interest gave a credibility to the old masters and permitted a return to the originals as works worthy, at least, of comparison with the more "decorous"

18th-century adaptations. Many romantic critics consequently jumped on the bandwagon of bardolatry, including the writer Leigh Hunt (1784-1859), who pays homage to Shakespeare with the following:

> Blessings on thy memory, thou divinest of human beings! who without either vehemence or want of enthusiasm, without partiality or want of deep affectation, without resentment against the most provoking mistakes of what is still human, left us a body of beautiful wisdom, in the spirit of which everything human is done justice to . . . . (198)

This new, often hyperbolic, wave of interest in the variety and complexity of Shakespeare challenged the mass of inferior material of the time, re-introducing products of quality to audiences over the entertainments of more current writers. But coming from a literary rather than theatrical background, these critics did nothing to modify the overworked, formalized, grand production styles of the stage's star system. In some ways, in fact, the high style of acting was supported by these critics--Lamb especially--because of their enthusiasm for and advocacy of formalized, poetic verse in drama, to the point that Lamb even preferred dramatic readings over any other kind of "performance."

Hunt and others did accurately identify the qualities in Shakespeare that have stood the test of time. But Hunt's praises notwithstanding, it seems that in the main this rediscovery of the old masters was made for the wrong reasons, favoring them seemingly more for their artifice and style than for any accuracy of depiction of human interchange. Lamb, for example, in his defense of Farquhar and Congreve, shows his admiration for the masters's artifice when he defends these Restoration playwrights for their various violations of 18th-century policies of decorum, including in this case failure to present a "moral" point. It isn't Farquhar or Congreve who are flawed, claims Lamb, but audience expectations. This claim appears to charge that 19th-century audiences expected a sort of moralistic drama stemming from sentimentalism, which in turn could lead to the charge that the sentimental leanings of audiences were too reductive. However, Lamb argues that a sentimental predisposition is not the problem; instead he attacks audiences for being influenced by another, more recent, source:

> We are spectators to a plot or intrigue (not reducible in life to the point of strict morality) and take it for all truth. We substitute a real for a dramatic person, and judge him accordingly . . . . We have been spoiled with--not sentimental comedy--but a tyrant far more pernicious to our pleasures which has succeeded to it, the exclusive and all devouring drama of common life; where the moral point is everything. (324)

Where one would expect Lamb to attack sentimental comedy and its artificial imposition of justice and morality, he attacks the "pernicious" influence of a growing theatre of "common life" directing audiences to judge all characters and actions by realistic standards, rather than allowing them to enjoy the wit and style of the works. Such a prejudice stems from a "morality" even more threatening than sentimental theatre's brand, according to Lamb. Drama of common experience is the threat.

The passage illustrates a very important point. Lamb's romanticism advocates artistic presentation of a world of the ideal and distant-- more Byronic than Wordsworthian, perhaps. As such, there seems to be in Lamb a distinct aversion to directly confronting social activity and interaction in favor of presenting discourses on "wit" or, at most, abstracted arguments on the human condition. So where Shakespeare and others could have been held out as examples of capturing true human interchange, he and the other masters are held out as examples of wit and artifice. The discovery of the old masters alone would not change theatre. Such advocacy, in fact, indirectly led to the intimidation of potential playwrights (those humble enough not to try to challenge Shakespeare) or to imitation of and "improvement" upon the masters by current playwrights (the less modest writers), with the result being continued, highly stylized, and artificial performances in the theatres.

But despite attacks by critics like Lamb, one essential element did derive from romantic theatre, what Donohue calls "its increasing emphasis on the character's mental state" (5). This is, of course, "a concept whose radical departure from the notion of character in the age of Shakespeare marks the change from which grew the drama as we know it today" (8). In general, however, the romantic period contributed little to the revitalization of playwriting in England. The spell of escapism, sentimentalism, and romanticism, too, would first have to be broken.

Perhaps the first critic to take this challenge seriously was George Henry Lewes (1817-1878), often considered England's foremost drama critic of the mid-19th century. Throughout his career Lewes championed what would eventually be called realism. In his book *On Actors and the Art of Acting* (1875), he clarifies his premises, arguing that theatre should be "of representation, not of illusion, [representing] character with such truthfulness that it should affect us as real, not to drag down ideal character to the vulgar level" (112-13). Dragging the "ideal character to the vulgar level" is exactly how Lamb would characterize Lewes's theatre of common life and what he would attack. But in an earlier essay, "Recent Novels: French and English" (1847), Lewes defends realism against such romantic charges: "Incidents however wonderful, adventures, however perilous, are almost as naught when compared with the deep and lasting interest excited by any thing like a correct representation of life" (687). And in an 1851 essay, Lewes directly attacks Lamb's revival of the old masters: "The greatest injury yet sustained by the

English drama was the revival of admiration for the Old English Dramatists" ("The Old and Modern Dramatists" 101). He continues:

> To appeal to the public tastes, to move the general heart of men, you must quit the study, and try to image forth some reflex of the world that all men know, speaking their language, uttering their thoughts, espousing their idealisms . . . . If they [Shakespeare and Racine] were born into this century they would not adopt the tone of two centuries past, but do what they did then--reflect their age . . . . [One] should not strive to revive defunct forms, but produce a nineteenth century drama. (103-104)

For this new drama a new form must be created. In *On Actors and the Art of Acting*, Lewes notes that "it is obvious that a coat-and-waistcoat realism demands a manner, delivery, and gesture wholly unlike the poetic realism of tragedy and comedy" (115-16). Of course, this "representation of life" can be and must be more than mere representation; it must be a refinement of real actions into "well-known symbols" (119) of particular actions so that the viewers, "recognizing these expressions, are thrown into a state of sympathy" (124).

It will be theatre "idealized of course, but issuing out of the atmosphere we breathe" ("The Old and Modern Dramatists" 102). The "atmosphere we breathe" should be the setting of drama, and the attendant "manner, delivery, and gesture" should be the natural form of expression. Lewes is demanding a new drama that more directly appeals to the actual conditions of a contemporary audience. However, his protests would go largely unheeded in England until the coming of Shaw at the end of the century.

In France, Emile Zola (1840-1902) was reacting against similar practices. Victor Hugo (1802-1885), the champion of French romanticism, was once the hope for contemporary theatre. But in France, too, romantic escapism and excess could only keep a temporary hold on audiences, a tenuous hold that led to renewed restlessness and a continued search for a new form. A counter-romantic movement was begun in 1843, actually prior to Zola's influence, with the production of the *Lucrece* of François Ponsard (1814-1867). From Ponsard and his followers came plays that were simple and direct in style--though still written in verse--and that addressed the particular concerns of the rising bourgeois classes, like duty to family and society. But this type of theatre too strictly adhered to an essentially neo-classical style--modeled after Racine--a fact which ran counter to the wishes of those wanting a true "new theatre."

Zola became the proponent of the new theatre. Like Lewes, Zola became an advocate of natural style with the intention of returning theatre to the realm of the "true." That entailed, as Lewes noted, using not just real events but realistic actions and realistic language. Zola's argument, similar to Lewes's, is delineated in "Le costume" and "Les décors" of *Le naturalisme au théâtre* (1881), where Zola makes the claim that to appeal to the truth that lies in today's world, one must depict the "milieu" as it actually appears.

Zola, however, takes this point a significant step further than Lewes does, claiming that clothing and surrounding and language *cause* people to act as they do, that these elements of "milieu" are influences and not just "color." This environmentalist conclusion actually rigidly links realism to a deterministic philosophy--scientific materialism--an important addition to Lewes's less prescriptive tenets. So in Zola's writing, one can clearly see the element of realism that Lewes foresaw: it is a form in which the writer "gives the facts as he observed them, suggests the point of departure, displays the solid earth on which his characters are to tread and the phenomena to develop" ("The Experimental Novel" 5). But to that common base Zola adds the following: "Then the experimentalist appears and introduces an experiment, that is to say, sets his characters going so as to show that the succession of facts will be such as the requirements of the determinism of the phenomena under examination call for" ("The Experimental Novel" 5). This is scientific materialism, a system inspired by the actual scientific methodology that Zola found in Claude Bernard's *Introduction à l'étude de la médicine expérimentale* (1865). Also of great influence on Zola were the writings of Hippolyte Taine (1828-1983), a man who, according to Zola, "made a science of criticism" ("The Critical Formula" 81). The following summarizes Zola's perceptions of Taine's work:

> [H]eredity provides the theme for all human manifestations, natural and instinctive, the products of which we call virtues and vices . . . . [M]ilieu and moment play the variations. Milieu and moment rise henceforth to their full stature as a spatial and temporal climate--a living stage of Darwinian proportions, made to order for the strong, treacherous to the weak. (Bede 15)

Predestination and fate have been reduced from religious or even romantic mystery to scientific inevitability and incorporated into Zola's theories.

Identifying the fundamental difference between Lewes and Zola basically identifies the difference between realism in general and what has been specifically coined naturalism. Realism, according to Lewes's presentation, assumes that close study and creative re-enactment of real life will guarantee accuracy and "truth" in art. It is an approach to drama whose flexibility theoretically can succeed at reflecting any of a variety of outlooks or perspectives on, and philosophies of, existence. Zola goes a bold step further, using realism in a specific and limited manner to present his adopted philosophy of scientific determinism, one founded on a belief in some basic rationality governing the universe that can be tapped and used to predict human events and behavior when applied to prior knowledge of genetic and social antecedents. In this case realism has been manipulated for one particular end. Though Zola saw his naturalism as the logical conclusion of realism, Lewes would argue against Zola, claiming that close observation of existence--that which is realism--does not necessarily demand that one has to believe that existence can be rigidly--scientifically--analyzed and consequently comprehended. Realism does not in itself presume a rational order in the universe, or a sense of genetic or social "fate." Zola's naturalism *does* presume such notions and has managed to fuse both realist technique and its own adopted assumptions into one, gathering and presenting common experience, but assuming precision in observation and deriving a sense of "inevitability" that Lewes's realism nowhere presumed.

For a 19th-century world riding a wave of scientific optimism, naturalism would seem the likely reflection of civilization's way of viewing existence. Scientific enterprise, after all, seemed capable of probing any issue, and with conclusive results. Naturalism, however, moved in a rather unexpected way, reflecting not optimism but a growing (perhaps inevitable) disappointment in what various artists perceived to be the hypocrisy and complacency of Western civilization, and the result was an urge to both reveal and work to correct that world. This element of naturalism would cause problems. Naturalism took what was commonly perceived as a positive attitude toward rational comprehension and produced a pessimistic tone. Having an indifferent, mechanistic, even Darwinian, fatalism governing natural (and social) affairs sufficiently explained the world to those classes in power and even justified the suffering of the lower classes. After all, the suffering that existed was an inevitable part of a grand design. Naturalism, however, worked to confront these abstractions, a confrontation that was, generally speaking, philosophically distasteful to the optimistic and forward-looking Victorian public. But having an art form--theatre--graphically exposing its audiences to these inequities and injustices was nothing less than revolting, especially considering the fact that theatre had generally served as entertainment or as a positive mirror of genteel behavior. In fact, the theatre world, comfortable in socially untroubling melodrama and easy entertainment, actively resisted this development to accommodate such controversial views and attitudes in the theatre. But drama had clearly taken up its role as social critic, and change did come.

As with Zola's work, the pioneering naturalist works of Henrik Ibsen (1828-1906) and G.B. Shaw (1856-1950) met with resistance, public outrage, and banning from public performance. The production history of Ibsen's *A Doll's House* (1879) is well known, as is Shaw's advocacy of Ibsen's work in general and his interest in presenting Ibsen to the English-speaking world. And just as with the literary and public uproar over Zola's works, the theatrical uproar over Ibsen's drama focused on his "degenerate" and "decadent" outlook on the world, an outlook whose exposure decent members of society would not tolerate. One critic responds to the English premiere of *A Doll's House* in 1889:

> It is all self, self, self! This is the ideal woman of the new creed; not a woman who is the fountain of love and forgiveness and charity . . . but a mass of aggregate conceit and self-sufficiency, who leaves her home and deserts her friendless children because she has *herself* to look after. (Scott 114)

The propriety of having Ibsen's outlook on life presented to the public was the critics' central point of contention during the period. Ethics and morality were debated more than aesthetics. This critical focus, in turn, diverted attention away from the issue of whether the machinations of naturalism constituted a viable new aesthetic form in theatre. And realism itself was only peripherally the issue.

But out of all this critical turmoil arose proponents of Ibsen's art, Shaw and William Archer perhaps being the most outspoken. Edmund Gosse, another defender of Ibsen, notes Ibsen's particular relevance to American audiences in his "Introduction" to *Lovell's Series of Foreign Literature: The Prose Drama of Henrik Ibsen* (1890). After pointing out American and Norwegian political and temperamental similarities, Gosse concludes with the following aesthetic observation, one free of moralizing expostulations:

> Ibsen has created a new form of drama, and until he is himself superseded by some still more vivid painter of actual life, we must look upon him as the first of dramatic realists. The impression of vitality, of actuality, which his plays give us arises partly from the truth of his dialogue, which is astonishing, and partly from the alteration of plan which he has introduced. (151)

At this point Gosse is clearly discussing the aesthetic attributes of simple realism in Ibsen. But no discussion of Ibsen is complete if realism alone is addressed, and Gosse does add an important consequent tenet of Ibsenism--its naturalism (though Gosse does not identify it as such). Concerning Ibsen's "alteration of plan," Gosse writes:

> All plays before his are built on the system of climbing up the hill to a crisis and then rushing downward. The "well-made" comedy of Scribe or of Sardou has reduced this Jack-and-Jill ideal of dramatic construction to a mechanical trick. The figures are drawn up to the apex of their intrigue with a string, and dropped down the inclined plane at a given signal. But with Ibsen the downward path has been taken before the play opens, and the velocity is cumulative from the first scene to the last. (151)

Gosse is pointing out the formal benefits of Ibsen's drama--that his works do not merely insert ingredients to create crises, but come with the necessary material for crisis "pre-packed," brewing from the opening curtain. Ibsen does technically follow a well-made play format in the majority of his work, but Gosse would argue that the various turns are less theatrical and arbitrary tricks than inevitable and impending events prescribed from the play's opening, in true naturalist form. And it is downward, as Zola himself would predict it to be. From a strictly realistic perspective, too, Ibsen's work has value. Realism has proven its worth as a thoroughly contemporary medium that can confront serious issues and engage its audience in something other than escapist or moralistic entertainment.

Besides merely urging Americans to open themselves to "Ibsenism," Gosse succeeded in transmitting the germs of realism and naturalism to the United States. Henry James, for one, became interested in Ibsen, thanks to Gosse, as early as 1889 (see James 94). The American turn to realism began in the Eastern literary circles of Henry James and W.D. Howells, finding its best, though far from perfect, dramatic expression in the works of James A. Herne (1839-1901). With Herne, American theatre worked to break with the past and enter the modern world of serious drama. The effort itself should be credited, though the result was perhaps less than satisfactory.

Herne is often labelled the American Ibsen. His plays today seem trifling and flawed, but his contribution to American drama in general and American realism in particular must be acknowledged. Despite being an actor and manager of the old theatre of melodrama, he was the first to experiment with the new dramatic form and the first to try to adapt it to an American idiom. In his book *The American Dramatist* (1925), Montrose Moses says of Herne,

> [H]e has never been given full credit for his pioneer efforts,--with the examples before him of Howells, whom he knew personally, and of Ibsen, whom he knew by reading,--to apply to American themes for the stage, the realistic treatment, of which in this century Howells was the arch-exponent in fiction. (210)

Margaret Fleming (1890) is Herne's first realist work, a tale of a man "gone wrong," loyally supported by a wife who comes to know the animal instincts in man. It is naturalist in design and execution, but finally fails to be "American" by doing little more than giving the stage "'transformed English characters' rather than native Americans," as critic William Winters put it (in Moses 208). In a recent study, Brenda Murphy notes that the play's "serious treatment of the double standard for sexual fidelity . . . won praise from some daring critics but was never accepted by the public. In short, the American theater was far behind the European in the serious depiction of contemporary life" (13). Herne's next work, *Shore Acres* (1892), goes a significant step further. Though coming dangerously close to melodrama with a relighting-of-the-lighthouse-beam scene, the play adopts an American (New England) setting, an American dialect, and works to infuse American ideals of optimism and self-determination into its plot. The play is the best early attempt to use common American events (like a New England family feast) to produce theatre. Despite faults of technique, the play is, as Moses notes, an

> illustration that the poignancy of our soil, of our native character,--the primal sweep of our American life--is to be found between great cities, not in them; that there are more native stamina, more distinctive folk passion in the small community than in the large. In some respects Herne's plays are folk dramas of the best kind. The abnormal community, where a mixture of all nations makes the civic body, does not encourage such interest as he showed in the simple people and their daily lives. (212)

Herne found his simple people and daily lives in rural communities. Others would find them there, too, while still others would find them tucked away in neighborhoods of the most imposing American cities, Moses's observations notwithstanding. The point, though, is that, starting with Herne, Americans had finally begun to find native sources of material and to use native idioms in their presentations. Whether in New England or New York, there was a wealth of material, not in the fantastic stuff of melodrama, but in the lives of common Americans. The dramatist was freed to find rhythms in daily events and to work to present those events on stage. Herne's works met with limited popular success, but he attracted important literary and critical admirers. William Archer was one. He introduced Herne to Great Britain as a writer with a knack for realistic accuracy and as a man who foresaw the possibilities of American realism. Archer reports his response to a 1906 production of the Herne play *Griffith Davenport* (1899):

> The curtain rose on a quiet domestic scene on a Virginia plantation, and I was instantly struck by the skill with which the old-fashioned dignity of the environment was brought home to us, along with the atmosphere and aroma of the South . . . . I felt throughout that here I was in the presence of what I had come to seek, and had not found elsewhere--original American art. (in Moses 221)

However, at this point in American dramatic history, popular leanings toward entertainment supported by theatre's attachment to the profit motive prevented full development of the form and acceptance by a broad audience. And various playwrights, apparently, were not fully sold on naturalism/realism either. Experimentation with various other forms resulted both within and outside the realms of realism.

Elmer Rice (1892-1967) is an excellent example of an American playwright searching for a form, experimenting with expressionism (*The Adding Machine*, 1923), melodrama (*Counsellor-at-Law*,

1931), and farce (*See Naples and Die*, 1929). *Street Scene* (1929), however, a very nearly "photographic" report of a New York neighborhood, is perhaps his most American, a work that captures the language and aspirations of a community of people in an urban world, as Herne did with his rural world.

Another experimentalist, John Howard Lawson (1894-1977), offered an essentially realistic play, *Processional* (1925), but introduced an innovative concept to the stage. The play is realistically set in West Virginia during a coal-mining strike and strives to capture the idiom of the region, but Lawson works to add to that idiom the unique American rhythm of jazz. In the play's "Preface," Lawson says:

> I have endeavored to create a method which shall express the American scene in native idiom, a method as far removed from the older realism as the facile mood of Expressionism. It is apparent that this new technique is essentially vaudevillesque in character--a development, a molding to my own uses, of a rich vitality of the two-a-day and the musical extravaganza. (ix)

Lawson is arguing that America not only has a "milieu" and language of its own, as is implied in other writers, but also an attendant vital rhythm of its own. The point is revolutionary, but Lawson's skills were not sufficient to develop this theory. Though a jazz model never fully develops, the concept of American rhythm does.

At this stage in America's dramatic development, two problems are evident. Where European countries have had centuries of literary and cultural heritage from which to draw, America had very little. So while Europe was struggling to develop a comfortable form of expression (and perhaps debating the value of its artists' perceptions), America was struggling with two concerns: that of developing a form and, perhaps more importantly, that of trying to discover itself. Two playwrights are instrumental in gelling the concerns of American theatre: Eugene O'Neill (1888-1953) and Clifford Odets (1906-1963).

Moses, writing in 1925 about O'Neill, well before the production of O'Neill's masterpieces, says of the playwright:

> O'Neill is not a pleasant accidental; rather he is a starting point in the history of the American Drama. One cannot consider him from the old angle. He is not as frankly experimental as Elmer Rice in "The Adding Machine", or as John Howard Lawson in "Processional", but his work is more persistently identified with his own personality. For a while this is interesting, but it sooner or later gets on one's nerves; sincerity becomes almost mannerism, rebellion becomes calculated. (432-33)

Moses is right about O'Neill at this juncture in his career. He was experimental and innovative, but finally not content with his experiments. What one does see, however, even at this stage, is the willingness to indulge in highly personal art, though Moses reveals a distaste for this brand of art as produced to that point in O'Neill's career. Travis Bogard agrees with Moses about the personal aspect, but, having witnessed O'Neill's later products, Bogard disagrees with Moses's final assessment: "Eugene O'Neill's work as a playwright was . . . an effort at self-understanding . . . . The extent, variety and quality of the work signals a rare creative energy, but the energy's source lay in his need to find a pattern of explanation by which his life could be understood" (xii). Though his early plays are highly personal, it is not until O'Neill made peace with his past through his last great plays that we see precisely the qualitative level his art could reach.

This extreme self-analysis succeeded in doing what Herne's rural research only nominally succeeded at doing. In fact, with these later works, American realism began showing signs of maturity. In them, O'Neill went beyond the superficiality of surface realism to a level of psychological realism never before achieved in American drama. Though O'Neill credits Strindberg with triggering this tack in his work, the fact that it is O'Neill himself who is the subject of study separates him from ever sounding European (in his mature works, that is). In fact, this examination of himself and his relationship to his Irish-American family roots becomes the means for O'Neill finally to evolve solid, original, distinctive American theatre, from his comedy *Ah, Wilderness!* (1932) through to his masterpieces *The Iceman Cometh* (1939) and *A Long Day's Journey into Night* (1939-41), and finally to *Hughie* (1941) and *A Moon for the Misbegotten* (1943). And they all develop after his early period of experimentation, when he finally settles on realism, giving his plays American surroundings, working with American idiom, and revealing psychological underpinnings of American characters. So though initially highly experimental in his art, O'Neill eventually turned to realist techniques to present his vision.

As was the case with Herne and the others, O'Neill made the scene on the cusp of the old and new theatre in America, creating, as Bogard observes, a dramatic "contour in time":

> O'Neill began writing at the end of a period when a flamboyant, semi-professional style of acting, one which placed a heavy emphasis on rhetoric and the stances of formal delivery, had held the stage for nearly a century. His father, James O'Neill, was almost the last of a long line of actors of romantic drama. Of necessity, O'Neill's heritage bound him to that theatre and its playing style. (xvii)

O'Neill's talent, however, greatly aided in American theatre's efforts to break from the old, continuing a movement toward the future that Herne had begun. Concerning O'Neill's final turn to realism, Bogard adds, "O'Neill's own dramaturgy did much to end the demand for such actors" as his father had been, but concludes that his dramaturgy "did little to aid the development which took its place" (xvii). Though

O'Neill is correctly regarded as being less than influential in changing dramatic technique, his works did give validity to American material, its immense, untapped wealth of depth and complexity. And he gave final validity to realism as the form to express that material. His work is naturalist in its portrayal of genetic and social entrapment, but that naturalism had become "American" through O'Neill, who proved its flexibility and adaptability to the American scene. George Jean Nathan notes that "O'Neill alone and singlehanded waded through the dismal swamplands of American drama, bleak, squashing, and oozing sticky goo, and alone and singlehanded bore out of them the water lily that no American had found there before him" (284).

While O'Neill succeeded in solidifying a concept of American theatre, the nation was invaded by another European influence--following Ibsen by some thirty years--one that was initially digested by playwright Clifford Odets in particular. That source was Russia and the works of Anton Chekhov (1860-1904), and ultimately the practical workings of Konstantin Stanislavski (1863-1938). The influence has been a very important and long-lasting one.

As with Ibsen, Chekhov initially was not well received by either the European or American communities. Critic Ashley Dukes argues the generally accepted early view of Chekhov, calling Chekhov's works "tragedies of disillusionment" and then adding:

> It must be said at once that Tchekhov can by no stretch of imagination be called a great dramatist. He cried "Open Sesame!" to actuality, but the reality behind was only vaguely outlined, and he died before he could perfect the new dramatic form which he attempted to create. (192)

Much can be said in defense of Chekhov, but what many early viewers generally missed in Chekhov, it seems, was the rich psychological element present in his works. The depth of psychological realism that exists in Chekhov's characters was not fully and consistently revealed until that realism was interpreted by Stanislavski and the Moscow Art Theatre.

Chekhov's plays were ideal works for Stanislavski's method, being plays that almost insist on a system of producing "actors capable of discovering the inner life of the man they portray, actors capable of building 'the life of the human spirit'" (Moore 10). The system as outlined by Stanislavski in *An Actor Prepares* (1936) is more of a philosophy than a practical method. The process includes:

1) Inner grasp
2) The through line of action
3) The super-objective. (264)

According to Stanislavski, the three steps together serve "the common purpose" (258) of avoiding "*all extraneous tendencies and purposes foreign to the main theme*" (262). Stanislavski demanded from his students an internal consistency aimed at a final thematic goal. But because Stanislavski's writing/teachings allowed for a variety of specific goals, his essentially realist methodology was open to a variety of particular interpretations. And in America in particular, the naturalists saw the method's acute suitability and co-opted it for their own specific designs. For example, Sonia Moore, a disciple of Stanislavski, notes that his teachings "form a science based on human functioning according to laws of nature. These laws are obligatory for all people . . . . Through the System, actors learn natural laws and how to use them consciously in re-creating human behavior on stage" (10-11). So with the help of Stanislavski's teachings, his desciples took the naturalism of Zola consciously into the realm of psychology, which in turn informed and determined the realm of action. A new acting style was created to accommodate the new form, one that gave internal psychological and emotional depth to its on-stage characters. In the 1930s Stanislavski's full influence was felt in America with the formation of the Group Theatre and discovery of Clifford Odets, events that converted Stanislavski's method into a full, rigorous program.

With this development of Stanislavski's method, Clifford Odets and the Group Theatre made that final break with past conventions that O'Neill first struggled to accomplish, and did with language what Lawson had tried to accomplish with musical rhythms. Odets found his best material in the same place O'Neill found it: in his own life. As O'Neill tapped the dynamics of the Irish-American family, so Odets tapped his own roots, the Jewish-American family. His best works-- like *Awake and Sing* (1935) and *Paradise Lost* (1935)--have the same distinguishing factors as O'Neill's, that is, autobiographical relevance which leads both to a deeper understanding of himself and consequently of the characters he presents. That in turn produces psychological depth--psychological realism--that gives a universal validity to his American experiences.

Primarily the result of his agit-prop play *Waiting for Lefty* (1935), Odets is remembered as a socialist, communist, political activist. But perhaps his most noteworthy contribution is the element that complements psychological realism--his dialogue. Where O'Neill was still somewhat tied to a declamatory style of the past, Odets bottled the idiom of the streets and used it for his own ends. Says Odets's mentor, Harold Clurman:

> It is an ungrammatical jargon--and constantly lyric. It is composed of words heard on the street, in drugstores, bars, sports arenas, and rough restaurants. (Odets used to cut out newspaper photos of faces to help him flesh the characters who might speak his language.) It is the speech of New York; half-educated Jews, Italians, Irish, transformed into something new-minted, individual, and unique. Above all it makes crackling theater dialogue . . . . It is not "English"; in a sense it is not "realistic" at all. It is "*Odets*." (xi)

Clurman is right that it is not strictly realistic in that it is not mere documentation of street language, but it is aesthetically realistic in its street-talk accuracy. And its cadence and rhythm, finally, produce what Lawson seemed to want in his own dramas, though he arbitrarily inserted rhythm rather than let rhythm flow out of the text, as Odets had done.

Odets succeeded in taking foreign dialects and making them "American" as O'Neill had taken general events and conflicts and made them American experiences. The fusion of the two men's efforts finally turned drama by Americans into recognizably American drama.

To present the sources of his dramas on stage, not only did Odets need to understand them, but so did the actors. And that is where Odets found the "method" of Stanislavski so useful, with the help of Lee Strasberg, Harold Clurman, and the Group Theatre. Stanislavski's work became for them a naturalist method that could tap the roots not only of Chekhovian despair but also Odetsian optimism. They had to tap, as Clurman notes,"[a]n all-enveloping warmth, love in its broadest sense, [which] is a constant in all Odets's writing, the very root of his talent. It is there in tumultuous harangues, in his denunciations and his murmurs" (xii). And they succeeded in tapping that optimism, a fact that proves the flexibility of the method. Sonia Moore supports the notion of Stanislavski's flexibility:

> The System . . . cannot be called a Russian phenomenon, and does not have to be "adapted" to American actors or to actors of any nationality. Through the System, actors learn natural laws and how to use them consciously in re-creating human behavior on stage. (11)

The method replaces the old style and produces actors who are receptacles for the realistic, fleshed-out characters to be produced in theatre throughout the world. The Group introduced the method to America, and the hold has been a solid one.

Tennessee Williams (1911-1983) was perhaps the foremost talent among the next generation of playwrights and one whose plays benefitted greatly from method-acting techniques (Marlon Brando and Elia Kazin being products of the Group). Like Odets, Williams's works were well suited to the Group approach, since they dramatized complex personal experiences from Williams's own experiences as a Southerner raised in a South quixotically clinging to old values. Williams is perhaps the most personal writer to date, drawing from his past in such a manner that the tragic vision of life returns to theatre And in presenting that vision, Williams utilizes lyrical language that often verges on the "non-realistic." In fact, in his 1945 "Production Notes" to *The Glass Menagerie,* Williams asserts that his play is not realistic at all, adding, "These remarks are not meant as a preface only to this particular play. They have to do with a conception of a new, plastic theatre which must take the place of the exhausted theatre of realistic conventions if the theatre is to resume vitality as a part of our culture" (7). Williams is arguing against realism here, noting that realism itself has already become outmoded. It is an argument that will be repeated, but only rarely heeded in America. In fact, with rare exceptions like *Camino Real* (1953), Williams's own plays continue to use realism as the essential form of presentation. Williams is making the same error in his assessment of realism that Clurman nearly did in his assessment of Odets's language. The raw material that becomes "realism" *can* and *should* be manipulated by the artist; realism is not just journalistic reporting or photographic recounting. We must remember the early assessment of realism by Lewes: realism must be more than mere representation; it must be a refinement of real actions into "well-known symbols" of individual actions so that the spectators, "recognizing those expressions, are thrown into a state of sympathy" (*On Actors* 124). Williams's use of music and lighting, for example, is a freedom that Lewes's realism in fact gives the playwright license to manipulate. Williams's sets may be highly symbolic, but they are still finally realistic. Additionally, no one can deny that Williams's characters are psychologically real, as the success of method acting in his plays attests. So though he reviles realism, Williams has nonetheless earmarked all his works with elements of realism. He has in fact added to the understanding of realism's flexibility, having given his works a sensitivity and fragility not approached by other artists. Finally what this addition has done is, not argue against realism, but argue for the flexibility of realism, even in its naturalist permutation.

Arthur Miller (b. 1915), like Williams, also skirts the non-realistic in several of his pieces, *After the Fall* (1964) being perhaps his most noteworthy. But works like *All My Sons* (1947) and *A View from the Bridge* (1955) are very clearly realist dramas. Even his masterpiece, *Death of a Salesman* (1949), though ostensibly a "dream" play subtitled "Certain Private Conversations," is essentially a realist drama. The dream flashbacks are perhaps an innovation but are presented as realistically as actuality in the drama. Here chronology is manipulated, but, given the primary concern of psychological realism, the manipulation demonstrates the flexibility of the form rather than warranting a new label for the form used. And though without the ear of an Odets or Williams, Miller too inserts a sense of the poetic in his speeches by common men while maintaining an essentially realistic posture.

American realism from Herne to Miller illustrates a great deal of flexibility as a tool for expression. Grounded in real existence, realism is nonetheless capable of lyricism, of studying deep recesses of the human psyche, and of capturing any of a number of microcosmic Americas. But despite this transformation of realism into an American idiom, this branch of realism never quite escapes the grasp of its naturalist philosophy. Robert Brustein, for example, observes that the tightly argued and constructed works of Miller "belong to the eighteenth century, which is to say the age of Newton, rather than to the twentieth, the age of Einstein . . . . [For Miller] every dramatic action has an equal and opposite reaction" ("The Crack in the Chimney" 148). And such endeavors as assessing guilt, a focus of much modern drama, can "usually be traced to a single, recognizable event" (145). In Stanislavskian terms, through line and super-objective have become trivialized and oversimplified.

Even our foremost playwright, O'Neill, is bound to that tight, deterministic process that so easily reduces the complexities of human interaction to simple patterns of cause and effect. Brustein notes that in O'Neill's *Long Day's Journey into Night*, "O'Neill proceeds to weave a close fabric of causality; every character in the play is suffering pangs of remorse and every character is trying to determine the root cause of his guilt" (145). Brustein explains the pattern of causality:

> The miserliness of the elder Tyrone is the cause of his wife's addiction, since it was the quack doctor he hired who first introduced her to drugs, and Edmund's tuberculosis accounts for his mother's resumption of her habit, since she cannot face the fact of his bad health. Jamie is plagued by the very existence of Edmund, since his brother's literary gifts inspire him with envy and a sense of failure; and his mother's inability to shake her habit has made him lose faith in his own capacity for regeneration. (145-46)

By far, the majority of American drama is heavily influenced by the naturalism of Zola's material determinism. Brustein's argument--and complaint--is a solid one.

But, much overdue, the trend is slowly shifting, the result of a long, painful process. In the 1950s a new world view was solidly introduced to the English-speaking theatre public that indisputably challenged the order of naturalism--absurdism, as digested by Samuel Beckett from French drama. Subtler early shifts in 20th-century drama were perhaps less readily accessible to the English-speaking stage than absurdism, but through this comparatively late movement, American sensibilities slowly evolved.

Where genetic and social determinism (as "proved" by Darwin) are the bases of naturalism, absurdism is an offspring of the theories of Einsteinian physics and modern psychology, which have "proven" little more than an unsure relativity of existence and a consequent sense of disjointedness with nature in general (not merely with social stricture). At best, the material placed before our eyes, in art or in daily existence, is insufficient material to determine future effect, unless of course a new epistemological framework is first developed and embraced. Given the current condition, however, if there is no comfortably perceivable and predictable order to the universe, how can any action be naturalistically assumed? Naturalism, it seems, has lost its philosophical and practical value.

But despite Beckett, the French absurdists, and existential philosophers, life does continue to function in a seemingly naturalist progression and certainly in a perceptibly real environment. Even in such a void as the absurdists present, Britain's "Angry Young Men" of the 50s and 60s succeeded at writing in the realist and often even in the specifically naturalist vein, and succeeded at convincing audiences that realism, at least, and possibly naturalism, was still a viable means of expressing existence. There was still *something* of value in our old systems of perception. Despite absurdists who argued abstractions that "proved" the contrary, empirical evidence apparently challenged those abstractions. The lines seemed drawn: either we use realism/naturalism as reactionary weapons to defend against a modern world picture, or we opt for experimental means to fathom the world and present new visions.

In America the controversy took a similar form. Either a writer opted for a realistic mode of presentation and its attendant naturalist philosophy, or moved to newer forms of expression to relate new philosophies. In the 60s in America an explosion of high-energy productions seemed to signal a revitalization of the theatre world and triggered a guarded sense of hope among its defenders that theatre would at long last move beyond naturalism to forms that could better relate current experiences of existence. The passage below, from an introductory drama book published in 1971, summarizes the conclusions of many during that period:

> In the last ten years several explosions have shaken the theatre, making it seem that the old theatre might be replaced by dynamic rituals of primitive intensity for a fully participating audience. Young enthusiasts deserted theatre buildings to be in the streets "where the action is," carrying masks and monsters in confrontations before draft boards and military-industrial headquarters. Or they gathered in old barns and warehouses to stage "happenings" or "love-ins," celebrating aggressive nudity, four-letter words, and drugs in joyous defiance of "hypocritical" restraints, exploring "total environment," surrounded by grotesque animated shapes, projected scenes on shaped screens, and dozens of loud-speakers each with a different sound track. (Kernodle 1)

Theatre was searching for new forms. In America, theatre was struggling to find a means of expressing itself, perhaps not exactly expressing a view of the absurd but at least something other than the ordered, Newtonian perspective of realism/naturalism that clearly did not present a picture suitable for the eyes and minds of the post-war nuclear age.

But the "traditionalists" had not given up the struggle. Coinciding with this period of rash experimentation in the American theatre of the 60s was also a surge of conventional vitality, a fact often overlooked. Robert W. Corrigan notes this fact in "The Search for New Endings: The Theatre in Search of a Fix, Part III":

> Just as the American theatre was taking off into what many thought was outer space in the early and mid 60s, our playwrighting establishment-- those writers whose work embodies the most significant achievements of the modernist theatre tradition--had a quite wonderful final flowering. I am referring, of course, to some of the remarkable plays that were first produced during this period: Williams's *The Night of the Iguana* (1961), Albee's *Whose* [sic] *Afraid of Virginia Woolf?* (1962) and *Tiny Alice* (1964), Miller's *After the Fall* (1964), *Incident at Vichy* (1964), and *The Price* (1968), Bellow's *The Last Analysis* (1964), and Robert Lowell's *The Old Glory* (1964). (154-55)

Though not all of these works are naturalistic, they do adhere to more conventional modes of presentation. As was the case in Britain, conventional theatre and even realism/naturalism clearly had not died completely.

Corrigan then argues that since that productive period, traditional theatre has failed to produce such quality material; even the above-cited writers lost their edge. Possibly the competitive element created by "alternative theatre" in the 60s created a turmoil that in turn finally led to self-doubt among the more conventional writers. Or more precisely stated, this direct confrontation finally succeeded at causing the traditionalists themselves to question the validity of the realist/naturalist format that had dominated American theatre for so long. As suggested earlier, Corrigan notes that the lack of a continued strong performance on the parts of these playwrights points "to a failure on the part of our traditional playwrights to give expression to the conflicts of contemporary experience, and also to a loss of confidence in the capacity of the traditional dramatic form to adequately address those conflicts" (155). Questioning the validity of realism-as-naturalism, it seems, finally did occur, and realism (with its naturalist affiliations) fell out of favor. Bernard Dukore does identify a group of 60s writers--Gelber, Brown, and Jones/Baraka, among others--as realists, even calling them "New Realists" (166). But for the most part the movement had lost its drive, and the realists that Dukore identifies are better remembered for techniques that lie outside the realm of realism.

Given that the traditional form Corrigan speaks of is strongly allied with naturalist tenets (though some, like Albee, avoided this hazard, but unfortunately have dropped from the scene), then Corrigan is certainly accurate: theatre does need a new fix. But the playwrights discussed in this study--among others--have risen out of the turmoil of the 60s and are not reasserting a reactionary program as Corrigan fears; rather they are doing what Brustein seems to hope for: redirecting traditional theatre to express contemporary concerns free of naturalist imposition. In a way the "new fix" has come from an unexpected direction.

Possibly taking their cues from the British Angry Young Men of the late 50s and early 60s, or at least springing from the same sentiments, these American playwrights have realized that empirically experienced existence argues more effectively than philosophical abstractions or theatrical vagaries. But unlike the Angry Young Men, these Americans are even less convinced of the veracity of naturalist assumptions and have opted for realistically presenting--empirically asserting--their own versions of what could be loosely called the absurdist situation. As Pinter, for example, has utilized British realism to argue absurdism--a step beyond the Angry Young Men-- so, too, are the new American realists taking the American realist idiom to present their own modified visions of the world, not precisely absurdist but definitely influenced by that movement. Where naturalism has used a rationally based argument for political and social change, these new playwrights are revealing that change must be made at far deeper levels, beyond surface modification of an already acceptable base. The base itself needs re-evaluation, and that is the task these new realists have undertaken.

Brustein, in *The Theatre of Revolt* (1964), argues that modern drama has been dominated by what he calls a spirit of revolt against modern civilization, a very broad movement that Brustein breaks down into three types: messianic, social, and existential (16). "Spirit of Revolt" does seem to fairly identify the mood of modern drama in general and has definite applications to drama even today. When Brustein speaks of the social revolt type of drama, he observes, "The emphasis of the drama shifts from radical [messianic] cures to careful diagnoses, with the patient taking the stage and the physician withdrawing behind the scenes" (22). This explanation of social revolt has clearly naturalistic overtones; in fact, Brustein notes that social drama is "frequently written in the realistic or Naturalistic style" (23). The label of social revolt can certainly be applied to the works of Odets, Miller, much of O'Neill, and early American drama in general. And noting that realism/naturalism is primarily concerned with social conditions certainly holds true as well. In fact, it has become standard to assume realism deals almost exclusively with social issues. But Rabe, Mamet, Shepard, and the others in this study have taken realism beyond this socially-oriented domain and have entered what Brustein would label the existential realm of revolt, that which presents "a cry of anguish over the insufferable state of being human" (26). In essence, these artists have moved beyond the traditional realms of realism/naturalism. Dissatisfied with results on the social level, they have moved beyond the social levels of revolt to presenting perspectives on the existential dilemma itself, a level not commonly considered the domain of realist drama. As a result, assumptions that realism is a form dedicated to social issues are assumptions that these new realists will have to overcome. And at times this obstacle is quite formidable. But if successful, then arguing the need for a "new fix" and looking for a revolutionary new form may be premature. At the very least, a "new realism" may be *an* answer if it isn't precisely *the* answer.

That new realism isn't exclusively *the* answer is demonstrated by the experimental works of such artists as Robert Wilson, Richard Foreman, and the members of the Wooster Group, which have succeeded at dramatizing late 20th-century views of existence accurately and innovatively. However, having a theatre that utilizes a basically realistic format seems to me essential for two reasons.

Given the concern for maintaining contact with a supportive and general public and maintaining, or regaining, its communal function, the theatre would benefit from a revitalized realism. Thanks to television and cinema, today's audiences come to the theatre "trained" in realism, given the fact that with the last few generations of audiences a circle has been completed--the theatre trained moviegoers and now movies train theatregoers. As a result, the doors of American theatre remain open to the widest spectrum of the American public as long as it offers a realistic format.

Perhaps a more important reason is that realism can and does remain vital even when divested of its naturalist consequences, for it does not merely present life-like photographs of reality, merely working Frigidaires and live elephants, as some claim it does. Though early realist drama, like that of some of Herne's, for example, may have merely celebrated success at having achieved "photographic realism," there is in fact more to realism than that. As noted in the "Introduction," Martin Esslin makes the following important but often ignored observation, shadowing Lewes's 19th-century claim:

> Reality itself, even the most mundane, everyday reality, has its own symbolic component. The postman who brings me the telegram which announces the death of a friend is also, in a sense, a messenger of death, an Angel of Death. Whether he is perceived in that symbolic sense is merely a matter of my own way of looking at him, my own awareness, my own mood . . . . What the stage gives us is an enhanced reality that itself becomes a sign, a metaphor, an image, a dramatic symbol. (9)

Everyone looks at real objects and actions and has the general ability to interpret them as meaningful symbols. So why "re-train" and therefore risk limiting potential audiences?

The counter-response, of course, to that question is that the symbols and signs of realism are insufficient as means of articulating the modern condition, and that they need to be replaced if that modern condition is ever to be dramatized properly (regardless of the risk of losing audiences). To the first part of that response, the new realist playwrights may in fact agree, at least in part. Those signs may be insufficient. But to that conclusion these artists would argue that those signs and symbols are, perhaps unexpectedly (and certainly unwittingly), perfect tools for demonstrating their own insufficiency, a self-reflective action, in essence. Those tools may in fact no longer be meaningful or dependable means of perceiving and/or communicating perceptions of the world around us, but these writers can at very least ironically use these tools to dramatically overturn our faith in those tools. And if they can challenge our faith in those tools, they can challenge our faith in the systems that created them. The source of the modern dilemma is thereby confronted: our misconceptions and delusions about "order" in our world are revealed to us.

These playwrights, simply enough, can and do utilize our commonly held sign/symbol preconceptions to reveal the modern failure of the systems we depend on for understanding and communication. *That* is precisely the design of the following playwrights. And in the process of realizing this end these artists, as Eric Bentley would say, are creating another species of the genus realism: "new realism."

Works Cited

Bede, Jean-Albert. *Emile Zola*. New York: Columbia UP, 1974.

Bogard, Travis. *Contour in Time: The Plays of Eugene O'Neill*. New York: Oxford UP, 1972.

Brustein, Robert. "The Crack in the Chimney: Reflections on Contemporary American Playwriting." *Images and Ideas in American Culture*. Ed. Arthur Edelstein. Hanover, NH: Brandeis UP, 1979. 141-57.

--------. *The Theatre of Revolt*. Boston: Little, Brown, 1964.

Clurman, Harold. Introduction. *Six Plays of Clifford Odets*. New York: Grove Press, 1979. ix-xiv.

Corrigan, Robert W. "The Search for New Endings: The Theatre in Search of a Fix, Part III." *Theatre Journal* 36 (1984): 153-63.

Donohue, Joseph, Jr. *Dramatic Character in the English Romantic Age*. Princeton: Princeton UP, 1970.

Dukes, Ashley. *Modern Dramatists*. London: Frank Palmer, 1911.

Dukore, Bernard F. "Off-Broadway and the New Realism." *Modern American Drama*. Ed. William E. Taylor. DeLand, FL: Everett/Edwards, 1968. 163-74.

Esslin, Martin. "The Stage: Reality, Symbol, Metaphor." *Themes in Drama*, Vol. IV. Ed. James Redmond. London: Cambridge UP, 1982. 1-12.

Gosse, Edmund. "Introduction to *Lovell's Series of Foreign Literature: The Prose Drama of Henrik Ibsen*." 1890. *Ibsen: The Critical Heritage*. Ed. Michael Egan. Boston: Routledge and Kegan Paul, 1972. 94.

Hunt, Leigh. "The Jew of Malta." *Dramatic Criticism, 1808-1831*. Eds. L.H. Houtchens and Carolyn Washburn. New York: Columbia UP, 1949. 195-98.

James, Henry. "Letter: 29 Jan., 1889." *Ibsen: The Critical Heritage*. Ed. Michael Egan. Boston: Routledge and Kegan Paul, 1972. 94.

Kernodle, George and Portia. *Invitation to the Theatre.* New York: Harcourt, Brace, Jovanovich, 1971.

Lamb, Charles. "On the Artificial Comedy of the Last Century." *Elia.* 1823. Menston, Eng.: Scolar Press, 1969. 323-37.

Lawson, John Howard. Preface. *Processional.* New York: T. Seltzer, 1925. i-xii.

Lewes, George Henry. *On Actors and the Art of Acting.* 1875. New York: Grove Press, 1957.

--------. "The Old and Modern Dramatists." *Dramatic Essays.* London: Walter Scott, 1896. 101-104.

--------. "Recent Novels: French and English." *Fraser's Magazine* 36 (Dec. 1847): 686-95.

Moore, Sonia. *The Stanislawski System.* Harmondsworth, Eng.: Penguin, 1965.

Moses, Montrose J. *The American Dramatist.* 1925. New York: Benjamin Blom, 1964.

Murphy, Brenda. *American Realism and American Drama, 1880-1940.* London: Cambridge UP, 1987.

Nathan, George Jean. "Our Premiere Dramatist." *O'Neill and His Plays.* Eds. Oscar Cargill, N. Bryllion Fagin, and William J. Fisher. New York: New York UP, 1961. 283-91.

Scott, Clement. "A Doll's House." *Ibsen: The Critical Heritage.* Ed. Michael Egan. Boston: Routledge and Kegan Paul, 1972. 114.

Stanislavski, Constantin. *An Actor Prepares.* 1936. Trans. Elizabeth R. Hapgood. New York: Theatre Arts Books, 1984.

Zola, Emile. "The Critical Formula Applied to the Novel." 1893. Trans. Belle M. Sherman. *The Naturalist Novel.* Ed. Maxwell Geismar. Montreal: Harvest House, 1964. 81-84.

--------. "The Experimental Novel." 1893. Trans. Belle M. Sherman. *The Naturalist Novel.* Ed. Maxwell Geismar. Montreal: Harvest House, 1964. 1-32.

David Rabe's *Hurlyburly*. World premiere production (1984) at the Goodman Theatre, Chicago. Pictured are Phil (Harvey Keitel) and Eddie (William Hurt).

Photo: Tom Lascher.

Chapter Two

David Rabe's Assault on Rationalism and Naturalism

Though naturalism is a relatively recent phenomenon in the history of Western art, its attendant belief that rationally perceived causal connections can explain human affairs has been the subject of debate in Western thought for centuries. In brief, philosophers and artists have had much opportunity to contemplate the limits of reason and to conclude that rational explanations alone trivialized human interaction, failing accurately to document existence as they had grown to perceive it. As a result, naturalism itself came under fire, even as it was developing. Its very practitioners expressed doubt, in fact, as early as in Ibsen's own *Master Builder* (see Brustein, "The Crack in the Chimney" 142-43). Robert Brustein, however, notes that American playwrights have persisted in following this time-worn naturalist creed after many other nationalities have long since dispensed with it. And with a few notable exceptions, Brustein argues, the persistence continues today--or at least to 1979, when he published his observations. Sam Shepard is, for Brustein, the central notable exception. But surprisingly, among the long list of "reactionaries"-- O'Neill, Miller, and Williams included--is the Shepard contemporary David Rabe (b. 1940).

I say surprising not because Brustein's opinion is unique, but surprising because Brustein has obviously sensitized himself to a critical distinction between "naturalist" realism and other possible forms of realism, and because he had access at that time to at least one Rabe play that clearly aligned Rabe with those on Brustein's short list of notable exceptions, *Streamers* (1976). But despite these points, Brustein failed to see and/or report Rabe's innovative approach to playwriting in America. Instead of *Streamers*, Brustein chose an earlier Rabe product, *Sticks and Bones* (1971), as his example, and, arguably, his assessment of that play alone supports the claim that Rabe is a reactionary from the "old school."

But if Rabe *were* from this old school of thinking, this newer product--*Streamers*--would likewise follow the path of naturalism. But it doesn't. It is a play that isolates several G.I.s in a barracks community, who, after striving to co-exist, become part of an eruption of violence leading to the senseless deaths of several buddies. As many theatregoers and critics can attest, the bloody, climactic conclusion is unexpected and finally rationally unsupportable. In this work, Rabe essentially asks his audiences to divest themselves of their naturalist prejudices and not assume that what is placed before their eyes is designed to substantiate assumptions that the world is rationally and causally ordered.

If *Streamers* failed to place Rabe at the forefront of this movement away from naturalism in American drama, then perhaps a more recent work, *Hurlyburly* (1984), may. With *Streamers* Rabe confronted the ordered and consequential naturalist world by using a straight realistic mode to present his own perceptions and having them overturn naturalist assumptions. Though this actual confrontation may have appeared inadvertent in *Streamers* and was consequently overlooked by many, *Hurlyburly* is a considered and conscientious effort to follow up on *Streamers*'s first assault.

Rabe's basic argument in all his work to date is that the irrational violence he witnessed throughout his experiences during the Vietnam conflict (Rabe himself is a Vietnam veteran) is not some localized anomaly but a fundamental fact of life that permeates all current American experience. Comprehending and accepting such irrational action can in fact produce a foundation of understanding that better explains the human condition than rationalist endeavors ever could. It seems, though, that many of the consequences of this argument--and often the argument itself--are either missed or misinterpreted by audience and critic alike. In fact, until *Hurlyburly*, a vocal segment of the theatre world looked at Rabe in a way echoed by Janet Hertzbach in the final words of her essay, "The Plays of David Rabe: A World of Streamers":

> Rabe's reflections on the interrelatedness of war, sex, racism, the family, past, and present as they define the contemporary American battlefield are frequently shocking and often provocative. His dramatic world of streamers is, however, all of a piece; and lacking texture and amplitude, it finally fails to convince. (185)

To understand the roots of this assessment and to see how Rabe has worked to overcome such criticism, Rabe's earlier plays must be considered as well as his later. His career illustrates a process that has moved from a more experimental phase to one--his current one-- that fully and completely utilizes realist techniques in a manner that ironically shows the shortcomings of naturalist presumptions inherent in our perceptions of realism.

Rabe first gained national attention through the double billing of *The Basic Training of Pavlo Hummel* and *Sticks and Bones* in 1971 at Joseph Papp's Public Theatre in New York. They are works that address the Vietnam experience as Rabe saw it, as does a third work, *Streamers*, which together are often considered Rabe's Vietnam Trilogy. But though the plays are set in worlds that are directly affected by the Vietnam experience and though they perhaps ostensibly comment on that experience, Rabe's plays are neither dated period pieces nor politically motivated anti-war tracts. In a response to a production of *Sticks and Bones* in the Soviet Union, for example, Rabe argues that the work is not an isolated commentary on the Vietnam War: "If you [the directors] find only the United States in it, then you fail to see it or fail to see yourselves. It is a play about sophisticated tribalism in which ritual is used to define the insiders and outsiders of the tribe and make the definition hold" ("Each Night" 3). Violence and an underlying prejudice against "others," in the broadest sense, is Rabe's focus.

The critic or audience is perhaps justified in seeing social commentary. After all, Rabe argues that the Vietnam War clearly revealed America's prejudices, particularly anti-Asian prejudices. But the critic or audience is also obliged to look beyond the setting and immediate context to more fundamental points in the plays. Rabe himself argues, "I don't like to hear them called antiwar plays. Works like that, like some of the social-action plays of the thirties, are designed for immediate effect" (Berkvist 3). Rabe's most notable early non-Vietnam play, *In the Boom Boom Room* (1973), provides support for these observations in that it captures violent, abusive tones similar to those of his trilogy but is set in Philadelphia. Vietnam may have helped mold Rabe's vision, but it is not simply Vietnam about which he is writing. It seems that an all-too-literal approach to Rabe's work has often left his audiences missing the more expanded observations that Rabe is presenting.

Though actually produced after *The Basic Training of Pavlo Hummel*, *Sticks and Bones* was written earlier, shortly after Rabe himself returned from a tour of duty in Vietnam. Written mainly in response to the indifference Rabe met upon his return to the States, the play focuses on David, a blinded veteran who also returns to a home that is indifferent to him, to the point of denying he is even part of the family. He is, as Walter Kerr notes,

> a maimed soldier, silent behind his dark glasses, a threat to their [the rest of the family's] peace of mind with his omnipresent tapping stick. They would rather have him dead than an accusing presence, a reminder of their bland indifference to whatever might hurt. ("Unmistakably a Writer" 1)

Samuel Bernstein adds, "it is his cultural ethos and spiritual vision that have changed, far more than his body and his physical vision" (22).

David is re-introduced to his family and hopes to be a catalytic force that will convert his naive though brutally prejudiced family, give them an insight into their own metaphorical blindness. Rabe is, in essence, striving to break down the tribal rituals that assert "difference," that confirm institutionalized concepts of prejudice. Documenting this conflict is the source of the drama; the focus, however, is not on David, but on his family and the culture it represents. Bernstein notes,

> Rabe employs David's physical condition and the new relationship with his family as a springboard for examining American values; the standards and assumptions by which we live, our motivation to go to war, what happens to those who go to war, the American ethos, and what hope we can have for the future. (22)

The family is set up as a microcosm epitomizing the American ideals and values of which Bernstein speaks. Rabe ingeniously re-creates the Ozzie and Harriet Nelson family of the 50s television show, a move designed to have that family encapsulate the seeming wholesomeness of American culture. And into this American dream David thrusts the war. The war, however, is important only inasmuch as it is a stimulus for more general re-evaluation of the conditions and attitudes among the family members, which in turn work to identify the "causes" that led to the war.

The play's logical intention is tight, and the conditions are seemingly appropriate for the family itself rationally to engage in such re-evaluation. But Rabe makes it clear that the events fail to lead to the logical ends one would expect. In the play, logic and rationality break down. In fact, the processes of logic and reason have been utilized ironically to inform against themselves. The superficial order and control that make the Nelson family appear so contented explodes into a chaos that finally leads the entire family to encourage David to commit suicide. The family members even help. What starts out seeming to be a "problem play" designed to identify and resolve conflict is taken over by the characters and turned into a vicious effort to deny and cover up fundamentally flawed perceptions of existence. Edith Oliver reports that prior to this suicide conspiracy, "Ozzie's jolly reminiscences turn acrid, and Harriet's doubts and fears and prejudices rise to the surface, as do Rick's moral callousness and destructiveness" (119). Between David's entrance and the final scene, the family reveals, for example, its shallow theology, materialistic ideals, and twisted sense of hero worship.

But central to the action in the play is the presentation of racial prejudice, an element of hypocrisy that for Rabe seems to summarize all the flaws and self-deception afflicting American culture. Kerr claims that "David most hates his family for its bias against 'yellow people'" ("David Has Never Been Alive" 3). Kerr adds:

> He [David] has had, briefly in Vietnam, a mistress whom he has not brought home, though her shadow enters at the door and lurks behind the

bedroom walls upstairs. He has not brought her home, apparently, because his mother knows that such people "eat the flesh of dogs"; she also feels sorry for a Eurasian couple that has spawned a "Chink child." "They have diseases, these girls" is a refrain that runs through the household, and the priest would like David to know that "sexual acceptance of an alien race" implies rejection of one's own. ("David Has Never Been Alive" 3)

Simply put, the two worlds clash, and what was once perhaps a noble calling--to defend an oppressed people--has resulted in only providing Americans horrifying glimpses of truth about American culture. The consequence of these glimpses is that Americans like the Nelsons have further hidden themselves behind what has been revealed to be thin and finally unacceptable walls of security supported by prejudice and hate. Rationality in the play has broken down, and the logical (and ethical) choice of accepting and overcoming prejudice is replaced by an undesirable but seemingly inevitable alternative: entrenching oneself even further in "wrong action." Finally, is expecting the world to be rational a naive notion? To this question Rabe would answer "yes." But as for a solution to the problem, he could not be as precise in his response, for he claims of his works, "All I'm trying to do is define the event for myself and for other people. I'm saying, in effect, 'This is what goes on,' and that's all" (Berkvist 3). Rabe has presented a condition but implicitly concedes that answers/solutions aren't easily extended. And in this case, as Rabe sees it, society is unwilling to accept rationally motivated solutions, instead preferring to use a twisted and poorly disguised "reason" to defend its current stand.

Bernstein makes a more direct claim for *Sticks and Bones*. His work *The Strands Entwined* (1980) discusses *Sticks and Bones* and seems accurately to observe that though Rabe is influenced by a realist/naturalist tradition, he is doing much more than creating a "slice of life" (or "what's going on") drama. He isn't submitting an overt thesis; he can't conclusively respond to the above urge for an answer. Rather there is a strain (or "strand," as Bernstein calls it) in Rabe's work that argues that existence is basically illogical or irrational, and this underlying philosophy of absurdism is what Rabe centrally portrays in his realistic format. So when Rabe says "this is what goes on," he is not merely describing superficial movement or specific social events, but is portraying an underlying rhythm that is not rationally governed or structured. Bernstein acknowledges one additional strand in the play, a surrealistic one (the presence of the Vietnamese mistress left behind and the flashbacks to foreign events), but argues that the play's major elements are realistic and absurdist in nature:

The elucidation of this distinction is crucially important in any critical response to the play, for it is the play's realism that creates an emotional framework for our responses, provides a background for the starkly

contrasting Absurdist strain, and lures us, through its familiarity, toward
the frightening and enlightening perceptions that inform the vision of the
poetic work. (31)

Bernstein's claim that realism is the backdrop to something other than
naturalist dogma is a claim that, possibly with the exception of *The
Orphan* (1973), applies to all of Rabe's major works, a fact that
Brustein and others seem to have missed.

Similar general confusion exists for Rabe's other Vietnam plays,
The Basic Training of Pavlo Hummel for example. The first work to
place Rabe in the national limelight, it is a play about a young man
looking for an identity and thinking that the military and its
regimentation is a niche into which he can fit. Harold Clurman
describes Pavlo, the central character:

> Pavlo Hummel is a dumb kid who doesn't wish to go to war but once
> there he wants to fight it "like a man" . . . . He's a fool, almost crackers,
> an amalgam of the innocent vices and stupid virtues of the universal
> unknown G.I. He's good-natured and atrocious. Around him are the other
> clumps of recognizable humanity, reduced to the point where they lose
> any identity except that of soldiers, food for slaughter, self-killers,
> ridiculous and terrible, victims who are also venomous. ("The Basic
> Training" 733)

The play makes it clear that Pavlo is deluded from the outset by a
misconception about what this institution can offer. One wonders
what any set of circumstances can offer him, a man looking for
external signposts to mark his identity when it is clear that there is
nothing in him that such signposts can signify. Society, in this case
represented by the military, offers him only an illusion of identity, and
he himself is unable to make any clear determinations as to what it
means to have an identity. Societal solutions to the "identity crisis" do
not bother to extend beneath surfaces. As Kerr notes of Pavlo, "He's
not really against the war; the war may give him an identity . . . . His
name isn't even Pavlo. It's Michael. He changed it because the father
who gave it to him deserted him; 'Pavlo' is his first try at being
someone else"("He Wonders Who He Is" 3). Peter Schjeldahl sums
up the dilemma Pavlo faces: "According to what models, and at what
cost, does one become a responsible man or woman--an 'adult'--in the
frustrated, disenchanted America of today?" (1). Vietnam may be a
focus, but a frustrated, disenchanted America is the actual topic.
There is no stability, no order, unless we are willing only to perceive
the surfaces.

Pavlo is looking for something he will not find. His dilemma--what
is it that makes a "good" soldier--amounts to being a more general
dilemma--what is it that makes a "good" man or woman. Society's
suggestions are clearly insufficient. In this play, more than in *Sticks
and Bones*, the fact that no answers are offered troubled many, Kerr
among them:

> If he [Pavlo] wonders who he is, so do we. If he dies before he can ever
> find out, so does the play. Long before a hand grenade gets him in a
> brothel, we have felt an indecision and inconclusiveness hovering over us.
> The play is like a current of air on a very hot night that teases us and then
> goes away. It lacks a discovery. ("He Wonders Who He Is" 3)

For Rabe there is no discovery to offer if "discovery" entails a
rationally outlined process. Rather Rabe is again showing us "this is
what goes on." If the word must be used, the "discovery" is that not
much *is* going on, at least not beneath the surfaces.

As suggested earlier, that these "war plays" are not just period pieces
reflecting the pains of the Vietnam experience is suggested by Rabe's
1973 play, *In the Boom Boom Room* (rewritten and produced 1974).
In the Boom Boom Room is an important work if for no other reason
than for the fact that it exhibits the same sense of hopelessness,
confusion, and despair of his Vietnam plays, but attributes this mood
to a central female character and sets the action in Philadelphia. The
result is that Rabe seems to be arguing that neither setting nor gender
distinctions have much bearing on the message of these works, though
Rabe is admittedly focusing on the lower social strata. Clurman
describes the work as "a rather crude but very real piece of writing,
angry and cruel, but true to the life of people at the bottom of the social
heap--which means a very considerable portion of our population"
("Boom Boom Room" 701). John Simon, however, restricts the
character's representative qualities much more severely:

> Chrissy, a troubled go-go girl scratching about for some meaning to her
> life, does not grow into the prototype of modern woman in search of her
> soul. Though some things about her ring touchingly true, she is
> inconsistent: sometimes too primitive, sometimes too sophisticated for
> the rest of her. Even her job is too specialized and quirky to anoint her
> readily as Everywoman; and the people she seeks comfort from are rather
> too spectacularly and excogitatedly unfeeling and exploitative. (62)

Though generally considered a failure, the efforts of the play reflect a
sense that lost souls pervade the modern American world and are not
restricted to one or the other gender; women as well as men can be
disenfranchised from and alienated by their America.

The play centers around Chrissy, a lost soul who, as Clive Barnes
summarizes,

> lives in the world of a sleazy go-go joint. She tries to get herself sexually
> together. She wonders whether she was ever sexually assaulted by her
> father or her uncles. (We never find out.) She tries to equate with men--
> she wants to be loved, and not just treated as a "hunk of meat." She tries
> to equate with an astrologically inclined square, a homosexual who works
> for a sperm bank, a truck driver and his mate, and has a lesbian flirtation
> with the dance captain back at the club. ("Boom Boom Room" 31)

Barnes concludes: "Nothing seems to work for her--and this seems quite clearly Mr. Rabe's fault," noting, among other things, "The dialogue aspires too frequently to the comforting jargon of T.V. serials" (31). Theatrically, the criticism *may* be sound, but thematically, such dialogue seems justified. This world is fraught with characters lost and confused, equipped only with such social tools as a medium like television can offer them.

Kerr also attacks *In the Boom Boom Room*, seeing the same faults in it as he saw in *The Basic Training of Pavlo Hummel*. In his review "We Leave the Girl as We Found Her," Kerr offers the following criticism, commenting about the staging first: "you are apt to notice at once how immobile, how unused, how *unnecessary* it is" (3). He adds, echoing Barnes's disappointment:

> The play won't budge because there is nothing that demands staging. Each solo passage, including Miss Kahn's [as Chrissy] bouts of soul-searching, would function as well on paper, or in a telephone booth. Indeed, we often feel that we are listening to one end of a phone conversation while another party is frantically, but vainly, trying to get through. When there is nothing to *watch* in a theatre, beware. The playwright's words must lack energy to provoke so little onstage response. (3)

This disappointment in finding no energy seems to indicate that Kerr is looking for some traditionally ordained growth and interaction in a play that is arguing that neither growth nor interaction are likely to occur.

These critics attack Rabe for putting together "an empty and poorly crafted play" (Barnes "Boom Boom Room" 31), and they are very likely correct in noting dissatisfaction with the untheatricality of the play--given their expectations. But it must be conceded that the very theme of the work forces Rabe into the dilemma either of compromising his "message" to include the expected theatrical elements of development and resolution or of remaining pure in his presentation and hoping his audience is willing to modify theatrical expectations. This latter strategy is not an altogether unreasonable expectation, given the anti-theatre and minimalist movements that have preceded Rabe's works and that have in fact been incorporated into mainstream theatre by many other writers. Rabe, though, seems willing to try to meet his audiences half way. Given this criticism of inaction in *In the Boom Boom Room*, Rabe chose an alternative course of action in *Streamers* (1976), moving away from fractured inactivity and turning to frenetic, though still fractured, action in the extreme.

With a few notable exceptions, most critics agree that *Streamers* is the play that Rabe's earlier works were leading up to. Alan Rich is a typical example: "*Streamers* is the great play that has been trying--in several guises and with several degrees of success--to burst out of

David Rabe in the five or so years he has been on the scene" (78). Gerald Weales suggests one reason for its success:

> The manipulative hand of the playwright can be seen occasionally . . . but not so obviously as in the earlier plays. This may be because *Streamers* is the most realistic of the Rabe plays, almost free of non-realistic devices of the earlier works which in effect invited the playwright on stage. ("Streamers" 334)

The audiences are presumably more comfortable with a straight realistic play, free of various experimental insertions such as the ghost of the Vietnamese girl found in *Sticks and Bones*. But as will become clear, such "simple" works become more subtle, and the work of the critic/audience becomes more demanding, something that in fact led to a sort of rebellion among certain audiences and a few notable critics as well.

At another level, though, Rabe's play, if not actually a complete success, at least makes one significant advance over his earlier works. *Streamers* expands the population he applies his philosophy to, reaching beyond the lower strata and embracing a full range of characters, thereby universalizing his vision as encapsulating a dilemma faced by all classes and groups of Americans. Brendan Gill describes the community, three enlisted men, that Rabe has brought together:

> They are Billy, a sympathetic, rather innocent fellow from Wisconsin; Roger, a black soldier who seems far more realistic and mature than the others and is a close friend of Billy's; and Richie, a well-to-do homosexual from Manhattan. (76)

The three men are living in harmony despite their culturally and geographically varied backgrounds; though not a complete cross-sample of American society, they do illustrate the fact that in America different lifestyles and backgrounds co-exist and must somehow comprise a single culture. Barnes notes, "they sound like stereotypes, and to an extent, probably to a deliberate extent, they are" ("David Rabe's 'Streamers'" 45). In this regard, these three men are representative of American culture. And as was seen in *Sticks and Bones*, Rabe's general thesis is that this culture can survive, almost thrive in its present state, but only when not really tested. Surface harmony initially exists in the play, as Gill reports: "Billy teases Rich some about his effeminacy, and Rich teases back; Roger does not quite believe it [that Richie is gay] or take it very seriously. None of his business anyway" (76). But in this play, as in *Sticks and Bones*, Rabe has clearly set up this initial harmony with the distinct intention of creating what Kerr saw was missing in the other two works-- development, resolution and possibly even self-awareness. First, as noted earlier, Rabe utilizes realistic techniques "almost free of the non-realistic devices of the earlier works" (Weales, "Streamers" 334). Barnes elaborates: "[H]is earlier produced work has always been of somewhat elusive symbolism and tricky time changes. Here he is telling a plain tale plainly" ("David Rabe's 'Streamers'" 45). The set itself is simply a barracks on a military post in Virginia in 1965, a time when "the worst of the war still lies ahead," as Gill notes, adding, "The room itself seems an oasis of civilization" (76).

Into this oasis first intrude two grizzled sergeants who build a certain degree of tension, which in turn sets the stage for the more threatening intruder, Carlyle. Gill describes Carlyle as "half out of his mind with anger and frustration after three months on K.P. He never lets up on Richie, and it is he who precipitates the terrible, bloody climax of the play" (76). The climax is the point at which Rabe's theme is revealed, but once again some confusion exists among critics and audiences. Carlyle physically attacks a verbally abusing Billy, who has discovered Carlyle and Rich sexually engaged on the barracks floor. Billy's verbal abuse seems justified and in turn may very well be a justification for a response of some sort by the other two men, in accordance with naturalist prescription. But Carlyle's multiple slashing of Billy is an overly violent response, an irrational and finally unjustified one. Blood flows. Added to this violence, Carlyle attacks one of the sergeants who, drunk and unaware, stumbles onto the scene. Nowhere in the play has the audience been prepared for this climax. Kerr reports that this carnage was enough to cause audiences angrily to leave performances of the play during its early run in New Haven. At the performance he attended, Kerr witnessed several among the audience unobtrusively leave during the first two assaults on Billy, but when the sergeant was finally attacked,

> the atmosphere in the auditorium changed radically, boiled over. A rather substantial portion of the audience got to its feet noisily, not hesitating to call out to companions to join them in leaving, stomping purposefully across the thin space that separates stage from spectators in this most intimate arena theater, venting their spleen openly. Some hurled their programs onto the acting space in a clear show of contempt. ("When Does Gore Get Gratuitous?" 7)

Rabe observes that part of the reason for such behavior could have been that audiences feared that Carlyle "was going to get them next" (Savran 202). Later audiences, forewarned, were less extreme in their reactions but experienced roughly similar discomfort. And critics almost invariably responded to the bloody climax by noting discomfort as well but usually also by defending that climax. Gill says, "This climax seems almost gratuitous, yet it is integral to the story; nothing is done purely for effect" (76). Barnes essentially agrees, but expands on why the climax may be labelled gratuitous and is more specific about what Gill calls "the story":

He [Rabe] is not above cheap effects--nor is Mr. Nichols [the director]--and neither eschews the obvious. The drama deliberately sets out to shock--it uses more tomato ketchup than a B feature gangster movie--and quite often its mixture of joshing playfulness and harrowing horror does seem over-contrived. It is a play and a production that seek to manipulate that audience--but deep at the back of it lies Mr. Rabe's metaphor of death as an accidental joke. ("David Rabe's 'Streamers'" 45)

Theatrically the climax is literally "overkill," though thematically it is consistent. But it seems with the following explanation, Barnes overzealously and inaccurately defends Rabe. He argues that the play is

a concatenation of events, a veritable domino reaction, that with the implacable tread of a Greek tragedy leaves two . . . dead, a third dying (of leukemia), and two others appalled and transfigured. ("David Rabe's 'Streamers'" 45)

Death as an accident cannot be illustrated "with the implacable tread of a Greek tragedy." If causality is in fact perceived, then Barnes contradicts himself and seemingly misinterprets the play. If, however, Barnes is arguing something less than inevitability and that the play's craftsmanship is such that it simply leads to the possibility of the actual climax--one of many possible climaxes--then his statement is defensible.

Kerr's assessment is less ambiguous, taking a stance critical of Rabe's craft, conceding that the climax is necessary, but not that he (Kerr) should like it:

[The play's climax] must repel for a reason, a reason that seems not to rear its head in hundreds and hundreds of other plays and films.

It repels because it promises no reward. By "reward" I certainly don't mean happy ending, a convenient sentimentalization of the situation, and ultimate moralistic statement that will square away everything. What the audience asks for is a pattern, a design, a shape that will embrace what they are now looking at and place it in significant relationship to what has gone before and what may come after. ("When Does Gore Get Gratuitous?" 7)

Kerr later adds, "[W]e aren't being prepared to accept the eventualities that take place as in any way necessary" (7). Kerr's major criticism of Rabe, as suggested above, is that Rabe has still failed to find a sufficient structure or stage metaphor that can capture his vision:

He has not yet found one that will say to us precisely what he sees. And so he has simply put death senseless on the stage. But the stage, with its ancient and constant urge toward ordering experience, will not entirely tolerate that. (7)

Barnes concedes that the play is heavy-handed but argues that it proceeds consistently and with a single vision to its inevitable climax. Kerr argues that the craft is lacking and that the play fails since it is so constructed as in no way to prepare the audience for the climax--it proceeds erratically. One reason the two critics come to such different conclusions is that neither critic, it seems, has fully drawn the necessary distinction between notions of craft used to conform to convention (as anticipated by the audience) and craft used for thematic realization. If, as Barnes argues, Rabe's craftsmanship acceptably captures Rabe's thematic bent, it does not necessarily follow that the play must lead irrefutably and fatally to its resolution, especially if the refutation of inevitability is the issue. Rabe seems to be arguing that this is the state of existence, that modern existence is such that it can never be assumed that one series of events will lead, predictably, to another. Barnes's allusion to the "implacable tread of Greek tragedy" inaccurately describes the very theme that Barnes himself attributes to the play--death as an accidental joke. The march of tragedy entails there being a guiding hand. Rabe does not see a guiding hand moving world events. If the world is governed at all, the word "govern" must be used ironically, and only then would Rabe be able to say it is governed by randomness and an attendant violence stemming from frustration that the world has been misrepresented as ordered and harmonious.

Where Barnes's failure to distinguish the concerns of theme and craft led to an inconsistent description of the theme, Kerr's similar failure has virtually led him to arguing that Rabe's theme is impossible to dramatize. If the play must be so crafted as *necessarily* to lead to its climax, then Rabe's theme, the randomness of action, cannot possibly be presented on stage because the events could not "follow" in a manner anticipated by the audience. It seems that both Kerr and Barnes (though Barnes to a far lesser degree), when confronted by an essentially well-made and realistic play, assume that tenets of necessity and inevitability must follow. And so it may well have been the assumption of *Streamers*'s earlier audiences in New Haven.

Kerr, however, does offer a valuable insight into the breaking down of these prejudices toward well-made, realistic plays. Kerr's above comments come from a February 22, 1976, review of the New Haven premiere of *Streamers*. On May 2, 1976, Kerr published a review of the Broadway opening of the play, a production he called "tighter, emotionally clearer" ("David Rabe's 'House'" 5). The polish is an important craft aspect that Kerr acknowledges, but possibly Kerr's modified position on the play is a result of being prepared for and therefore more willing to modify his expectations. At the heart of his criticism of the earlier production is his initial unwillingness to accept various of the play's metaphors as relevant, thematically unifying factors. Of the New Haven experience he writes:

[T]he blow, when it comes, is a blow beneath the belt, gratuitous; the characters don't deserve it, the audience doesn't understand it.

Symbols offered along the way don't help. The title, for instance, refers to parachutes that fail to open, hanging "like big icicles right straight up above" the men falling to their deaths . . . . But which of the characters is victim of the mechanical failure, and why? The Vietcong soldier trapped with a grenade in a closed pit sounds like a possible symbol for suppressed homosexuality; is it, and if it is not, what *does* it mean to be given so much talking-time? ("When Does Gore Get Gratuitous?" 7)

Rabe has included these "signposts" for a reason, and finding answers to the above questions would most likely help one to evaluate the play as a whole and even to conclude that the play *is* finally crafted in a "tighter" and "clearer" manner than Kerr first thought. Several critics have in fact come to conclusions about the symbols, conclusions that provide valid answers to Kerr's questions. Barnes suggests that the "streamer" metaphor answers a key question the play poses:

What is violence? . . . No, not in Southeast Asia, but in the ordinary, deadly practices of everyday life? What are the promptings of seemingly illogical murder--the moment when mind and hands become derailed and irrational? . . .

Mr. Rabe's purpose is to show the face of violence. He takes the interlinking themes of two minorities--homosexuals and blacks--and indicates the sudden awful pressures that can detonate a disaster.

He offers as his symbol the army parachutist who careens to the ground when his parachute--for no apparent reason--fails to open . . . . We are all, Mr. Rabe is suggesting, subject to streamers as people and--remember the moral pattern of the Vietnam trilogy--as a nation. Violence is, indeed, as American as apple pie. ("Streamers" 38)

So for Barnes, it has become less important to ask Kerr's question, "[W]ho is the victim of the mechanical failure, and why?" than it is to notice that the unpredictable and random nature of the experience is a pervasive fact of life for all.

And Weales offers an explanation for the anecdote about the grenade. The drunk Sergeant Coker, in the final scene,

tells again the story of how he rolled a grenade into a hole and sat on the metal lid while the enemy soldier inside tried to get out before it exploded. It was like an old comedy, he says, with Charlie Chaplin as the man in the hole, but he didn't know who he was. The listening soldier suggests that he, too, may have been Charlie Chaplin . . . . *Streamers* offers a world of clown killers and clown victims in which, eventually, everyone's parachute refuses to open. ("Streamers" 335)

For Weales, then, the anecdote is not a symbol for suppressed homosexuality, as Kerr proposes. It is a symbol of the cruelty and pervasive inhumanity that one risks experiencing by merely being human.

In his review of the "tighter" New York production, Kerr seems at least implicitly to acknowledge the above metaphors as actually saying something similar to what is explained above, but he adds to these thoughts: "What I think he [Rabe] is saying is simple, simpler than the multiple symbols he keeps offering us to explain the bloody violence he invariably arrives at" ("David Rabe's 'House'" 5). Kerr continues:

> The actual message, if I read it correctly, is this. We are all--black, white, straight, queer, parents, children, friends, foes, stable, unstable-- living together in the same "house." And we can't do it . . . .
> In "Streamers" . . . three buddies and one interloper reach out to one another in a variety of ways; but the variety is too varied for comfort or safety and, in this smallest of small worlds where adaptation should be feasible, a knife is suddenly drawn to turn the "house" into a slaughterhouse. (5)

Kerr has fairly hit on Rabe's theme. This barracks set as a whole is a violently failed community that is a microcosm of the nation.

Seeing and accepting the theme of the play, Kerr then re-evaluates what he saw of audience responses. He first makes one important note: "Though the mass desertion that startled me the night I saw 'Streamers' in New Haven now proves to have been an isolated occasion, there are still solo escapes taking place"(5). Perhaps the New York audiences were more accommodating and less predisposed to an opinion than those in New Haven, but audience discomfort still existed. They experienced what Kerr argues even he still felt: "The wantonness takes us aback, insults our sense of dramatic coherence" ("David Rabe's 'House'" 5). But he acknowledges that the play effects Rabe's end, for

> that [wantonness], in turn, forces us to face up to Mr. Rabe's sense of life, of our joint occupancy of the "house." Our attempts to live together in this universe with some chance of ultimate harmony are hopeless. For our flare-ups are irrational, in excess of any possible motive. We violate one another at random simply because we *are* here and because we are what we are. We *cannot* coexist. Or so the pits of our stomachs tell us as we sit in numb horror. (5)

Finally, the "symbols" that Kerr criticizes are symbols that support his own claim. Streamers themselves suggest that nature randomly and cruelly destroys, and the grenade anecdote shows that humanity has perversely chosen to imitate nature.

Rabe's work is a pessimistic one, and this element, Kerr concludes, is what upsets him. In fact he feels it is the same factor that has caused general audience discomfort. So it seems that Kerr has accurately concluded that it is not Rabe's craft that disappoints as much as it is the effects of the theme which that craft presents. What causes discomfort is not merely that Rabe fails to adhere to naturalist techniques, but rather that he challenges an audience that is comfortable and secure in naturalist ways of viewing the world. Finally, the problem is less merely a theatrical one than it is a philosophical one. Kerr ends his review with the following summary:

> That we cannot coexist, that man cannot make a home of the universe, may be true. It is not a customary dramatic truth. Normally, no matter what ghastly things men and women may be seen doing to one another, we assume a possible rectitude, a natural inner harmony that has been temporarily and intelligibly shattered but can nonetheless be restored; we may not always see it restored in a play, but we are permitted to scent its return, accept its existence as a postulate.
> Not here. And so, to the degree that we admire the play, to the degree that we believe in it, we despair. We may take a considerable admiration home with us, as I do. But how many of us are willing to make a bedmate of despair? (David Rabe's 'House'" 5)

Kerr longs for an ordered vision reminiscent of classical tragedy and even seems to echo the mistaken assessment of Barnes: Kerr longs to see the "implacable tread of a Greek tragedy." And in the scientific, modern world where classical tragic perception is outdated, naturalist dogma has been created to fill the void. But increasingly, we see that such perceptions of order are inaccurate. Rabe's works are efforts to make us see the inaccuracies, and in making us see, he must shatter our biases. With *Streamers*, it seems, the opposition is softening.

Goose and Tomtom followed, produced at the Public Theatre (New York) in 1982. For various reasons Rabe disavowed this production, which Mel Gussow called "an impecunious caper comedy" (17). It is a play about two small-time crooks that moves from a realistic to a surrealistic mode, almost without warning. Though the play went through rehearsal again in 1986, it has still not been given full public exposure in a manner that has satisfied Rabe. For all its theatrical imperfections, however, the play continues to pursue Rabe's earlier general thesis, even going as far as having a *deus ex machina* pronounce Rabe's vision:

> We suspected that we were not the center of all territories, but we lived as if we were . . . . From those of us who squatted to pee, duplicates of ourselves would sometimes drop, squalling and clinging up into the secret place where divinities mingled with entrails and the cord of life ran backward as if through all time to the mystery . . . . We struggle to explain ourselves to those we destroy and we are dismayed. (116-117)

Goose and Tomtom has not proven to be the vehicle Rabe had hoped, but, as with the rest, it seemed to help him better develop the means to articulate his vision.

Though Rabe's earlier works may have failed for one reason or another, his strengths increased. With *Streamers* Rabe subjected his perceptions of the world to direct confrontation with the world he was challenging--the naturalist world--by using a straight realistic mode of presentation. His work rattled a complacent and confident theatre world into re-evaluating its social as well as theatrical biases. Rabe's next major work, *Hurlyburly* (1984), follows up on *Streamers*'s first assault, and it received critical acclaim in the process. As noted above, until *Hurlyburly*, a vocal segment of the theatre world looked at Rabe as a writer who, "lacking texture and amplitude . . . fails to convince" (Hertzbach 185). But *Hurlyburly* adds texture and amplitude to Rabe's body of work. For one, Rabe focuses on a character, Eddie, who thrives on rationalist endeavors, naturalist assumptions. The effect of giving such a predisposition to a central character is that the audience is given a sort of spokesman on stage, capable of voicing dismay when various disjunctions in action occur. Rabe has given a character the audience's tools to try to work through the actions of the play, and when/if those explanations fail, Rabe then works to demonstrate why. Such a design may in fact be a response to criticism such as Barnes and Kerr voiced about Rabe's earlier efforts; whatever the specific motive, however, this adjustment in Rabe's craft seems a conscientious effort to clarify former misconceptions.

Another way that Rabe adds texture and amplitude is by creating a contemporary American "battlefield" free from trappings of uniforms and war so customary in his earlier works. The set of *Hurlyburly* is a "civilized" and "sophisticated" upper middle-class Hollywood bungalow, a seeming bastion of security from the ravages of war. An audience will experience no confusing signals prompted by a Vietnam backdrop. If violence presents itself in these surroundings, the source (Vietnam in most other cases) cannot be so comfortably and mistakenly identified as a physical location geographically distant from our front doors. Violence and chaos may be expected and integral ingredients in war, on a military post, and maybe even in a Philadelphia slum; but in *Hurlyburly* Rabe argues that there is no basic difference between an army barracks (or a sleazy strip joint) and a community that houses an industry that produces America's image of itself--Hollywood. In essence, Rabe has come one major step closer to arguing the indigenous pervasiveness of such hostility throughout American culture.

His very choice and description of the set in *Hurlyburly* suggests that interconnecting the two worlds is his intention. After describing the interior of the bungalow that will serve as the set, Rabe adds to the description: "The house is completely surrounded by wild vegetation, which is visible through greenhouse-like windows in the living room and kitchen" (13). Frank Rich notes the significance of this aspect, as he saw it in its New York production:

"Hurlyburly" is set in the Hollywood Hills--seemingly a world apart from the Vietnam-era Army base of the last Rabe-Nichols [the play's director] collaboration, "Streamers." But the tropical villa designed with seedy elan by Tony Walton might as well be a barracks, and the battles haven't entirely changed. (3)

With this change of venue, Rabe can avoid what often plagued his earlier works, the mistaken notion that it is merely proximity to war and violence that propagates even more war and violence. Now he is clearly arguing that violence is human baggage that one carries wherever one goes. The war is as severe at home as it is when exported abroad, though perhaps less overtly perceptible. It is a symptom that identifies the very irrational element in American culture which so many strive to deny. Rational posturing has deluded us into believing we are somehow following a scheme of responsible behavior.

Added to this invitation to comparison by the set is a specific statement of design by Rabe in the play's "Afterword": the play is to confront naturalism directly, complete with the attendant philosophy. Rabe states that one of the reasons he wrote *Hurlyburly*

was an impulse to venture near at least the appearances of the so-called "realistic" or "well-made" play, which in my view is that form which thinks that cause and effect are proportionate and clearly apparent, that people know what they are doing as they do it, and that others react accordingly, that one thing leads to another in a rational, mechanical way, a kind of Newtonian clock of a play, a kind of Darwinian assemblage of detail which would then determine the details that must follow, the substitution of the devices of logic for the powerful sweeps of pattern and energy that is our lives. (162)

His play will by "appearances" be realistic, he says. In fact his play *is* both realistic and well-made, but it carries none of the naturalistic conviction that he above identifies as realism. Causal connections, etc., are what he plans to undermine. In essence, without clearly drawing the distinction in terms (as noted earlier, a problem in itself), Rabe claims that he plans to attack naturalist philosophy, and he is going to use realism to do it. Rabe wants to show the failings of the old assumptions and find a form that is free from the trappings of old ideas. *Hurlyburly* strips Darwin and Newton from realism, which in turn ironically illustrates the fact that realism itself is exactly the form that Rabe has been looking for to portray those new ideas.

For *Hurlyburly*, the key term in Rabe's above discussion of realism is "logic," or more specifically the phrase "substitution of the devices of logic for the powerful sweeps of pattern and energy that is our lives." The terms "logic" and "logical" are used in the play no less than twelve times, and related terms like "syllogism," "induction," and "deduction" are used throughout as well. They comprise the common vocabulary, in fact, of all the characters, with the exception of Bonnie, a drifter not yet part of the Hollywood scene. The characters constantly explain or analyze their actions in logical terms, often aligned with weak Freudian speculations. Appeals to "common sense," "reason," and "dialectic exchange" abound. This world, where the inhabitants are self-described as "sophisticated," is founded on the belief that the "devices of logic" explain and even control action and events. Philip C. Kolin notes, "In their [the characters'] 'California speak,' an amalgam of post-Freudian snippets and convoluted constructions, they ask an endless series of questions hoping to stumble onto meaning, groping to find the answer that makes the question worthwhile" (67). In the play, language itself is a focus and eventually becomes Rabe's focus of attack. In essence, Rabe attacks the "logic" of language, which in turn undermines the foundation of logic itself, which is itself the cornerstone of Darwinian and Newtonian reason and which, finally, have provided the key sources of ideas upon which naturalism is founded. What Rabe confronts seems nearly unmanageable, but his attack clearly extends to all these elements.

Hurlyburly additionally presents a world clouded by drugs and dominated by television, which upon first inspection, may seem to be the focus of the play. Kolin, for example, notes that "*Hurlyburly* may win an award for presenting more 'pharmaceutical experiments' on stage than any other American play" (65). Drugs certainly do pervade the play, and attention must be given to their effects. But Rabe uses the play to point out more than an unfortunate pervasiveness of drugs in our culture. He places drugs in such a dominant position to set up a parallel point that takes center stage by the end of the play, namely that in a world muddied by these various forms of self-deception, the belief in logic and reason is the ultimate and perhaps most dangerous form of self-deception, far more dangerous, finally, than drugs themselves.

As was the case with Chrissy (in *In the Boom Boom Room*) and Pavlo Hummel, the characters in *Hurlyburly* appear to be losers who lack the qualities to be deemed representatives of any "normal" universal condition. Speaking of Eddie, the central character, Michael Feingold observes that Rabe wanted the character

> to carry the weight of a tragic hero . . . , wrecked at the end by his lotus-sniffing inability to save the friend he loves from destroying himself, all of which is supposed to carry some moral meaning having to do with American society and the neutron bomb--two things of which I doubt any L.A. casting director has ever heard. (96)

According to Feingold, Rabe's lofty goals are not achieved in *Hurlyburly*. But to that criticism that the characters fail as representative (and conscientious) Americans, Rabe could argue that they *are* representatives, though perhaps extreme examples of what can happen to any of us. The two roommates of the bungalow, Eddie and Mickey, are intelligent and ambitious, full of the material that typically makes for success stories. But their private lives--and the lives of all in the play--have crumbled, and their professional existences lack any harmony whatsoever. Though they all use drugs, it's not counter-culture chemicals of a lost generation that attract them; it's the sleek, fast-lane items, of which cocaine is king, and without which business is rarely conducted. So though human frailty may be one source of their failure, the shortcomings of society must once again accept at least partial responsibility. These people, after all, aren't working outside the social fabric but are operating very much within its confines. Rabe, in fact, works to make the point clear that the root of the characters' overall problems is that they've bought into societal prescription of certain behavior, defended by a manipulation of seemingly logical explanations. In the case of *Hurlyburly*, the study centers on men. Rabe explains:

> It's such a weird thing society asks of men . . . . It asks them to go into a domestic thing and yet it nurtures this other thing. Most guys are given the double message by the society. "Be hard, think clear, don't let emotion muddy your thoughts, sleeping around is a good thing." And at the same time, you're told to have your feelings available, be a good father. So you take the guys in this play [*Hurlyburly*], who have all been flung out of their marriages. They're all back in this adolescence. They have the bitterness and disappointment of having failed. (Freedman, "Rabe and the War at Home" 13)

Society no longer extends a sense of security to these men who have failed by doing more or less what society prescribed for them. Cast adrift, such men are equipped with tools that society now rejects as insufficient in dealing with the world. They must adapt or perish in a forbidding, strange, new world that they somehow entered without even having taken a step from their own neighborhoods.

Part of the critics' failure to see or accept these intentions stems from problems with the Broadway production itself, according to Rabe. Rabe notes that director Mike Nichols "blocked the play so that his story was different from the story of the text" (Savran 200). The central character, Eddie, is a man debating the virtues of the world views of two friends, Phil and Mickey. But, according to Rabe, Nichols "made a play that put Eddie in the Mickey role. He cut everything about Phil that could make him interesting or complex or vulnerable and tried to turn him into a total creep" (Savran 200-201). Through such a move, the dramatic tension in the play was reduced to a struggle among aimless antagonists, none of whom displayed any genuine concern about conditions into which they were thrust.

In the "Afterword" to the play, Rabe abstracts his purpose, outlining goals that the production failed to highlight:

I remember beginning *Hurlyburly* with an impulse that took its shape, at least partly, in a mix of feelings spawned in my own experiences and also from my observations of the prices some men were paying from within their varied armored and defended stances--the current disorientation and accompanying anger many feel at having been flung out from the haven of their sexual and marital contexts and preoccupations . . . . Around me, and within myself, I felt I saw the wild reactions of creatures who had been recently given the good news that they had brutalized large portions of themselves for a disreputable cause, and now, if only they would quickly change, they would find fulfillment. Trained to control their feelings and think, they must now stop thinking and feel. (161)

The men are trapped in actions that forbid fulfillment, and are victims of logical devices that continue to uphold and defend such actions, with violence even, if necessary. Though Nichols's production reduced the conflict to a sort of "lotus-sniffing" inertia, the text of the play itself does dramatize these failings much more particularly than his other works have, and does so mainly through the insertion of a conscience-ridden Eddie. Finally, this play has an immediacy that is less confused by such peripheral distractions as the Vietnam War; the play works to engage its audience rather than shock and alienate it; and through that engagement, the play uncovers/uproots specific misconceptions instilled in the audience, as evidenced by its desire for naturalist-rooted explanations.

The characters in the play are also the products of these various misconceptions, men and women who have assumed their roles--in the extreme--as prescribed by society. And these extreme personalities, testing the system to the extreme, illustrate the failings of that system which typically functions well when left untested. The opening scene of the play illustrates the system at work, one mastered by Eddie. Phil, the first to accept his "lost soul" status comes to Eddie's bungalow to talk to and get advice from Eddie about a fight Phil had had with his wife, Susie. Phil is distraught, cannot imagine how he will survive if Susie leaves him. But before he fully describes the fight, Phil inadvertently confesses that Susie said she hated Eddie as well. Surprised that Susie does not like him as he had thought, Eddie, now personally involved, is absorbed into the discussion, not to help Phil but to uncover Susie's actual opinion of himself. His ego has been challenged, and he must find an explanation that upholds his socially prescribed behavior and reveals the flaws in Susie's thinking. Up to this point Eddie has shown a cool, abstract interest in Phil's very real anxieties and concerns, but upon the discovery of Susie's hatred of him, defenses are activated and Phil's serious problems are forgotten, Eddie's interests heightened. Eddie instantly attacks: "I mean, what is she, a goddamn schizophrenic, here? Is this a goddamn psychotic we've been dealing with here?" (16). Delving for a possible psychological explanation, Eddie moves into an analysis of the situation:

I mean, did she have a point of reference, some sort of reference from within your blowup out of which she made some goddamn association which was for her justification that she come veering off to dump all this unbelievable vituperative horseshit over me--whatever it was. I wanna get it straight. (17)

Looking for answers, Eddie has completely forgotten the emotional plea of Phil and in fact sweeps Phil into his own frame of mind. Eddie first goes into his own "logical" generalization of the situation: "She's sad. They're all sad. They're all fucking crazy" (18). And then, literally first to introduce the term "logic" into the play, Phil explains: "We're friends. You know. So she thinks we got somethin' in common. It's logical" (18). They then turn to attack Susie, using their insights about logic and logical fallacies, fallacies they themselves have emotionally become victim to (hasty generalizations, for example). Phil explains that the reason for the fight had something to do with a drug-induced scheme to beat the odds in Las Vegas that he was explaining to her. Eddie, still absorbed, begins the following exchange:

EDDIE: But it would be logical that if this petty, cheap-shot animosity was in the vicinity of Vegas, it would have to do with Vegas. THAT WOULD ONLY BE LOGICAL.
PHIL: EXCEPT SHE AIN'T LOGICAL. (22)

Having identified the fallacy in Susie's thought as he perceives it, Eddie concludes, "She hates men," explaining, "She hates you, she hates me. She hates men. I don't know what else to think. It's a goddamn syllogism. Susie hates Phil, Susie hates Eddie. She hates men" (22). He further describes what he sees to be Susie's reasoning:

The fucker's irrefutable, except that's not how it works, GODDAMNIT . . . . You go from the general to the particular. I'm talking about a syllogism, here . . . . What the hell goes the other way? . . . You start from the particular in something. (22)

Then he hits upon it:

Oh my god, do you know what it is? . . . Science! What goes the other way is science, in which you see all the shit like data and go from it to the law. This is even better. We have just verified, and I mean scientifically, the bitch has been proven to basically hate all men. She doesn't need a reason to hate me in particular--she already hates me in the fucking abstract. (22-23)

Eddie's logic has exonerated him personally from any blame, and he concludes, "Now that I understand the situation, the hell with her. The bitch wants to go around hating me in the fucking abstract!" (23). He has taken the experience and manipulated it into a logical framework which in turn allows him to keep his strangely ordered view of experience intact. Of course, the logic has been perversely--and comically--twisted in this instance. But the point remains, that the tools are used to uphold a system, in this case one of sophisticated machismo (Eddie being the paradigm). In fact, the men have been trained to believe that one serves the other. And if the men hadn't twisted the logic to their satisfaction, then a true crisis would have arisen and a solution not easily found. In that case, the conclusions could either have been that logic is flawed or that their insulated lifestyle is delusion. Either choice would shatter the fragile harmony of their lives, so the comic outcome bypasses a crisis, at least at this point in the play.

Unlike Eddie, Phil has conceded that he has lost control of life. This concession in turn leads Phil to search for some means of re-establishing order, or of at least gaining some understanding. Seeing Eddie surviving comfortably behind his logic, Phil tries to understand its power. But Phil's passions cannot be harnessed by the old systems, and as a result, he is, involuntarily, rather ironically, the one who infuses a troubling but very real vitality into this artificially constructed world. The other male characters are virtual zombies compared to the life-engulfing turmoil found in Phil. For these others, the answer seems to involve reducing life experiences to conform to their systems of understanding rather than, like Phil, engaging life experiences and looking for alternative ways to understand them. But if Phil is perhaps more "primitive" a character than the others, far less adequately adept on a social level, at least he is truer to himself as a result.

Though Phil is a man prone to "absurd" bursts of violence, losses of control that he cannot explain, he wants and needs to understand, to be able to explain. Attaching himself to the secure and controlled Eddie, Phil, too, has bought into--or wants to buy into--the system. He admits to having received psychological help when he was once imprisoned for an outburst of violence, but to no avail. Finally, it seems neither form of reason--pure, though now twisted, logic nor the application of logic through analysis--can help Phil. At another crisis point (one included in the published text, but not in the Broadway production), Phil confronts Eddie looking for answers and shakes the foundation of Eddie's ordered world with his own insights:

PHIL: . . . . I mean, we got these dark thoughts, I see 'em in you, you don't think you're thinkin' 'em, so we can't even nail that down, how we going to get beyond it? They are the results of your unnoticed inner goings-on or my gigantic paranoia, both of which exist, so the goddamn thing in its entirety is on the basis of what has got to be called a coin toss.
EDDIE: I can figure it, I can--It's not a goddamn coin toss.
PHIL: You think I'm being cynical when I say that? Nothing is necessary, Eddie. Not a fucking thing! We're in the hands of something, it could kill us now or later, it don't care. Who is this guy that makes us

> just--you know--WHAT? . . . THERE'S A WORD FOR IT--. . . . IT'S
> LIKE A LAW. IT IS A LAW. WHAT'S A LAW? WHAT THE FUCK
> IS A LAW? (70)

Phil has come to the conclusion, it seems, that the end of reason leads itself to the conclusion that reason does not exist, except as artifice. Certainly the logic that Eddie utilizes has become little more than self-justifying artifice. For Phil, if inevitability exists as a law, it is paradoxically governed by randomness, stripping the term "law" of any conventional meaning. Phil ends his speech:

> The fucking thing is without a clue, except the mess it leaves behind it,
> the guts and gore. What I'm sayin' is, if my conclusion is contrary to
> your wishes, at least give me the fucking consideration and respect that
> you know that at least from my point of view it is based on solid thought
> and rock hard evidence that has led me to I have no other choice. (70)

"Rock hard evidence" is Phil's foundation, life experienced rather than, say, existence neatly packaged. This attack silences Eddie. Ironically the argument itself that the world is chaos may not convince, but a more disconcerting argument built into the speech may. Logic, a tool designed to reveal "truth," has just been manipulated not to find *the* truth but one variation of truth--apparently one of many. The belief that logic can deduce truth is challenged; it has become a tool in this case used to support two points of view, which by extension suggests it can defend virtually any prior conclusion submitted. Logic is revealed to be an insufficient tool in gathering what both men seem to desire. Where Phil concedes this point, Eddie thus far remains adamant about the objective usefulness of his logic.

Eddie's roommate, Mickey, is a character who seems to have deferred finding meaning in life, instead deciding to manipulate the chaotic situation for personal gain. He has apparently long since reached a point about truth and logic that Phil has just reached, and he is thriving at this stage in the amorality that ensues from such a revelation. For example, having taken out Eddie's new girlfriend and spent the night with her, Mickey delights in taking a logical stance against Eddie to defend an otherwise clearly unethical act:

> I just--I mean, from my point of view, the point is--the main point is, I
> asked . . . . That--in my opinion--is the paramount issue, the crucial
> issue. And I don't want it forgotten . . . . Couldn't you have categorically,
> definitively said "no" when I asked? But you said--"Everybody's free,
> Mickey." That's what you said. (32)

Mickey has used the logic to justify a seemingly unjustifiable action. Unlike Phil, Mickey has come to revel in a world that claims a logical structure and refuses to admit it does not correspond to experience or even to some "pre-rational" sense of morality. It is exactly this discrepancy that traps Eddie. Eddie is upset with Mickey but can do nothing. Eddie has already stoically asserted that he is not seriously attracted to the girl, dispensing with feelings in a manner that allows Mickey to manipulate Eddie's logical abstractions and macho dispassion. At this point Eddie cannot, or refuses to, admit that his rational conclusions do not correspond to his feelings. He argues with Mickey, but within the parameters they have established, Eddie is doomed to lose the argument, though shortly after winning, Mickey cunningly returns the girl. Where Phil struggles with his discovery about the world and man's system to understand it, and where Eddie refuses to see the "new" world, Mickey has adapted and thrives with his new-found powers to manipulate this apparent period of transition.

Eddie remains wedded to his world of logic and reason, even in his relationship with the girl, Darlene. Where the context forbids him to confess his "irrational" affection for her to Mickey, a similar barrier separates Eddie and Darlene. Darlene is a woman who has bought into the Hollywood business as none of the men's wives and ex-wives have. As such, the relationship between Eddie and Darlene differs from any of the men's prior relationships. Where the other relationships failed presumably because the men rationally controlled their emotions, this relationship fails because Darlene, the "new woman," has foolishly become little more than a female version of the men, in order to "succeed." She analyzes her emotions as abstractly as the coolest of male logicians. Speaking of an earlier pregnancy and not knowing which of two lovers was the father, she describes the trauma:

> I liked them both. A lot. Which in a way made the whole thing even more confusing on a personal level, and you know, in terms of trying to figure out the morality of the whole thing, so I finally had this abortion . . . . I kept thinking in my mind that it wasn't a complete baby, which it wasn't, not a fully developed person, but a fetus which it was, and that I would have what I would term a real child later. (131)

Like the men in the play, Darlene's mind is cluttered with rationalizations and abstractions similar to the men's, though she articulates them differently than they do. Feeling is subverted to enable her, superfluously, to "think in her mind" (136). And psychological analysis has apparently further cluttered her mind. She attacks Eddie for his "Paranoia . . . . Be alert. Your tendencies are coming out all over the place" (136). And she defends herself for not being able to decide whether to dine at a Chinese or French restaurant because they are not really different "in my inner subjective, emotional experience of them" (136). If it is at all possible for her to feel, her language has forced her to reduce her expressions of those feelings to formulaic phrases.

That neither Eddie nor Darlene can relate to each other, and that the relationship is doomed to failure comes in what Frank Rich calls "Mr. Rabe's *pièce de résistance*," scene 3 of Act I, where "the couple's ever phonier declarations of sentiment are belied by ever lewder acts of disrobing" (3). As they disrobe, they declaim:

> DARLENE: . . . I think I was, you know, into some form of obsession about you . . . some form of mental loop . . . . I mean a year ago, I was a basket case. If we had met a year ago, I wouldn't have had a prayer.
> EDDIE: Me, too. A year ago, I was nuts. And I still have all kinds of things to think through. Stuff coming up, I have to think it through.
> DARLENE: Me, too . . . . We both need space.
> EDDIE: And time. We have to have time.
> DARLENE: Right. So we can just take the time to allow the emotional space for things to grow and work themselves out.
> EDDIE: So you wanna fuck? (55-57)

Despite the distance between the two, there is a strong hint that Eddie needs Darlene, but much later when he confesses his despair over the relationship to a third party and is asked to explain, he takes the offensive yet again:

> Is that some sort of arcane, totally off-the-wall, otherworldly sentiment that I am some oddity to find distressing so that nobody to whom I mention it has any personal reference by which they can understand me? What is going on here? My girlfriend doesn't love me. (119)

Even his twistedly formal syntax argues against his expressions being the result of heartfelt emotions. Emotions may be (and apparently are) there, but expression of that feeling is at best incomplete.

Mickey can at least momentarily thrive in the disjunctive world he experiences and feels no need to find a fuller understanding than to accept its chaotic pace. Phil needs much more and cannot accept seeing the world as Mickey sees it, but he hasn't the capacity to succeed. Eddie insists on making the world fit his preconceived constructs, still believes in them if for no other reason than the fact that they are the only constructs he has.

Eddie's world view having failed to convince Phil, and Mickey's world view being unacceptable to him, Phil turns to Artie, another friend, Jewish, who explains the world of destiny as found in the system of karma: "You have debts and credits and you have to work your way out from under the whole thing" (83). Not convinced because it is not "particularly useful" (82), Phil responds, "You make it sound like the cosmos is in your opinion this loan shark" (83). Destiny, fate, and "the pattern in the randomness" (89) are all bantered about throughout the rest of the scene, but no "hard data" (82) are recorded. Finally Phil gives up the quest, and in total despair, he kills himself. Far exceeding a safe speed, he hurls his car over a cliff.

This suicide provides the crisis that has so often been avoided throughout the play. On the day of Phil's funeral, a letter is delivered to Eddie, written by Phil and sent before his death, a single statement and signature: "The guy who dies in an accident understands the nature of destiny. Phil" (142). Predictably, Mickey calls it a "fortune cookie" (142) and expresses contempt for Phil and a total lack of interest in the message:

> He had somethin' to say he could a give us a phone call; he could have stopped by; our door was open. He wants to get some information to me now, he's going to have to bridge the gap directly . . . . Stay away from this shit. He's dead: He didn't want to discuss it before, I don't want to discuss it after. (143)

Mickey adds, with ironic truth, that the note is "part of his [Phil's] goof, you know, that he was a rational human being, when he wasn't" (144). Mickey's view of the world allows him to maintain an aloofness. His perception of the world has planted him firmly as an agent of amorality, bent on self-gratification, and anything that imposes on his attitude is ignored.

Eddie, though, wants to understand, so he goes about trying to unlock the "mystery" in what has become typical Eddie fashion. The comic tone of the play, however, no longer glosses the fact that Eddie's efforts are painfully inadequate. He tries to uncover an anagram in the note; he uses logic, however, to eliminate the likelihood of its being an anagram, since

> if it is an anagram, it wouldn't be cryptic. The cryptic element would have been, you know, more than handled by the fact that it was in a fucking anagram to begin with, right? . . . [F]ollow the logic of what I'm saying. It's logical. (149)

He has already made the next move, having grabbed a dictionary and plugged definitions into the corresponding slots in the note:

> "Accident: a happening that is not expected, foreseen, or intended . . . ." And "destiny," we have, "The inevitable or necessary succession of events. What will necessarily happen to any person or thing." So, if you die in a happening that is not expected, foreseen or intended, you understand the inevitable or necessary succession of events. (146)

Mickey, though, despite his aloofness--possibly because of his aloofness--gets more to the point. Ignoring Eddie's games, he casually explains Phil's suicide: "It's not that big a deal . . . you shift your point a view a little and what was horrible [the idea of death] looks okay. All the necessary information that might deter you gets locked away" (147). Mickey continues, offering his own explanation of the note. The above offers an explanation of "accident," as Mickey sees it in the note--not an unforeseen happening at all. The following explains "destiny." Hurling the car over a cliff,

> You've handed control over now, it's gravity and this big machine, which is a car, who are in charge now. Only it's not a car anymore. It's this hunk of metal rearranging itself according to the laws of physics, force and reaction, stress and resistance; heat, friction, collapse, and then you're gone, who knows where. (147)

Accidents entail giving up control, and destiny is a force of nature, blind and with no conscious sense of particular results.

Mickey can actually find justification for his amoral beliefs and practices in Phil's actions, since Phil "proved" that nature is an unconscious, conscience-less force that mechanically operates by a given set of "laws" and that giving up personal control to forces of nature (e.g., feelings or emotions) will lead to destruction. Phil verifies for Mickey that he must continue maintaining some sort of personal, even artificial, control over his life, for if Mickey were to describe the force, he would describe it as destructive and therefore to be avoided. As a result, Mickey has simply taken this belief in a malign amorality into account and modified his rationalism to order his desires, finally dispensing with any concern for ethical or moral judgments. If any such judgments are to be made, they will be governed by coldly and manipulatively rational considerations of personal gain and will be shrewdly glossed over as ethical choices.

Mickey may be able to find justification for his own egotistical actions in Phil's death, but Eddie, more probing and inquisitive, is no longer willing to delude himself about his system. It has failed to answer his questions, and the strain of holding back emotions is taking its toll. Unlike Mickey, Eddie genuinely struggles to salvage a manageable world view, even when it leads to the "sophisticated" (a term he regularly uses to describe himself) conclusion that his business world is absurd (see 82) or that life is like television, a "vague, you know, hurlyburly, this spin-off of what was once prime time life" (113). ("Spin-off," incidentally, was the original title of the play.) Eddie is much less of the glorifying heathen that Mickey is and despite his "sophistication" cannot reduce himself (or elevate himself) to living that life. Perhaps unwittingly, he looks for love, not just physical contact. He looks for attachment with Darlene, for example, and he does nurture attention and affection from his male friends, though the manifestation of the bonds may be perversely displayed. But he is so caught up in the value of reason and logic that he hasn't the ability to distinguish their "sophisticated" functions from the perhaps more "primitive" functions of giving in to nature and relinquishing control, and thereby possibly gaining even fuller insights into the "nature" of nature. Perhaps Phil's death, a genuine emotional blow to Eddie's world, can help Eddie recall that ability to distinguish.

Typically, Rabe leaves the ending, as he must, unresolved. The final conversation in the play is between Eddie and a 60s flower-child throwback, Donna, who responds to his "[H]ow'm I supposed to feel about it [Phil's death]?" with, "You have total, utter, complete freedom on that score, Eddie, because it doesn't make a bit of difference" (156). Donna herself has survived by giving up certain controls and has basically found the impulse of nature to be benign, unlike any of the other characters, too afraid to try. The end of the play suggests that perhaps Eddie's fears of losing control and being destroyed can be allayed. Perhaps he will no longer need to hide behind his language, logic, or machismo. Perhaps letting down the defenses won't result in annihilation, as he and Mickey both fear. Defeated and confused, Eddie quietly embraces Donna as the lights on the final scene go down.

To live in this world, one must either become a manipulative, self-serving, amoral (immoral?) Mickey, or a blind, self-deceiving character such as Darlene and the early, confident Eddie. Or one can commit suicide. A final option is to accept the errors of one's impressions about the world rather than to continue violently and aggressively to challenge/deny that world. Eddie may eventually choose that final option. The play leaves the options open.

The system of reason and logic, and society's endorsement of them, have effectively limited these people, cut them off from the non-rational element of emotions. Ethical questions, for example, have been cut off from their natural emotional foundations and have been turned over to rationally self-justifying logic. *Sticks and Bones* and the other plays illustrate this loss of a deeper emotional base by showing how our culture strives on surfaces, on artificial bonds, and defends itself by establishing premises--often false ones--leading to sound defenses of "wrong action." *Hurlyburly* clarifies the earlier plays' intentions, showing how rationally based, socially enforced systems of thought and behavior isolate our actions from more natural instincts. And that isolation in turn allows us to hold onto unjust, immoral codes involving racism, sexism, etc., provided of course that they permit our materialist surfaces to thrive. The simple failure of interpersonal relationships is one result of this "sophisticated" abstraction from the natural sources of bonding and interaction. And the dependency on such artifice (e.g., male "roles") reveals a more general and equally unfounded faith in reason's ability to unearth and order all meaning.

All of Rabe's work to date has shown American culture to be out of touch with its roots. Happy with superficial "progress," it has violently opposed change and enforced its will by continually "proving" itself through rational and logical defenses. But the defenses are showing cracks; the foundations of our culture are becoming undone because the naturalist assumptions on which they were laid are losing or have lost their power to convince.

Rationalism and logic--as expressed in naturalism--fail to explain the broad sweeps of energy that surround and affect our lives. With *Hurlyburly*, Rabe has written a realistic work that has striven to attack the naturalist assumptions standardly attributed to that mode. He has taken a form and separated it from its prior thematic implications by portraying characters whose own assumptions on life are essentially naturalistic, and whose assumptions are subsequently dashed by the onslaught of contradictory evidence. If Rabe provides any really hopeful insights, it is at the end of *Hurlyburly*. There he suggests that if we can break through the surface tyranny of reason, perhaps we can then re-establish contact with a truer, purer perception of reality and return reason itself to its rightful position of being one of many complementary tools of comprehension rather than *the* tool.

David Rabe does belong to that anti-naturalist movement that Brustein earlier discussed. Perhaps because of the self-reflexive actions of Eddie, the play met with less resistance than his earlier works. Rabe has in effect guided his audience through an assault on naturalism, and many have responded favorably. *Hurlybury*, however, did have its detractors. Nightingale, for example, applies a typical criticism of Rabe in general to *Hurlyburly* in particular: "There are occasions when one feels that severe moral opinion, not plain human observation, is responsible for 'Hurlyburly'" (3). And others feel he confused issues by highlighting the drug aspect of the culture. Taking the various criticisms into account, the play may finally best be assessed as a work that shows Rabe's growth rather than one that demonstrates a fully realized potential. Hopefully the growth will continue. But through it all he has begun to win a growing audience; among those he's converted is Brustein himself, whose review of *Hurlyburly* states the following:

> I had not been kind toward some of Mr. Rabe's previous work, characterizing it as formally linear, thematically manipulative, morally self-righteous--smug mechanisms for producing guilt. This new play was either a major departure for Rabe or I had been wrong in my previous assessment. ("Painless Dentistry" 27)

If in 1979 Brustein was perhaps mistaken about Rabe, it is quite possible that others, too, were/are mistaken. Perhaps a reassessment of the playwright is in order. If that can be done, then there is an even stronger chance that out of all this hurlyburly Rabe's battle may still be won.

Works Cited

Barnes, Clive. "'Boom Boom Room' by Rabe at Lincoln Center." *New York Times* 9 Nov. 1973: 31.

--------. "David Rabe's 'Streamers' in New Haven." *New York Times* 8 Feb. 1976, sec. 2: 45.

--------. "Streamers." *New York Times* 22 April 1976: 38.

Bennetts, Leslie. "Rabe's New Play Due Next Month on Upper West Side." *New York Times* 11 May 1984, sec. 2: 2

Berkvist, Leslie. "If You Kill Somebody . . ." *New York Times* 12 Dec. 1971, sec. 2: 3+.

Bernstein, Samuel J. *The Strands Entwined.* Boston: Northeastern UP, 1980.

Brustein, Robert. "The Crack in the Chimney: Reflections on Contemporary American Playwriting." *Images and Ideas in American Culture.* Ed. Arthur Edelstein. Hanover, NH: Brandeis UP, 1979. 141-57.

--------. "Painless Dentistry." *New Republic* 6 Aug. 1984: 27-29.

Clurman, Harold. "The Basic Training of Pavlo Hummel." *Nation* 7 June 1971: 733.

--------. "Boom Boom Room." *Nation* 28 Dec. 1974: 701.

Feingold, Michael. "Moving Experiences." *Village Voice* 9 Oct. 1984: 96.

Freedman, Samuel G. "Rabe and the War at Home." *New York Times* 28 June 1984, sec. 3: 13.

Freedman, Samuel G. and Michaela Williams. "The Craft of the Playwright: A Conversation Between Neil Simon and David Rabe." *New York Times Magazine* 26 May 1985: 37+.

Gill, Brendan. "Trilogy's End." *New Yorker* 3 May 1976: 76-77.

Gussow, Mel. "'Goose and Tomtom' Opens." *New York Times* 8 May 1982: 17.

Hertzbach, Janet S. "The Plays of David Rabe: A World of Streamers." *Essays on Contemporary American Drama.* Eds. Hedwig Bock and Albert Wertheim. Munich: Max Hueber Verlag, 1981. 173-85.

Kerr, Walter. "David Has Never Been Alive." *New York Times* 12 Mar. 1972, sec. 2: 3.

--------. "David Rabe's 'House is Not a Home.'" *New York Times* 2 May 1976, sec. 2: 5.

--------. "He Wonders Who He Is--So Do We." *New York Times* 30 May 1971, sec. 2: 3.

--------. "Unmistakably a Writer--Why, Then, Does His Play Stand Still?" *New York Times* 14 Nov. 1971, sec. 2: 1+.

--------. "We Leave the Girl As We Found Her." *New York Times* 18 Nov. 1973, sec. 2: 3.

--------. "When Does Gore Get Gratuitous?" *New York Times* 22 Feb. 1976, sec. 2: 1+.

Kolin, Philip C. "Staging *Hurlyburly*: David Rabe's Parable for the 1980s." *Theatre Annual* 1987: 63-78.

Nightingale, Benedict. "David Rabe Explores a Different Kind of Jungle." *New York Times* 1 July 1984, sec. 2: 3+.

Oliver, Edith. "Twice Hail." *New Yorker* 20 Nov. 1971: 114+.

Rabe, David. "Each Night You Spit in My Face." *New York Times* 18 Mar. 1973, sec. 2: 3+.

--------. *Goose and Tomtom.* New York: Grove Press, 1986.

--------. *Hurlyburly*. New York: Grove Press, 1985.
Rich, Alan. "Streamers." *New York* 10 May 1976: 78.
  Rich, Frank. "Hurlyburly." *New York Times* 22 June 1984, sec. 3: 3.
Savran, David. *In Their Own Words: Contemporary American Playwrights*. New York: Theatre Communications Group, 1988.
Schjeldahl, Peter. "Pursuing a Bogus 'Manhood.'" *New York Times* 11 July 1971, sec. 3: 1+.
Simon, John. "Three Fizzles, A Sparkler, and a Slow Burn." *New York* 23 Dec. 1974: 62.
Weales, Gerald. "Pleasant Dreams: Diagnostic, Not Curative." *Commonweal* 19 Oct. 1985: 558-60.
--------. "Streamers." *Commonweal* 21 May 1976: 334-35.

David Mamet's *Glengarry Glen Ross*. American premiere production (1984) at the Goodman Theatre, Chicago. Pictured are Aronow (Mike Nussbaum) and Roma (Joe Montegna).

Photo: Brigitte Lacombe.

Chapter Three

David Mamet's
Dis-Integrating Drama

David Mamet (b. 1947) is a writer interested in studying what man has become as a result of his social surroundings. But unlike the old realists and more like his contemporary, David Rabe, Mamet is less concerned with social issues per se than he is with uncovering how these social concerns have actually taken over and corrupted/destroyed the men and women of that society and then cut them free. Mamet himself argues, "The purpose of the theater is not primarily to deal with social issues; it's to deal with spiritual issues" (Nuwer 9). William Herman notes that "Mamet's obsessive themes are broken relations, the failure to form relations, the impossibility of forming relations, and yet the endless pursuit of these relations" (130). Mamet has turned to uncovering a spiritually lost culture and showing that it has lost the means to recapture the essence of life it has allowed to slip away. And Mamet has found his own unique way of dramatizing that experience, again by beginning with realism to present surfaces and working to illustrate the cracks in those surfaces. To that task he brings his own talents, which have flourished at least partly as a result of current conditions in the theatre world. Walter Kerr, in a 1976 article entitled "Easy Does It Playwrighting Comes of Age," summarizes what he considers the modern playwright's condition and standing:

> Formerly, if Moss Hart knew that he didn't know how to write his next play and that he'd have to go to the mat with it to learn its private tricks through contact, he at least knew what a comedy, or a farce, looked like . . . . He may have had problems, but he wasn't going to fall off the edge of the world.
> And then we all fell off the edge of the world. With the coming of Beckett and the Absurdists and Grotowski and Peter Brook (let a few names stand for the many), every traditional shape was challenged, the

> very notion of form dissolved. The last crutch was no longer available; it wasn't thinkable now to write a Kaufman farce or a regulation "suspense" play; put something together that so much as looked like William Inge and you'd be tagged out-of-date before you got your front porch nailed up. (5)

This observation is a prelude to Kerr's review of the works of two new playwrights, David Mamet's first New York efforts among them (Chicago is his home), works that, as Kerr argues, are not "what would have been called a play when plays wore familiar faces" (5). Mamet himself agrees with Kerr's general assessment: "I think it's a great time to be a young person in the theatre. All bets are off, as in such times of social upheaval as the twenties in Germany, the sixties in Chicago, the period from 1898 to 1920 in Russia" (Savran 143-4).

Kerr notes that this new breed of playwrights has met the challenge of the new era, not shrinking away from a profession that offers no crutches. Instead, they are "perfectly prepared to construct outside and inside simultaneously, reaching for whatever fits and blithely dismissing past habits" (5). In the particular case of Mamet perhaps a more precise assessment would substitute the phrase "reaching for whatever fits" with "concentrating on unique skills," for it seems more likely that a profession that offers no direction in fact offers greater freedoms to those confident enough in their own talents to take advantage of the situation. Applying "unique skills" seems to be the case with Mamet, whose particular strength lies in his use of language; it is language that controls and finally structures many of Mamet's plays. Kerr notes this fact in his assessment of *Sexual Perversity in Chicago* (1975), stating that it

> makes its shape out of the way words are used, out of an over-arching cadence that replaces the structural authority narrative would once have imposed. Narrative here is elliptical, unimportant, not much more than lightning-flash glimpses into the sexual enthusiasms and hostilities briefly generated by two young men, two young women. But the language in which real and imagined relationships are boasted of, regretted, mocked, makes use of rhythms that are self-starting, then nonstop, finally overriding. You can't fight with an express train. (5)

Mamet has granted narrative or plot no more than a secondary role in the great majority of his works, spotlighting dialogue instead, and thereby shifting from a sort of Aristotelian philosophy that argues humans reveal themselves through their actions to one that argues humans reveal themselves through speech. C.W.E. Bigsby notes that for Mamet "[a]ction is character; action is also a language whose rhythms, tonalities, intensities and silences generate and reveal crucial anxieties" (*Mamet* 14). The conventional sense of action, translated into plot, has been given only secondary consideration to what for Mamet is the more intriguing "action" of language. When a plot is clearly discernible, as in later works like *Glengarry Glen Ross* (1984), language is still the central element, the events in the plot little more than incidental action.

In turn a closed structure for Mamet becomes a matter of artifice rather than a statement of "order." In a 1986 interview, Mamet justifies utilizing a "well-made" plot with the following claim:

> I'm sure *trying* to do the well-made play .... I like this form because it's the structure imitating human perception .... This is the way we perceive a play: with a clear beginning, a middle, and an end. So when one wants to best utilize the theatre, one would try to structure a play in a way that is congruent with the way the mind perceives it. (Roudane 77)

But though he accepts and defends the human "need" for a well-made frame, his earlier works resist being informed by such patterns. Even in *Glengarry Glen Ross* the plot that establishes it as "well-made" is little more than an event into which Mamet infuses his more central concerns. The form is established, it seems, more as an incidental overlay for his works, a glue that binds the more important elements of his works, which are themselves necessarily disjointed. In essence the form of drama that Mamet chooses has become a forum to reach beyond the superficialities of action and even intention, to reach a level of reality which reveals that beneath a seeming harmony (if in fact even that can be assumed) lies a disjointed social order where human contact and interchange are in constant struggle against an infringing chaos. So when Mamet uses the well-made structure, it is simply a convenience that works to console or set at ease the audience--a sort of compromise with the audience--which is about to be assaulted by a perhaps unexpected process within that form.

Mamet works in a realistic mode, one in fact often considered reminiscent of early naturalist works. And occasionally the confusion is understandable. In a 1976 *Village Voice* interview, for example, Mamet himself expresses a debt to Stanislavski: "That's when I first learned the correlation between language and action, that words *create* behavior . . ." (Wetzsteon 101). But Mamet uses Stanislavski for his own ends, proving in fact that Stanislavski need not be restricted to naturalist enterprises. Dennis Carroll notes that Mamet's main exposure to Stanislavski came through Sanford Meisner, whose adaptation avoided "excessively internalised techniques such as 'emotion memory' and 'sense memory'--and any techniques which unduly emphasised self-involvement at the expense of contact" (6-7). Stanislavski's method has helped Mamet to understand and relay the fact that surface behavior and language reflect psychological states. But rather than immersing these psychological creations into a rationally comprehensible, naturalist world, Mamet works them into what he sees to be a "truer" picture of the world than that which can be depicted through full naturalist methods. Literal realism is less important than artistic consistency. It is less important, finally, to be true to naturalist perceptibility than to what Mamet calls "the aesthetic integrity of the play" (*Writing in Restaurants* 130). Choices made in writing or in staging, he argues, should be made "in favor of an idea more specific to the play than the idea of 'reality'" (131). Speaking specifically of Stanislavski's system, Mamet continues:

> The purpose of the system was, and is, to *free* the actor from extraneous considerations and permit him or her to turn all of his or her concentration on the objective [Stanislavski's "super-objective'], which is not "this performance," but the *meaning* of the play. (132)

Truth in art is necessarily linked to empirically ascertained reality, but it is not strictly controlled by that reality. And neither is it strictly controlled by naturalist means of perceiving that reality. The "necessity" of an action is controlled by the intended "meaning" of the play, not by some prescribed mechanism of scientific inevitability. And Mamet's message is not one that argues inevitability; it is *not* naturalistic in its intention. As Carroll notes, for Mamet "no subject for drama is a fit subject which does not involve a possible choice" (20).

Specifically, Mamet has taken Stanislavski beyond naturalistic inevitability to show the unnecessary entrapment of humanity by the last vestiges of a failed order that needs somehow to be overhauled; it is not merely the result of some breakdown of a worthy structure/order that merely needs to be re-established or fine-tuned. In this regard, too, Mamet is more like Rabe and less like the early naturalists who were clearly willing to accept and work within the system rather than challenge the system itself as fundamentally flawed. Mamet's plays give us the raw material, the remains of a lost world, for us to study. And language in particular is the material that he studies. For Mamet, as for Rabe, understanding the chaos that language has created may lead us to understand the chaos apparent throughout our society in general. Fundamental means of perception and interpersonal contact must first be modified in order to reclaim our lost "spirituality," as he would identify the situation. And only then can more sweeping changes be expected. Bigsby notes that Mamet's "plays stand as a consistent critique of a country whose public myths he regards as destructive, and whose deep lack of communality he finds disturbing" (*Mamet* 12). As such, his works are not arguments for social change, but are arguments for individual awakening on a broader scale. By moving away from social commentary to a more fundamental ontological concern, Mamet has moved away from O'Neill or Miller. Mamet focuses on what Herman calls "ontological weakness" (130), dealing with what Mamet says "can't be dealt with rationally" (Savran 139). Mamet adds, if actions and events "can be dealt with rationally, they probably don't belong in my theatre" (139). But he is willing to concede, "There are other people who feel differently and work that way brilliantly. One of them is Arthur Miller" (139). However, it is not the way Mamet proceeds. For him, the fundamental spiritual malaise must first be addressed before social and rational/conscious concerns can be confronted. And language is the obvious instrument through which to address this spiritual isolation and disintegration.

So in this regard, the focus of Mamet's language directly conflicts with the work of 30s naturalism as well. Odets, America's early master of American dialects, wrote what Clurman calls "lyric afflatus which . . . is perhaps somewhat forced . . . but the overall effect is youthfully energetic and arousing" (Introduction ix). Clurman further notes George Jean Nathan's assessment of Odets, that "Odets wrote some of the finest love scenes to be found in American drama. An all-enveloping warmth, love in its broadest sense, is a constant in all Odets's writings, the very root of his talent" (Introduction xii). For Odets language unites; it harmonizes situations. There is, finally, a faith in the healing powers of language, founded on an optimism that the social fabric, when damaged, can be repaired through the conventions epitomized by language. Mamet's view of language, on the other hand, is that it widens the breach, that language has reached a point where it fails to function as desired and fails ultimately not only in allowing people to communicate but also in permitting individuals even to "communicate" to themselves. It has become an unwilling, unintentional means of self-deceit. Such perspectives has led Weales to conclude that "Mamet has a more sophisticated sense of language than Odets had" ("Clifford's Children" 16). And not only is Mamet's general conception of language more sophisticated, but even Mamet's manipulation of language simply as a tool is more sophisticated. Says Weales:

> Despite Odets's sense of the connection between the speaker and the spoken, I can think of only one instance--Marcus Hoff in *The Big Knife*-- in which a character is conceived primarily as a pattern of words. Mamet, on the other hand, builds his characters verbally. (16)

Mamet has essentially updated both the perspective on language and the use of language, making his aesthetic form fit his philosophical content.

To dramatize his claim of isolation and alienation, Mamet utilizes detailed analysis of social interaction among very select--and not necessarily overtly "representative"--groups. One reason he feels free to pursue such a course (and a large part of the reason he is different from his 30s predecessors) involves influences:

> Pinter was probably the most influential when I was young and malleable . . . . "The Homecoming," "The Basement," especially his revue sketches. I felt a huge freedom because of Pinter's sketches--to deal in depth and on their own merit with such minutiae. Beckett and Pinter--of course I'm influenced by them. (Gussow "The Daring Visions" 13)

His style is Pinteresque in its efficiency and spare use of language, and his material bears the Pinter mark as well in that it uses characters that seem to have fallen or forced their way through the safety net of polite society and found themselves faced with the harsh realities of existence. But though not overtly representative, the characters find themselves in spots and under conditions that differ only in "environment" to situations in which anyone is liable to become involved. We may not live in a Chicago slum, but we may easily fall victim to the type of greed, for example, that we find in that slum.

Despite the debt to Pinter (and Beckett), Mamet's works are not British in flavor, for other influences include his native Chicago's Second City and playwright Sam Shepard, specifically Second City's energy and Shepard's "use of contemporary materials," as Gussow puts it ("The Daring Visions" 13). The combination has made Mamet a modern American dramatist unafraid of experimentation on stage. In a 1976 interview, Mamet explains what he plans to do with his skills:

> In the theater today we're beginning to recognize ourselves as Americans. In the 60's we rejected pride in being American. In the 70's the theater is saying that being American is nothing to be ashamed of. But we have to learn how to deal with it. We need to take a look at certain taboo aspects of ourselves. (Gottlieb 4)

The culture's institutions need to be overhauled, and the standard means of contact need to be re-evaluated. Conforming to the American business ethic is a focus of criticism for Mamet, but so are other patterns prescribed by society. Working to break from an ineffectual order, Mamet realizes that his own dramatic efforts must struggle against conformity. He gives his views about his profession in that regard:

> Theatre is the very area of the evanescent. The very nature of theatre is always to be dying. By that I mean the theatrical urge is the very antithesis of the urge toward institutional survival. You see it ineluctably throughout the history of drama--form outliving its original aesthetic impulse. (Wetzsteon 101)

Consequently, as Kerr noted, Mamet's early works break from form as much as possible and present raw material--language--in a fashion unique to his needs. Even in *Glengarry Glen Ross,* where Mamet acts in a less non-conformist way, he blends his content into a "well-made" form only as a means to hold the same essential "stuff" that had been presented in his non-conforming early works. His central aim is to present a world where language is deceptive, unreliable; it often increases rather than bridges the gaps that separate individuals. And since he is concentrating on the spiritual over the social, Mamet himself insists on looking at drama "as a primordial instinct, rather than an intellectual exercise" (Gottlieb 1).

The above "instinct vs. intellect" comment suggests another approach to Mamet's material, one which entails a darker view of existence. It is possible to view his works as arguing beyond social chaos and claiming that such chaos is the result of an inherent flaw in humanity itself: not just that society's dictates are detrimental merely to the social aspect of human interaction but that humanity itself has fundamental inherent flaws that are illustrated by its language and that have been incorporated into the social order it has created. These perceived flaws in the social order are actually symptomatic of deeper flaws in the human animal itself. This would be a vision of the absurd on a more expansive, metaphysical, level. To a point Mamet himself hints that this vision of the absurd is the one he is presenting. *Sexual Perversity in Chicago* is a play that dramatizes the failure of males and females to interact on a meaningful level. If society itself were the reason for this failure, then Mamet would have, on at least one level, a "reason" to offer. His work should be able clearly to point to a naturalist-based "cause." However, when given an opportunity to explain himself, Mamet asks but leaves unanswered the question, "Why don't men and women get along?" (Wetzsteon 103). The interviewer, critic Ross Wetzsteon, offers the following: "One reason, the play suggests, is because men, in both their language and behavior, regard women as objects of conquest, as beings who possess what men want, yet refuse to yield it" (103).

But is this "cause" societally motivated or rooted in some deeper, primal source? And, finally, can reason itself overcome either source of this antagonism? Neither Mamet's interviews nor his works point to a clear preference. But whatever the source, it is clear that the machinations of reason alone won't give us the solution. Mamet, however, does give us a general direction in which to look for "solutions." In the same interview Mamet also discusses *American Buffalo* (1976):

> What I was trying to say in "American Buffalo" . . . is that once you step back from the moral responsibility you've undertaken, you're lost. We have to take responsibility. Theatre is a place of recognition, it's an ethical exercise, it's where we show ethical interchange. (103)

Ethical or moral responsibility may well be the means to regain control; finding a sub-rational (super-rational?) root is the hope.

As noted earlier, to illustrate the perceived dilemma, Mamet focuses "on the rhythm of language--the way action and rhythm are identical" (Wetzsteon 101). Mamet continues:

> Our rhythms describe our actions--no our rhythms *prescribe* our action. I became fascinated--I still am--by the way, the way [sic] the language we use, its rhythm, actually determines the way we behave, more than the other way around. (101)

Language *causes* action; it doesn't just illustrate or narrate action. But unlike earlier playwrights like Shaw, for example, for whom the argument that language is action holds true, for Mamet language has become a sort of inaction. So like Rabe here, too, Mamet's works are observations recording the irrationality of human existence muddied by a warped, self-supporting logic built into the language and designed to justify actions--which have become inconsequential or counter-productive and which actually have no justification. As Kerr suggested earlier, it may in fact be true that initially refusing to impose an arbitrary structure on a work may be a "sign of the times," but in Mamet's case the new freedom seems particularly useful, becoming an integral element to Mamet's own ambivalence as to why such events as he puts on stage occur. If there is some "logic" to this existence, it cannot be neatly packaged and labeled. And by extension, neither can his dramatic material. It may be a later transformation in Mamet's concept of audience that leads to the well-made play *Glengarry Glen Ross,* but that use of an established form finally means less than many assume. And turning to that practice involved a rather lengthy evolution that reaches back to Mamet's earliest works.

Richard Eder summarizes his impression of Mamet's first New York offering:

> "Sexual Perversity in Chicago" is a glittering mosaic of tiny, deadly muzzle-flashes from the war between men and women among the filing cabinets and singles bars . . . . At the start, "Sexual Perversity" looks as though it is going to be a series of blackout skits, funny and painful digs at the fantasies and distances of the contemporary sexual game. This is the form of it, and much of the substance too, but Mr. Mamet has woven his bits into a jumpy fabric. ("Mamet's 'Perversity'" 29)

The play is episodic, jumping from event to event and forcing the audience to make what connections it can. As such, it suggests the very fragmentation that the characters in the play experience. Furthermore, it is unconventional in that finding the narrative becomes the work of the audience while the playwright focuses on the language. Edith Oliver comments on the plot, observing, "the subtly pointed incidents are so unobtrusively put together that for quite a while the audience is unaware that any story is being told at all" (135).

Concerning theme, Gussow makes the following comment, one that suggests the play is not merely attacking current societal practices: "The four-character comedy deals with the mating habits of young people today--which seem not so different from the mating habits of young people any day" ("Two Pungent Comedies" 15). The action of the play is at once unique in its applicability to contemporary culture and universal in its relevance to human mating habits in general. The story is an old one "about male and female bonding." Gussow summarizes:

Romance put a strain on friendship. Bernard masks his envy with derision and Deborah's schoolteacher roommate is above the battle but not above being abusive. They know the affair is going badly--and they can hardly wait. ("Two Pungent Comedies" 15)

The power of the play, of course, comes from the language, which from the opening scene works as a signpost announcing the doom of any heterosexual relationship in the play, given the character of its participants. The play opens:

DANNY: So how'd you do last night?
BERN: Are you kidding me?
DANNY: Yeah?
BERN: Are you fucking kidding me?
DANNY: Yeah?
BERN: Are you pulling my leg?
DANNY: So?
BERN: So tits out to here so.
DANNY: Yeah?
BERN: Twenty, a couple years old.
DANNY: You gotta be fooling.
BERN: Nope.
DANNY: You Devil.
BERN: You think she hadn't been around?
DANNY: Yeah?
BERN: She hadn't gone the route?
DANNY: She knew the route, huh?
BERN: Are you fucking kidding me?
DANNY: Yeah?
BERN: So *wrote* the route.
DANNY: No shit, around twenty, huh?
BERN: Nineteen, twenty.
DANNY: You're talking about a girl.
BERN: Damn right. (9-10)

And the following exchange between Joan and Debbie in scene 2 of the play illustrates the character of the opposition, a cynical defensive pair:

JOAN: Men.
DEBORAH: Yup.
JOAN: They're all after one thing.
DEBORAH: Yes, I know. (Pause)
JOAN: But it's never the *same* thing. (18)

The two older characters, Bernie and Joan, are experienced in relationships but have refused to or are unable to learn from those experiences. Their respective protégés, Danny and Debbie, are handed down the twisted lessons of their elders and are finally unable themselves to grow in and learn from either their elders or their own personal experiences. Mamet himself summarizes:

> All the characters in "Sexual Perversity" are losers. To me, it's a play about insight. Insight not acted upon leads to all our impedimenta . . . . To me, it's a play about four different ways of dealing or failing to deal with insight. Joan intellectualizes everything. Debbie uses catch phrases. Danny jokes things away, and Bernie tries to overpower everyone. (Wetzsteon 103)

Their language has become a defense against right action and in fact works to discourage right action. As for Rabe (in *Hurlyburly* in particular), Mamet has here dramatized a world where language aggravates human interaction, only superficially uniting isolated groups in their efforts to rationalize more significant failures. Language for Mamet is the center of attention, and sexual confrontation is merely the forum through which an even deeper crisis is illustrated.

A companion piece to *Sexual Perversity in Chicago,* an early work entitled *The Duck Variations* (first staged 1972 and then co-produced in 1975), offers an example of a stable, working relationship. With this double-bill, Mamet illustrates his argument that choice exists, that we aren't inevitably bound to a foundering system. But in order to establish such stability, the two characters essentially break from any strict dependence on language as the central means to communicate. Mamet's focus, however, is still on language, having his characters conduct what Gussow calls "[t]heir freewheeling conversation [which] is basically about the natural world--ducks vs. the blue heron, the barnyard rules of order, animal misbehavior" ("Two Pungent Comedies" 15). But it is less important to follow the meaning of their conversations than it is to follow the significance of the interchange. As Oliver notes,

> There is a marvellous ring of truth in the meandering, speculative talk of these old men--the comic, obsessive talk of men who spend most of their time alone, nurturing and indulging their preposterous notions. There is more here than geriatric humor; there is also imagination and understanding, as these old parties grow impatient with each other, quarrel, make up, reveal their need for each other, and talk glorious nonsense with impassioned solemnity. (136)

It is a play of fourteen short scenes between two men in their sixties. Like that of *Sexual Perversity in Chicago*, the structure itself complements the fragmented nature of the dialogue. But according to Steven Gale,

> In spite of the fast delivery of short one-line dialogue, the characters know each other well enough to communicate, sometimes responding to

> unfinished thoughts, though ironically, too, sometimes not being able to pick up the most obvious clues. (208)

The play shows at once the hopeful belief that relationships can exist and healthily thrive but also that in order to exist they must struggle to transcend the barriers of language. Gale continues:

> [U]ltimately the importance of their conversation lies not in occasional insights but in the fact that they are conversing. When they come together it is clear that they know each other and that they have met here [on a park bench] previously, perhaps for years. They are familiar and they use their familiarity as a basis for much of the mental gymnastics that they engage in. They have achieved a stable relationship, one that is vital to their mental well-being. (208)

It is curious that Mamet chose two elderly males to break through the language barrier, suggesting that such success comes with time and prolonged effort combined with a minimum of outside resistance. For example, given the fact that it was chosen as a companion to *Sexual Perversity in Chicago*, there is the hint that such understanding is even more difficult between the sexes. The miscommunication still exists between these two men on a verbal level, but the effort reveals that genuine need and a period of exposure can in fact lead to some form of "understanding."

Several later minor works by Mamet are additional variations on *The Duck Variations* theme. *Reunion* (first staged 1976 and in New York 1979) dramatizes a reunion of a father, 53, with his daughter, 24, after a twenty-year separation. And *The Woods* (1977) involves an extended exchange between two young lovers on a vacation retreat. All three plays depict relationships where the parties need someone and somehow find a glue that binds. As the character Emile says in *The Duck Variations,* "A man needs a friend in his life" (97), and so do the characters of the other plays. Gale reports that in *Reunion* "[t]he conversation realistically bounces from thought to thought about the past and present. The two are not sure what they have in common or whether the other will reciprocate emotionally" (216). Gussow adds: "This short bittersweet play . . . is wistful, enveloping us in the isolation of two lonesome people. Their mutual need is almost as strong as their inability to make contact" ("Reunion" 3). The father finally offers the daughter a bracelet that unfortunately has an error in the inscription. It is a fitting symbol of a flawed language struggling to communicate. The gesture itself, though, combined with the mutual and natural need for human contact, salvages a situation and reunites a family. The cast of characters may be different, but the need is there and a relationship is given a chance, though only after breaching barriers that have been reinforced by language.

Similarly, in *The Woods* elements of miscommunication and basic misunderstanding must be overcome. Two lovers on retreat come to know each other, as best they can, but only after countless false starts. It is not language that finally succeeds, but the dogged determination to continue trying. Richard Eder notes: "The words are important in themselves. They are there to reveal, through the intersecting and fearfully separate fantasies of Ruth and Nick, not character but brute need" ("Mamet's 'The Woods'" 15). After extended miscommunication leads to qualified self-understanding between the two lovers, the play ends, as Gale observes, "with them hanging on, partly in love and partly in a desperate need to be together" (221).

Gale termed *Reunion* "realistic," and to a great degree it is very realistic, almost documentary in style. But it is also a play that uses, as Gussow notes, "everyday language, distilled into homely poetry" ("Reunion" 3). The two critics have together touched on the essential qualities of Mamet. He captures the rhythms of the ordinary in a pattern that is ultimately poetic in nature. In his review of *The Woods,* a play which has essentially the same poetic ingredients as those of *Reunion,* Eder argues that Mamet transcends a mundane brand of naturalism/realism and reaches for a heightened realism:

> What Mr. Mamet has made is not a naturalistic play but a poetic one. The couple's continual talk, with its vaguenesses, its erratic leaping quality, its half-irrelevant sequences, sounds highly realistic; but in fact it is a highly charged super-realism, possessed by the most concentrated kind of emotion. ("Mamet's 'The Woods'" 15)

Mamet's language is both realistic and poetic, accurate in its everyday rhythms to the degree that it can be called "homely poetry." With this realistic format Mamet has portrayed the daily struggles of common individuals in their drive to make contact. And in his more complex works, this "poetic" realism continues to reveal its theme of disjunction among human beings.

In *American Buffalo* (1975-76), Mamet's next major work to follow *Sexual Perversity in Chicago*, the playwright does include the kind of relationship highlighted in these minor pieces, but places them in the larger public context of American enterprise, strongly suggesting that the flaws inherent in the American Dream are the cause of, first, the breakdown of language and, secondly, the inability to establish solid relationships in our culture. In *American Buffalo* a delicately balanced personal relationship is destroyed by a business compact that brings with it a cruel and corrupting ethic couched in a convincing but ultimately sterile jargon.

In essence, *American Buffalo* extends the theme of Mamet's other works, asking, "What are the boundaries, the rules of behavior?" (Gussow "The Daring Visions" 13). Mamet answers his own question: "Law is chimerical. Rules are anarchistic. Whenever two people have to do something they make up rules to meet just that situation, rules that will not bind them in future situations" (Gussow "The Daring Visions" 13). And nowhere better than in the business world, the cornerstone of modern American society, do we see this conclusion illustrated. June Schlueter and Elizabeth Forsyth note that the play's junkshop set, "with its piles of once treasured, now rejected cultural artifacts, proves to be a powerful image for an America in which the business ethic has so infiltrated the national consciousness that traditional human values have become buried under current values of power and greed" (499). Mamet summarizes the play's theme in specific terms: "The play is about the American ethic of business . . . . About how we excuse all sorts of great and small betrayals and ethical compromises called business" (Gottlieb 4). These business betrayals in turn make ethically questionable compromise easier in other interactions, and, as Mamet argues, "[O]nce you step back from the moral responsibility you've undertaken, you're lost. We have to take responsibility." (Wetzsteon 103). Gale develops the point, noting that the play's title interconnects the two themes that most involve Mamet, one which focuses on the business world, the other on its affect on human relationships:

> It might . . . refer to American business, which because of its excesses may be on the verge of extinction, as the buffalo has been. Or it may have significance in reference to the characters, for buffalo are large, bumbling, fairly unattractive animals and normally we do not attribute to them the same emotions and sensitivity that we might project onto other creatures. (213)

These bumbling personalities are three characters who Clive Barnes describes as "small-time crooks. But they like to think of crime as a business, and that instead of being hoods they are big-time businessmen pursuing the legitimate concerns of free enterprise" (50). The implications are obvious. Business fails to act responsibly, and this criminal neglect essentially makes business the work of criminals. Mamet's own observations support the point:

> There's really no difference between the *lumpenproletariat* and stockbrokers or corporate lawyers who are lackeys of business . . . . Part of the American myth is that a difference exists, that at a certain point vicious behavior becomes laudable. (Gottlieb 4)

The play then extends this vicious behavior of the business ethic to personal relationships in the play, going beyond the relatively limited "business is criminal" claim to one arguing that this business ethic afflicts all interaction once it has infected the business fabric of our culture. This combination of claims seems to be Mamet's central argument. The business ethic is vicious enough *in* the business world, but it alters those in it to the point that they adapt it to *all* situations.

The relationship that comes into jeopardy in the play is the one between Don, the junk-shop owner, and Bob, a junky who is almost a surrogate son to Don. To execute a planned burglary of a coin collection from a local collector, the two men include Walter Cole, known as Teach, in their ring. Teach takes charge, turning the heist into a twisted form of business transaction. Frank Rich notes,

> [Teach] spouts dim-witted syllogisms about the nature of business, loyalty and friendship, yet his behavior is so itchy that we always realize that Teach neither knows nor means what he says. He only wants to cut his friends out of the action. ("Al Pacino in 'American Buffalo'" 3)

The men have adopted a business attitude for the caper, a posture that has no room for the loyalty and friendship that Teach speaks of but disregards. Rich again makes a point: "Though they like to believe, as one of them puts it, that the 'free enterprise system' has saved them from savagery, they are allowed no such salvation" ("Al Pacino in 'American Buffalo'" 3). Ironically the play's point is that the "free enterprise system" actually encourages savagery, under a guise of civilized conduct, and these three men's actions illustrate the point.

Among these three incompetents--the burglary is never realized or even attempted--Bob is the least competent. His various assignments are blown, and in his mind these mistakes have cost him his friendship with Don. Teach, more because of greed (the root of all business) than anything, convinces Don to exclude Bob, arguing:

> What are we saying here? Loyalty . . . . You know how I am on this. This is great. This is admirable . . . . It turns my heart the things that you do for the kid . . . . This is fantastic. All I mean, a guy can be too loyal, Don. Don't be dense on this. What are we saying here? Business . . . . [D]on't confuse business with pleasure. (*American Buffalo* 33-34)

The tenuously held-together relationship all but collapses and Bob, in complete despair, tries to buy his way back in. The offered payment for friendship is a gesture that illustrates total absorption into the business ethic at the expense of a true relationship, no matter how frail. Finally, the plans having collapsed, the volatile Teach strikes Bob with a piece of junk, and the play ends with Teach and Don preparing to take Bobby to the hospital.

Several have criticized Mamet's ending in particular and the play as a whole for dramatic flaws. Gussow, for example, argues, "The final outburst of violence seems to have strayed from a different work" ("Mamet's 'American Buffalo'" 30). And Kerr doesn't even bother to be specific in his criticism: "Nothing at all happens in 'American Buffalo,' which is what finally but firmly kills it as a possible event in the theatre" ("Language Alone" 3). Clurman takes a similar stand: "The situation hardly matters: hence the lack of dramatic fiber" ("American Buffalo" 313). However, rather than simply condemning, Clurman perceptively adds: "The fragmentation and vagueness of the play's plot and dialogue constitute its meaning. The characters' lines have no 'body': their behavior is a series of obscene spasms, all of them abjectly pathetic" ("American Buffalo" 313). The play, and the final scene, must work as it does, or the theme is compromised and the true focus missed. This debate over the dramatic viability of inaction and unanticipated violence echoes the complaints made of Rabe's art. However, as was the case with Rabe's works, Mamet's use of inaction and irrational behavior is, quite simply, a thematic necessity, illustrating an overall state of disjointed stagnation.

As Clurman implies, the true focus for Mamet is embedded in the dialogue which shows more than even the play's *in*action can. For example, consider one much commented on scene in the play, the end of Act I, when Don and Teach depart:

TEACH: Anybody wants to get in touch with me, I'm over the hotel.
DON: Okay.
TEACH: I'm not the hotel, I stepped out for coffee, I'll be back one minute.
DON: Okay.
TEACH: And I'll see you around eleven.
DON: O'clock.
TEACH: *Here.*
DON: Right.
TEACH: And don't worry about anything.
DON: I won't.
TEACH: I don't want to hear you're worrying about a god-damned thing.
DON: You won't, Teach . . . .
TEACH: Then I'm going to see you tonight.
DON: Goddamn right you are.
TEACH: I am seeing you later.
DON: I know.
TEACH: Good-bye.
DON: Good-bye.
TEACH: I want to make one thing plain before I go, Don. I am not mad at you.
DON: I know.
TEACH: All right, then.
DON: You have a good nap.
TEACH: I will, Don. You know I will. [Exits]
DON: Fucking business. [Lights dim to black] (54-55)

The scene shows Teach's own sense of facility with the language, comfortably omitting words that rhythmically fail to fit his speech. And it shows Teach's concerted effort to control Don. If Don fails to respond with "okay" or "right" or "I know,"--all submissive accessions--Teach repeats himself, waiting for what is expected. When Don responds with "Goddamn right you are," Teach firmly undermines the strength of the assertion by twisting Don into mouthing the desired, weaker response. And when Don offers the kindly "You have a good nap," Teach offers no thanks, but a curt, "You know I will." Mamet grants Don the last words, but they are offered only to an empty stage. Mamet notes the following in relation to the above passage:

> Have you ever listened to two people trying to say good-bye on the phone? Especially in a business situation. They just *cannot* say good-bye. And their language is so revealing of their relationship. All those quid pro quos. Who owes what to whom? They can end up saying "okay, okay, okay," for half an hour. (Wetzsteon 101)

The inaction in the play is only a symptom of a deeper problem. Activity itself is supplanted by a search for the tool to initiate that lost action. But that tool, language, has lost its power to initiate such action. Since it fails as a tool to assist comprehension and to help improve conditions, it has been reduced to a weapon used to dominate and even control current, stagnated conditions.

For an audience or critic to allow Mamet's works to present his thesis means to be willing to modify expectations. Kerr, who lauded Mamet's early works for their rich language, has by *American Buffalo* lost patience with this focus:

> God knows I have nothing against the use--the richest, most profligate use conceivable--of language in the playhouse. Been campaigning for it for years. But when words become an end in themselves, when they tend to constitute a playwright's entire stock in trade, when we are asked to hail a newcomer because he "has such a good ear for the way people really speak" though he lacks eye and appetite for the way people behave, then, I think, we've got trouble right here in River City. ("Language Alone" 3)

At this point Kerr has disregarded his own earlier argument that form must be re-analyzed in this post-Beckett world of the theatre. It is interesting to note that Gale suggested a subtitle be given to Act II of *American Buffalo*, "Waiting for Fletcher" (212), Fletcher being a potential partner who presumably could bring the deal to fruition but who never shows. The act of waiting, obviously, is not conducive to dramatic translation in a traditional sense, as Kerr seems to want, but there does seem to be a need to realize, as Bigsby argues, "that a play's energy may subsist in more than the unwinding of narrative logic" (*Mamet* 14). Bigsby's observation notwithstanding, Kerr's complaint seems to be one that Mamet worked to accommodate in later works. Mamet's later works do include more pronounced plots but continue, for the most part, to insist on highlighting language. As illustrated in the previous chapter with Rabe, the development of a playwright almost necessarily entails modifying one's plans to accommodate an audience. Mamet does work to accommodate; however, he rightly refuses to abandon his essential intentions or his fundamental means of presentation, as Rabe also refused to do.

Another criticism must be taken into consideration here, too. Some critics question whether *American Buffalo* really succeeds as an indictment of the American business ethic, Gale among them: "The play definitely can be read in this light [that it succeeds], and it makes sense, though it is not sufficiently developed or epic enough to be as convincing as it might be" (212). In the face of this criticism, Mamet himself defends the play by pointing out audience responses: "Businessmen left it muttering vehemently about its inadequacies and pointlessness. But they weren't really mad because the play was pointless . . . they were angry because the play was about *them*." (Gottlieb 4). Mamet at least believed that his audiences felt a more universal relevance in his play. His observation, however, is by no means conclusive.

Possibly taking criticism such as the above to heart, Mamet does produce a more "epic" work in *The Water Engine* (1977) and later in *Glengarry Glen Ross* (1984). But before achieving these more "audience-pleasing" and epic designs, Mamet wrote *Reunion, The Woods*, *Dark Pony*, and other shorter works. As noted earlier, they are dramas that focus very specifically on select human relationships-- between a father and daughter or man and woman, for example. Perhaps the most *popularly* successful of this type was *A Life in the Theatre* (1977). Several critics suggest that its popularity was due to its subject matter, the theatre, but it must be conceded that the dynamics illustrated in the relationship presented, between a veteran actor and a newcomer, plays a significant role in the play's gaining acclaim.

It is a play comprised of twenty-six scenes which, more than the other fragmented plays, works as an interesting experiment in manipulating conventional temporal considerations. As Gale notes, "while there is no specific indication of the passage of time, taken together the scenes create a time-lapse montage that is sufficient to trace the stages of development in the relationship between the two men" (219). The relationship moves from that of a student-teacher type, through various crises, into a secure and mature relationship based on understanding, once again despite language. Many themes are touched on--a variation on *theatrum mundi*, for example--but the key is less its traditional thematics than its structure. As Kerr congratulated Mamet on finding a working form for the material in *Sexual Perversity in Chicago,* so should he have congratulated Mamet for *A Life in the Theatre*. The play is chronologically ordered, one must assume, but it freely dispenses with actual day/date considerations, and the episodic structure--as in *Sexual Perversity in Chicago*--does succeed at providing a framework for material while dispensing with the busy-ness of filling in or explaining away time lapses. One central theme, for example, is that life is fleeting and must be enjoyed for the moment--the *carpe diem* theme. Eliminating concrete time (to force life in the present) and choosing an episodic form enforce the theme and formally capture the essence of the elder actor's musings, "Ephemera! Ephemera!" Gussow suggests, "Acting is for the moment, and Mr. Mamet has captured moments that add up to a lifetime" ("Illusion" 3). If there is a unifying thread that binds the scenes, it is finally up to the audience to produce it, as was required in *Sexual Perversity in Chicago*. Life is episodic, Mamet suggests, and it is human artifice that insists on linking them and even on fossilizing them for understanding and for posterity. Mamet comes very close in this play to producing a work of raw material, then asking we put it together.

There was of course criticism of the play, namely that the characters and actions were stereotypical and clichéd, but given the choice of form, the characters and events could never be as developed as they would have been if given a more conventionally narrative approach. It is very likely that such was Mamet's intent, an argument that what we look at as "personality," whole and consistent, is rarely if ever experienced in the real world.

Another successful work in this period is *The Water Engine* (1977), which Eder congratulates for having "both more overt and more complex" action ("David Mamet's New Realism" 42), and he calls it Mamet's "most beautiful play" (47). Originally a radio play reworked for the stage, *The Water Engine* is, superficially at least, a 30s-type melodrama pitting an innocent, naive inventor of an engine fueled by water against a vicious and corrupt business world bent on silencing the inventor rather than marketing a product whose fuel it can't manipulate for profit. The play is subtitled "An American Fable," and according to Bigsby, it is "about the invention of America and the invention of art" (*A Critical Introduction* 275). Perhaps more importantly, Bigsby adds that the play "probes behind the bland and confident surface of the American dream" (275) which sets the stage "to penetrate the fiction which is America" (275).

The play works to depict the same self-delusions about America and American business that *American Buffalo* does, utilizing a grand scheme (forty characters, for example) to produce a play concerned, as Bigsby notes, with "national myths of commercial enterprise and imperial strength" (*Mamet* 89). But Gale adds that it is "B-grade Odets . . . . almost like a Charlie Chan movie" (215). Weales says it comes from a "borrowed genre" ("Stronger Than Water" 244), and Clurman, among others, agrees with Gale's general assessment: "[I]t is not, as it is widely and feverishly proclaimed, a consummate achievement" ("The Water Engine" 92). Though it may indeed be more accessible to an audience--Weales calls it "perfect for a serious theatre organization's initiation into cabaret" ("Stronger Than Water" 244)--it is not vintage Mamet. It lacks, for one thing, the interpersonal element that pervades Mamet's other works, and the richness of language is noticeably missing, perhaps the result of the former absence. But the work does appear to be a concession to those who claim Mamet works to avoid rather than include action. He has produced an action play, but has also illustrated that action of this sort, complete with logical interconnections and tight narration, is produced at the expense of what Gale describes as "emotional intensity and involvement" (215), which are trademarks of Mamet's work.

A Life in the Theatre took a popular theme, one unusual for Mamet, and dramatized it using Mamet's unique style. *The Water Engine* took a Mamet theme and dramatized it in a popular style uncharacteristic of Mamet. Both plays were successes, which doubtless Mamet welcomed, but they aren't vintage Mamet, and one must be wary that the success may be less due to the plays' intrinsic value than due to some extrinsic cause. Clurman makes a point about *The Water Engine*, that it

> has been accorded "Parthenon" quality and greeted with such hosannas as were never bestowed upon O'Neill, Odets, Williams, Miller, Albee or David Rabe at the start of their careers. Mamet is not to be blamed for any of this hawking and puffing: it merely indicates the state of most of our journalistic theatre criticism--if one can call it that. ("The Water Engine" 92)

And in another review, Clurman attacks *A Life in the Theatre* for the same reason:

> I disliked *A Life*. But I soon realized that my annoyance was not induced by the fact that it was a trifle (talented artists are permitted their piffle) but by the gush with which it has been received by most of the press-- celebrated as if it were the best of Mamet. ("A Life in the Theatre" 504)

Both works have merit, but neither deserves the unqualified acclaim that many have given them.

One other important work that preceded *Glengarry Glen Ross* and that did receive critical acclaim is *Edmond* (1982), an episodic presentation of one character's odyssey into the bowels of a city and its sub-culture. It did not, however, command a popular response in America, but the message is clearly Mamet's, and the play's failure is unfortunate. In this work, Mamet has created a victim who sees a bleaker truth than any of his characters previously revealed:

> You can't control what you make of your life . . . . There's a destiny that shapes our ends . . . . And people say it's *heredity*, or it's environment . . . . but, but I think it's something else . . . . I think it's *beyond* that . . . . I think maybe in dreams we see what it is. (100-101)

The references to heredity and environment indisputably attack naturalism, an articulation found nowhere else in Mamet's drama. Very simply put, the sources of despair are not subject to rational correctives. According to the play, adjustments are necessary *beneath* the surfaces that reason occupy, or utter despair is the result. The message is Mamet's in the extreme, uttered by a completely destroyed man, Edmond, in the closing scene of a despairing play. It is perhaps this bleakness and total failure of a man that discouraged audiences. Perhaps it is the overall absurdist sense of helplessness, unadulterated by more assuringly familiar elements, that led to the play's popular failure in America. Whatever the exact reasons, Mamet would not present as stark a vision in his next work, at least not without including familiar touchstones to comfort his audiences.

The waters had been thoroughly sounded for Mamet's *Glengarry Glen Ross* (1984; Pulitzer Prize 1984), which better deserves the plaudits received by *The Water Engine* and *A Life in the Theatre,* and which seems to have benefited from the lessons of *Edmond* as well. *Glengarry Glen Ross* returns to the business world, but instead of focusing on abstractly epic characterization or distilling bleak visions of doom for the stage, Mamet returns to a realistic setting and captures characters driven and torn by the social conditions they are thrust into. Theatrical metaphors and B-grade Odets styles are discarded, as is the more European-influenced absurdist or expressionist style. And from those extremes Mamet seems to have developed a technique that includes a fleshed-out exterior action without detracting from the focus of the work--dialogue and the themes it reveals--thereby at least nominally satisfying those who consider a narrative action essential, but still being true to his theme and unique style. However, some observers still fail to see the full implications of Mamet's style of playwriting. In his study of Pulitzer Prize-winning plays, for example, Thomas Adler notes that "Mamet's work [*Glengarry Glen Ross*] is finally . . . a slight drama, remarkable more for its extreme realism, for the almost cinematic conciseness and swiftness of its first act . . . and for its pervasive odor of despair than for any startling new insight" (107). From a perspective of a Pulitzer tradition (consider Miller), perhaps, the approach may *appear* slight, but understanding the significance of appearance is of course itself the issue, which Adler sems to have overlooked.

As Bigsby notes, the play is one which "pursues the implications of *American Buffalo* to a logical conclusion" (*A Critical Introduction* 286). The two plays simultaneously deal with the business ethic and the interrelatedness of language and action. But *Glengarry Glen Ross* moves from the seedy back-alley world of *American Buffalo* into the seedy mainstream world of big business, the real estate world in particular. The transactions conducted in *Glengarry Glen Ross* are accorded at least nominal public approval, and, though "criminal" in many respects, the official business at hand is no longer forced into alleys and back rooms. That the *chosen* places of business are just as seedy, however, is more than coincidence.

Gussow recounts a Mamet experience that triggered the play's particular bent:

He [Mamet's wife's stepfather] described one incident in which an older salesman was so terrified about making a presentation that he had a heart attack on the spot, "and the new president of the company stepped over his body to leave the room." ("Real Estate World" 19)

Out of this formative incident, Gussow notes,

That callous act started the playwright thinking about other professions, including both politics and theater, in which there were similar pressures. "To me the play is about a society based on business," he said, "a society with only one bottom line: How much money you make." (19)

What is presented in the play is based on real experience and very clearly focuses on the business ethic, but it is a much broader topic that Mamet is addressing--the decaying of America as a result of this ethic, not just in business, but throughout. To accomplish this end, Mamet does indeed present a very specific business world, and lays out a plot that should please those interested in such development. Nightingale summarizes the play:

It happens in and around a real estate office in Chicago, a jungle-within-a-jungle where the only unalterable law is starkly Darwinian. Sell and survive; fail, and be fired. Invisible to us, but ever-present in the characters' minds, is a graph known simply as "the board." This shows which of the four hustlers we meet is ahead in a contest whose first prize is a Cadillac, whose second is a set of steak knives and whose third and fourth are the sack. It also explains why the four-letter word most often on their lips, apart from one not quotable in a family newspaper is "lead." This is the identity and address of the mug who is to be chivvied, browbeaten and caressed into buying a slice of Florida sod with the name designed to evoke stags at bay, kilted troglodytes throwing cabers, and other such Scottish exoticism. In the world of "Glengarry Glen Ross," a good lead brings the hope of a good placing on the board. A bad lead might as well be a one-way sign pointing over a cliff. (5)

If it so wishes, an audience may become involved in following this contest and is given the added opportunity of trying to solve a crime (robbery) conducted between Act I and Act II, the clues of which are received in the first act. The play is still rather spare in its actions, but Mamet does seem to concede that they are at least nominally necessary, nominally in that though included, one leaves the theatre feeling it was only incidental. The first act, for example, uses three scenes in which the characters--in various combinations--sit and discuss their respective dilemmas. It is without question the richest half of the play, leaving the mystery-plot second act little chance to be anything but anti-climactic, though it satisfies a well-made plot formula, presumably appeasing those looking for such closure.

The play opens with Shelly Levene, one of three aging salesmen, begging Williamson, the company manager, for decent leads, a scene reminiscent of the cashiering of Willy Loman in *Death of a Salesman*. Williamson tries to walk out on Levene, but Levene holds him with his pleas:

> LEVENE: John . . . John . . . John. Okay. John. John. Look: (Pause) The Glengarry Highland's leads, you're sending Roma out. Fine. He's a good man. We know what he is. He's fine. All I'm saying, you look at the *board*, he's throwing . . . wait, wait, wait, he's throwing them *away*, he's throwing the leads away. All that I'm saying, that you're wasting leads. I don't want to tell you your *job*. All that I'm saying, things get *set*, I know they do, you get a certain *mindset* . . . A guy gets a reputation. We know how this . . . all I'm saying, put a *closer* on the job. There's more than one man for the . . . Put a . . . wait a second, put a *proven man out* . . . and you watch, now *wait* a second--and you watch your *dollar* volumes . . . You start closing them for *fifty* 'stead of *twenty-five* . . . you put a *closer* on the . . .
> WILLIAMSON: Shelly, you blew the last . . .
> LEVENE: No. John. No. Let's wait, let's back up here, I did . . . will you please? Wait a second. Please. I didn't "blow" them. No. I didn't "blow" them. No. One kicked *out*, one I closed . . .
> WILLIAMSON: . . . you didn't close . . .
> LEVENE: . . . I, if you'd *listen* to me. Please. I *closed* the cocksucker. His *ex*, John, his *ex*, I didn't know he was married . . . he, the *judge* invalidated the . . .
> WILLIAMSON: Shelly . . .
> LEVENE: . . . and what is that, John? What? Bad *luck*. That's all it is. I pray in your *life* you will never find it runs in streaks. That's what it does, that's all it's doing. Streaks. I pray it misses you. That's all I want to say. (15-16)

The language is spare, vintage Mamet. Williamson's silence in this scene--plus his continued motions to leave--illustrates his control of the situation, while Levene's attempts at domination through conversation (unlike Teach's in *American Buffalo*) at once illustrate Levene's illusion of being in control as well as the fact that his language--and his personality--has lost its power to win over or to charm. Being "well liked" *is* essential in this world (it is not an illusion), and Levene has lost his edge. In this world, when the glitter fades, no amount of personal urgency can replace it.

Finally Levene tries to bribe Williamson, but because Levene can't come up with the money, Williamson leaves him. Even Williamson is vulnerable to unethical offers; it is almost a matter of business. And if Williamson, seemingly the only scrupulous character in the play, is lost in this world, all seems destabilized, a fact that further distances such a world from an ethical norm. The business ethic itself is of questionable virtue, but since it seems a matter of course to abuse the ethic, moral responsibility slides even deeper into the quagmire.

Scene 2 sets up the plot to burglarize the office in order to steal the leads by the two other aging salesmen, one more overbearing than the other. In this case, Moss still has the power to dominate, at least to dominate his colleague, Aaronow:

MOSS: They're going to ask me who were my accomplices.
AARONOW: *Me*?
MOSS: Absolutely.
AARONOW: That's ridiculous.
MOSS: Well, to the law, you're an accessory. Before the fact.
AARONOW: I didn't ask to be.
MOSS: Then tough luck, George, because you are.
AARONOW: Why? *Why*, because you only *told* me about it?
MOSS: That's right.
AARONOW: Why are you doing this to me, Dave. Why are you talking this way to me? I don't understand. Why are you doing this at *all* . . . ?
MOSS: That's none of your fucking business . . .
AARONOW: Well, well, well, *talk* to me, we sat down to eat *dinner*, and here I'm a *criminal* . . .
MOSS: You *went* for it.
AARONOW: In the abstract . . .
MOSS: So I'm making it concrete. (45-46)

They never execute these plans, though, and it becomes a scene reminiscent of *American Buffalo*, fraught with explanations and justifications that range from minor technical misinterpretations of the law to bold and direct lies to rationalize away any moral culpability. The burglary is to be a business transaction with a twist.

The one character who thrives in this Darwinian wasteland is Roma, younger than the other three and much more polished in comparison. Scene 3 has him warming up to a lead. He philosophizes about trains, food, women, life in general. In this scene Roma completely controls the exchange in a manner that Levene is unable to sustain in scene 1. The scene concludes with Roma preparing to enter into his actual sales pitch, the introduction seemingly having worked:

James. I'm glad to meet you. (They shake hands.) I'm glad to meet you, James. (Pause.) It might mean *nothing* to you . . . and it might not. I don't know. I don't know anymore. (Pause. He takes out a small map and spreads it on a table.) What is that? Florida. Glengarry Highlands. Florida. "Florida. *Bullshit*." And maybe that's true; and that's what *I* said: but look *here*: what is this? This is a piece of land. Listen to what I'm going to tell you now: (50-51)

The scene ends, and the actual pitch is not seen, but we see that through Roma's complete dominance of the dialogue, he has disarmed the lead, gained his sympathies, and set up the illusion that it will be the lead's decision to buy. And in Act II, we learn that the lead does buy. In this instance language has served its user's end, but the end is unscrupulous and illustrates the unethical dimension of the business ethic that profit is all.

But if the leads are victims in this world--and they are--the play clearly shows that the agents are, too. That world has turned on them just as viciously, leaving them victims of age and their growing infirmity. It is a world of jackals, as several critics have termed it, and only he who stays ahead of the pack can survive.

There is, however, a glimpse of what might be or what possibly once was. Weales summarizes:

> [T]here is a revealing scene in Act II in which Shelly [Levene], at the insistence of the only other salesman who understands the art of con [Roma], recounts his moves, his thoughts, his sense of triumph in closing a most unlikely sale. These men are jackals, for whom customers are fair game, but in Shelly's tale there is a glimpse of the possibility of achievement, of professional pride. ("Rewarding Salesmen" 279)

Even in this world the need to connect exists, and these two men do find a connecting thread, one similar to that found in *Duck Variations,* among others of Mamet's works. In Act II Levene works to help Roma keep the Act I lead, who has come to the office to back out of the deal. Levene is offered no monetary incentive to help Roma, but the sheer joy of working the deal provides sufficient impetus. Levene assumes the role of an affluent investor who Roma must immediately drive to the airport to catch a flight. The scheme falls apart when Williamson, an obvious uninitiated office man, innocently interferes. And it is Levene, not Roma, who confronts Williamson with the event:

> WILLIAMSON (Brushing past him): Excuse me . . .
> LEVENE: .·. . excuse you, *nothing*, you be as cold as you want, but you just fucked a good man out of six thousand dollars and his goddamn bonus 'cause you didn't know the *shot*, if you can do that and you aren't man enough that it gets you, then I don't know what, if you can't take *some thing* from that . . . (Blocking his way.) you're *scum*, you're fucking white-bread. You be as cold as you want. A *child* would know it, he's right. (Pause.) You're going to make something up, be sure it will *help* or keep your mouth closed. (Pause.). (98)

Williamson gets revenge in the end, though, refusing to drop charges against Levene when it is discovered that he, Levene, is the one who in fact burglarized the office, not Moss and Aaronow. The loyalty that Levene showed toward his colleague, Roma, is a loyalty that Williamson is oblivious to and that simply is no longer standardly exercised in the business world, as illustrated by the very format of the competition set up by the firm. Levene is taken off by a police officer while the true violent action of the office contest continues. The law ignores, even defends, the true crime. Levene, quixotically, is struggling in a world that functions in a way that can't accept even his minimal expectations of and need for community. He and his type are lost, even destroyed. No thread can be established at all, much less an ethical one.

With *Glengarry Glen Ross* Mamet has found a plot and subject matter to illustrate his point, but still it is less the plot development than Mamet's language that succeeds in capturing the essence of his themes. Mamet argues that current conditions are such that it is futile to even as much as *consider* ethical action on a large and consistent social scale. We need first individually to establish much more basic bonds. But since language, the manifestation of the bond in question, has lost its power, current conditions have reached a point where even the most sincere individual efforts (note, especially, the earlier works) meet with incredible resistance. And any effort less than total is doomed to failure. Frank Rich offers his impressions of the language in *Glengarry Glen Ross:*

> In the jagged rifts of coarse, monosyllabic words, we hear and feel both the exhilaration and sweaty desperation of the huckster's calling. At the same time, Mr. Mamet makes his work's musical title into an ugly symbol of all that is hollow and vicious in the way of life his characters gallantly endure. ("A Mamet Play" 17)

The play's lyric but finally hollow language is a reflection and symptom of the lives these men lead, indicators of inevitable behavior, cruel and uncaring. We may sense in many characters the longing to break out, but finally all we see is the inability to do so, perhaps because there is no escape. These men are trapped in their worlds, and their words are trapped in their culture.

Nightingale sums up the culture Mamet presents:

> B.F. Skinner himself could not have invented a system better calculated to unsettle the human rat and drive him to desparate expedients. When these salesmen aren't manipulating and exploiting the customers, they're likely to be manipulating and exploiting each other. (5)

That we can be so cruel to each other is what Mamet finds repulsive and despairing. Like Rabe, Mamet seems to be attacking standard assumptions that humans somehow need to operate in such an environment and in such a manner. He dramatizes a naturalist/Darwinian perception of order so he can unearth the subtle horrors of the social structure that it has produced. And the horrors aren't some isolated phenomenon, either, but are a pervasive element of our culture, affecting not just the few who have slipped through society's welfare net, but even including the most successful and secure representatives of that social order. No one is safe. And given the fact that the problems are so deep-rooted, much more than cosmetic treatment or fine tuning is necessary. The very underlying assumptions of that culture need to be re-evaluated.

Typically, realistic portrayals reveal surfaces and attendant surface problems, but Mamet's brand of realism digs beneath the surface, thematically and aesthetically. Rich notes, with admiration, "Mr. Mamet's talent for burying layers of meaning into simple, precisely distilled, idiomatic language" ("A Mamet Play" 17). The language *seems* to communicate but does nothing of the sort for the great majority of interchanges. So, too, our society's structures *seem* to be working--and on the surface they do--but beneath them we see their failings. Bigsby makes a similar point: Mamet "tends to locate his plays in an ostensibly realist environment only to deconstruct the assumptions of realism as they relate to plot, character and language" (*A Critical Introduction* 287). Mamet takes material that has the flavor of myth--the American Dream, for example--challenges its assumptions and brings into question all that hangs from those assumptions. Once the surfaces are shattered, an emptiness is left, one reflected in his works' many pauses and one that often calls up images of Pinter. (*Glengarry Glen Ross*, incidentally, was dedicated to Pinter.) It is finally this combination that makes Mamet the unique voice that he is in contemporary theatre. He is a man who has taken form and content that has been handled for decades, but has managed to mold both in his own way to present a modern vision with a unique means of presenting that vision.

Glengarry Glen Ross has quite often been compared to another classic attack on American business, *Death of a Salesman*. The themes are of course similar. But Mamet triumphs on one level where Miller tried and, many agree, failed. Mamet's experiments with language has brought him closest to developing a poetic voice for the theatre in a period when many have failed to find such a voice even outside of realist restrictions. And that fractured, disjointed voice *reflects* a frustration in all modern conventions and institutions. Miller's rational, generally coherent prose, on the other hand, implies an ultimate faith in current systems, a belief that wounds will eventually heal or be healed. Mamet's plays reveal complex psychological constructs that can't be analyzed through strictly rational, or cause-and-effect means. For Mamet there is no affair with a secretary, for example, to identify as a cause. And the choice of escaping to a simpler lifestyle cannot be made either, for as all his works illustrate, Mamet argues that the roots of the dilemma pervade the American soil itself. Mamet refuses to simplify causes or tidy them up with reductive explanations and romanticized solutions, simply because they *can't* be categorized or explained and because there aren't any easy correctives for the problems observed.

Mamet's latest product for the stage, *Speed-the-Plow* (1988), follows David Rabe into Hollywood, producing a perhaps even harsher critique of America's "dream factory" than Rabe presented in *Hurlyburly*. Frank Rich reports: "Even as Mr. Mamet savages the Hollywood he calls 'a sinkhole of slime and depravity,' he pitilessly implicates the society whose own fantasies about power and money keep the dream factory in business" ("Mamet's Dark View" 17). Every corner of American culture, finally, has been touched by the spiritual malaise Mamet identifies.

With *Edmond* we see the influence of the European absurdists and existentialists in full view. *Glengarry Glen Ross* and Mamet's other works reflect that influence as well as the influence of other recent writers, like Pinter. To return to Miller's frame of reference would entail ignoring this new tradition, and Mamet chooses not to ignore it. Instead he utilizes that tradition, simultaneously using an American idiom to reveal that underneath rationalist surfaces lie problems potentially more despairing than naturalism ever imagined, more despairing because reason itself can no longer remedy the problem. And where writers like Rabe essentially *argue* the point, Mamet's particular triumph is that he *reflects* the point, offering us an *experience* of his world, both the despair and the "comedy" of such an existence.

With Shepard the form continues to expand.

Works Cited

Adler, Thomas P. *Mirror on the Stage: The Pulitzer Plays as an Approach to American Drama.* West Lafayette: Purdue UP, 1987.

Barnes, Clive. "Skilled 'American Buffalo.'" *New York Times* 17 Feb. 1977: 50.

Bigsby, C.W.E. *A Critical Introduction to Twentieth-Century American Drama,* Vol. 3: *Beyond Broadway.* London: Cambridge UP, 1985.

--------. *David Mamet.* London: Methuen, 1985.

Carroll, Dennis. *David Mamet.* London: Macmillan, 1987.

Clurman, Harold. "American Buffalo." *Nation* 12 Mar. 1977: 313.

--------. Introduction. *Six Plays of Clifford Odets.* New York: Grove Press, 1979. ix-xiv.

--------. "A Life in the Theatre." *Nation* 12 Nov. 1977: 504-505.

--------. "The Water Engine." *Nation* 28 Jan. 1978: 92.

Eder, Richard. "David Mamet's New Realism." *New York Times Magazine* 12 Mar. 1978: 40+.

--------. "Mamet's 'Perversity,' Mosaic on Modern Mores, Moves." *New York Times* 17 June 1976: 29.

--------. "Mamet's 'The Woods' Redone at Public." *New York Times* 26 Apr. 1979, sec. 3: 15.

Gale, Steven H. "David Mamet: The Plays, 1972-1980." *Essays on Contemporary Drama.* Eds. Hedvig Bock and Albert Wertheim. Munich: Max Hueber Verlag, 1981. 207-24.

Gill, Brendan. "The Lower Depths, Glengarry Glen Ross." *New Yorker* 2 Apr. 1984: 114.

Gottlieb, Richard. "The 'Engine' That Drives Playwright David Mamet." *New York Times* 15 Jan. 1978, sec. 2: 1+.

Gussow, Mel. "The Daring Visions of Four New Young Playwrights." *New York Times* 13 Feb. 1977, sec. 2: 1+.

--------. "Illusion Within an Illusion." *New York Times* 21 Oct. 1977, sec. 3: 3.

--------. "Mamet's 'American Buffalo.'" *New York Times* 28 Jan. 1976: 30.

--------. "Real Estate World a Model for Mamet: His New Play Draws on Life." *New York Times* 28 Mar. 1984, sec. 3: 19.

--------. "Reunion,' 3 Mamet Plays." *New York Times* 19 Oct. 1979, sec. 3: 3.

--------. "Two Pungent Comedies by New Playwright." *New York Times* 1 Nov. 1975: 15.

Herman, William. *Understanding Contemporary American Drama*. Columbia: U of South Carolina Press, 1987

Kerr, Walter. "Easy Does It Playwrighting Comes of Age." *New York Times* 15 Aug. 1976, sec. 2: 5+.

--------. "Language Alone Isn't Drama." *New York Times* 6 Mar. 1977, sec. 2: 3+.

Mamet, David. *American Buffalo*. New York: Grove Press, 1976.

--------. *Edmond*. New York: Grove Press, 1983.

--------. *Glengarry Glen Ross*. New York: Grove Press, 1984.

--------. *A Life in the Theatre*. New York: Grove Press, 1977.

--------. *Sexual Perversity in Chicago* and *The Duck Variations*. New York: Grove Press, 1978.

--------. *Writing in Restaurants*. New York: Viking Penguin, 1986.

Nightingale, Benedict. "Is Mamet the Bard of Modern Immorality?" *New York Times* 1 Apr. 1984, sec. 2: 5+.

Nuwer, Hank. "Two Gentlemen of Chicago: David Mamet and Stuart Gordon." *South Carolina Review* 17 (Spring 1985): 9-20.

Oliver, Edith. "David Mamet of Illinois." *New York Times* 10 Nov. 1975: 135-36.

Rich, Frank. "Al Pacino in 'American Buffalo.'" *New York Times* 5 June 1981, sec. 3: 3.

--------. "A Mamet Play, 'Glengarry Glen Ross.'" *New York Times* 26 Mar. 1984, sec. 3: 17.

--------. "Mamet's Dark View of Hollywood As a Heaven for the Virtueless." *New York Times* 4 May 1988, sec. 3: 17.

Roudane, Matthew C. "An Interview with David Mamet." *Studies in American Drama, 1945-Present* 1 (1986): 73-82.

Savran, David. *In Their Own Words: Contemporary American Playwrights*. New York: Theatre Communications Group, 1988.

Schlueter, June, and Elizabeth Forsyth. "America as Junkshop: The Business Ethic in David Mamet's *American Buffalo*." *Modern Drama* 26 (1983): 492-500.

Weales, Gerald. "Clifford's Children: or, It's a Wise Playwright Who Knows His Own Father." *Studies in American Drama, 1945-Present* 2 (1987): 3-18.

--------. "Rewarding Salesmen: New from Mamet, Old from Miller." *Commonweal* 4 May 1984: 278-79.

--------. "Stronger than Water." *Commonweal* 14 Apr. 1978: 244+.

Wetzsteon, Ross. "David Mamet: Remember That Name." *Village Voice* 5 July 1976: 101+.

Sam Shepard's *Buried Child*. World premiere production (1978) at the Magic Theatre, San Francisco, directed by Robert Woodruff. Pictured are Bradley (William M. Carr), Halie (Catherine Willis), Tilden (Dennis Ludlow), and Shelley (Betsy Scott). *Photo: Ron Blanchette.*

Chapter Four

Sam Shepard's Realistic Drama

The originality and ingenuity of Sam Shepard (b. 1943) have placed him among the top of America's list of playwrights, and his recent venture into realism has resulted in greatly expanding the potential of that form. But as with Rabe and Mamet, because Shepard has adopted a form and developed a style that are often misinterpreted, the plaudits are usually offered with reservation. For example, in the words of Robert Brustein, Shepard "may be . . . America's leading playwright" ("Love From Two Sides of the Ocean" 25), and in the words of Leo Sauvage, Shepard is a man who "seems to have achieved a status near the top in American theater" (21). But even these plaudits refrain from conclusively labelling Shepard "foremost"; note the qualifiers "may" and "seems." Among the more academic justifications for such reservation are charges that Shepard's work lacks polish (he rarely rewrites or edits) and that his plays are too short fully to develop character or theme. Rarely if ever, though, is he charged with being untalented or with not "showing promise," but critics argue that he has been writing since the early 60s, and they are getting impatient waiting for him to "give us a fully thought-out masterwork, untrammeled by the self-indulgent digressions that merely scatter his talent" (Sauvage 22).

Given such mixed reactions, it is perhaps justified to remind these critics that, as with the previously discussed playwrights, Shepard is sitting on a cusp in dramatic history not unlike that of an earlier playwright, Eugene O'Neill, and that O'Neill's career was also checkered with notably controversial works of a fairly experimental nature. Like O'Neill, Shepard has been forced to search for a form to accommodate his content; and it is a search that has recently led Shepard to move further and further away from experimentation and seemingly closer to convention in his search for an accommodating form, closer to realism, in fact. His, however, is not O'Neill's realism. It is the new realism that accommodates a 1970s-80s vision and that necessarily differs from O'Neill's. As Bigsby notes, Shepard's work reveals a "1960s desire to make fragments cohere and the 1970s belief that truth may ultimately lie in those fragments" (221). Because of the different times in which they write, the experiences of O'Neill and Shepard differ, and so do their brands of realism. As noted in Chapter One, Robert Brustein argues that O'Neill's masterpiece *Long Day's Journey into Night* exhibits a one-to-one cause-and-effect correspondence of action that oversimplifies the actual complexity of the relationships portrayed: "Each separate action radiates outward into myriad branches of effects, and characters interlock, imprisoned in each other's fate" ("The Crack in the Chimney" 145). The use of tight causal connections reduces a complex reality to a set of conditions in an attempt to uncover "guilt" within the system, a technique that Brustein argues is endemic virtually to all products of American realism. But Brustein further argues, favorably, that Shepard disintegrates causal connections and re-evaluates the "sources of guilt" (154) that so obsess American playwrights, a notable break from past traditions.

One point that Brustein did not foresee of Shepard's later works is that in Shepard's effort to disintegrate and re-evaluate American drama, he would soon turn to focusing on those same "sources of guilt and on the painful confrontations between parents and their children" (Brustein 146)--the disintegration of the family, in essence-- that Brustein himself saw in earlier writers like O'Neill and that Brustein labelled peculiarly American, making the parallels between O'Neill and Shepard even more pointed. Shepard himself explains why he turned to "family" in his dramas, in a 1980 interview:

> I felt it [disintegration of the American family] was exploited in the past by writers who didn't have anything else to write about. But then I felt that, rather than try to avoid it, I might as well try to meet it head on. The other thing is, my family is so idiosyncratic it verges on the bizarre. (Coe "Saga" 58)

Shepard's impression of past motives (that they had nothing else to write about) may be inaccurate for some of that early group of writers, but the point is that Shepard feels that the intricacies of such relationships have yet fully to be dealt with. His plans are not to exploit the issue but to confront it from a fresh perspective. Among the above observations, perhaps most telling is the implication behind the final, rather flip, observation that translates into Shepard resolving finally to confront his ghosts. For the last decade his plays have focused on peculiar dilemmas of his own family, including what he calls plainly enough his "family trilogy" of *Curse of the Starving Class* (1976), *Buried Child* (1978), and *True West* (1980). Two others have continued addressing the theme, *Fool for Love* (1982) and *A Lie of the Mind* (1986). So though superficially similar to O'Neill's works in that they address the "American" themes of family disintegration and the attendant sources of guilt, Shepard's plays are unique in the way they perceive the issues.

The significant point of departure between Shepard and O'Neill, finally, is Shepard's modified approach to these common themes. These two playwrights' means of presentation may be basically realistic, a form, according to Lynda Hart "that has historically been most conducive to the exploration of familial themes" (3). But Shepard's realism is invaded and rejuvenated by lessons of the 60s and 70s and molded to fit the new perceptions in a manner that the older form was not able. The search for a rationally perceivable causal thread has been abandoned in an attempt to uncover other types of coherence acceptable to a late 20th-century frame of mind. Shepard has moved away from probing rationally informed social concerns and toward a deeper probing of man's existential concerns.

Some observers have seen an ulterior motive behind Shepard's turn to realism, William Herman among them:

> As Shepard got on in the theatre--as he got more and more involved with actors and submitted more and more to their ethos--a not-so-subtle change came over his work. Actors who hate roleless roles--roles that do not permit them to flesh out the lines of the script with stage activities that create plausibility, enabling them to exhibit their lifestyles, so to speak-- actors, including Shepard the actor, had their way with him, and he began to produce the plays of his last period, the so-called realist works. (29)

Shepard's realist drama, however, doesn't provide fully drawn characters, as Herman charges, at least not in the conventional sense. And such charges of capitulation to commercial theatre pressures are finally unfounded. Shepard's realist work *has* attracted for him larger audiences and greater popularity, but within this realist format, his unique style of probing existential concerns remain essentially the same. Michael Smith of *The Village Voice*, reputed to have "discovered" Shepard, makes the following assessment of a 1964 Shepard double-bill of *Cowboys* and *The Rock Garden*:

> The plays are difficult to categorize . . . . Shepard is . . . working with an intuitive approach to language and dramatic structure and moving into an area between ritual and naturalism, where character transcends psychology, fantasy breaks down literalism, and the patterns of ordinariness have their own lives. His is a gestalt theatre which evokes the existence behind behavior. ("Theatre" 13)

The assessment can easily be applied to Shepard's latest works, not merely to his early efforts.

Through the turbulent and exciting time of the 60s and into the 80s, Shepard's interests have indeed remained consistent. In a 1981 interview Shepard makes the following comment about the 60s' influence on his impressions:

> To me the influence of the sixties and off-off Broadway theatre and the Lower East Side was a combination of hallucinogenic drugs, the effect of those drugs on those I came in contact with, the effects of those drugs on my own perceptions, the Viet Nam war, and all the rest of it which is gone now. The only thing which still remains and still persists as the single most important idea is the idea of consciousness. (Shepard "American Experimental Theatre" 212)

Consciousness remains the central concern, including awareness of self and awareness of surrounding. And the experience of a Shepard play goes beyond developing consciousness in the character to one that develops the same for the audience. Smith makes this particular observation of a 1966 Shepard product, *Red Cross*, noting the special achievement of Shepard's effort: "What matters in a Shepard play is not the life behind the stage actions, not the reality that is represented, but the life and reality that are shared by actors and spectators in the theatre during the performance" ("Theatre Journal" 19). Shepard creates this special relationship through the "charm" of the text, something that occasionally gets him in trouble with critics and that Smith warns Shepard against abusing: "He has discovered a bright stylistic trick, but his use of it again and again seems self-indulgent. Charm is fragile and tends sometimes toward cuteness; style if simply repeated turns into empty formalism" (20). The warning is double-edged. On one level, Smith is warning against simple trickery; on the other, he warns against subject-less material.

Given the trendiness of the 60s, trickery was indeed a risk Shepard ran the danger of becoming victim to, but such urges toward theatrical self-indulgence would soon be overcome. For example, Shepard himself attacks the superficial experiments involving the invasion of theatre action into the audience, in a 1981 interview:

> The myth is that in order for the audience to be actively participating in the event that they're watching they have to be physically sloshed into something, which isn't true at all. An audience can sit in chairs and be watching something in front of them, and can be actively participating in the thing that's confronting them, you know. And it doesn't necessarily mean that if an audience walks into the building and people are swinging from the rafters and spaghetti's thrown all over them, or whatever the environment might be, that their participation in the play is going to be any closer. In fact it might very well be less so, because of the defenses that are put up as soon as that happens. (Chubb 13)

Shepard is expressing a distaste for the facile sense of community that naive innovations claimed to achieve in the 60s and an equal distaste for innovations that were instituted simply for innovation's sake. What such innovations claimed to attain could be achieved in more subtle and substantial ways, even if it meant returning to the conventional..

Shepard's own classic work *The Tooth of Crime* (1972) was subjected to such an "environmental" treatment, by Richard Schechner and his Performance Group. Shepard's assessment is not favorable:

> He [Schechner] feels that he wants to experiment with the environment of theatre, which is okay, I've nothing against it. Except when you write a play it sets up certain assumptions about the context in which it's to be performed, and in that play they had nothing to do with what Schechner set up in the theatre. You can take that or leave it. It can be okay--the playwright isn't a holy man, you know. Except I'd rather that the experimentation took place with something that left itself open to that--a play that from the start defines its context as undefinable, so that you can fuck around with it if you want to. (Chubb 13)

The above could of course be interpreted as being an example of a playwright longing for control over his product, but it seems more appropriate here to consider the fact that if Shepard were in fact inclined toward experimentation without qualification, such a production would have been received with more of an open mind. It was not. And most critics agreed with Shepard that Schechner's production detracted from rather than contributed to Shepard's work, Clurman among them: "[T]he experiment I might most appreciate would be one in which Shepard's written stage directions were scrupulously followed on the highest level of competence" ("The Tooth of Crime" 412). In this case, at least, Shepard was in agreement with the critics. Subsequent productions have succeeded in bringing the outstanding qualities of *The Tooth of Crime* to the fore, revealing that Shepard's work has its own more subtle brand of unconventional and innovative techniques.

Most of Shepard's output prior to 1976, in fact, was experimental in nature, pieces that experimented with forms that grew out of the material Shepard was creating rather than having the material conform to pre-established forms. In no way, however, could they have been considered content-less formalism. In this respect, they were less reminiscent of 60s happenings than might at first be expected. Unlike 60s- and 70s-bred experimenters like Robert Wilson, Richard Foreman, and even Schechner, Shepard was not looking at theatre as simply a tool to awaken audience sensibility; he was not merely trying to move it from "the world of signs . . . to . . . a world of perception," as Foreman put it (Bigsby 152). Shepard goes beyond trying to retrain an audience to "let the sun shine in," beyond exposing an audience to new means of perception, because for Shepard even a new world of perceptions is entwined with a world of signs--perhaps new signs, but signs nonetheless. And if the new signs have no substance, then they are little better than the current ones. So Shepard seems to turn his attention to recapturing some sense of what has been lost by showing, in effect, that what has been lost in past systems may perhaps once again be recaptured, albeit in modified ways.

Many recent approaches to Shepard have focused on his manipulation of audiences or on his meta-theatrical devices. Shepard himself acknowledges that "the power of words for me isn't so much in the delineation of a character's social circumstances as it is in the capacity to evoke visions in the eye of the audience" ("Visulaization" 53). As a result, many critics have found particular value in studying Shepard's methodologies, often almost exclusive of content. Ann Wilson, for example, observes that "Shepard is concerned not with producing meaning but with the production of meaning in the theatre" (46). And Sheila Rabillard argues that Shepard's works can be seen as "explorations of theatricality" (59). Steven Putzel follows a similar line, discussing Shepard's means of developing "audience complicity," but noting that in recent works (the realist phase) "the nature of audience complicity . . . may be disintegrating" (158). Though these meta-theatrical approaches lead to valuable assessments, they fail to place in the proper perspective the fact that Shepard uses such effects as means to an end rather than as ends in themselves. So a play like *The Tooth of Crime* may manipulate, awaken, and stimulate an audience, but it also communicates an effort to recapture or restore a sense of meaning.

The Tooth of Crime is in fact a consummate example of Shepard's earlier work, a play pitting two characters, rock stars, in mortal combat against each other in a setting variously described as surreal and expressionistic. The aging star, Hoss, loses out to the rising star, Crow, and the result is the fall of a code, replaced by empty but dazzling style, meaningless but catchy language--a hollow aesthetic. Shepard reports:

> The character of Crow . . . came from a yearning toward violence. A totally lethal human with no way or reason for tracing how he got that way. He just appeared. He spit words that became his weapons. He doesn't "mean" anything. He's simply following his most savage instincts. ("Visualization" 56)

In light of Crow's victory, Hoss's lost code at least nominally signifies a sense of substance behind action, while the replacement has abandoned even an attempt at rooting itself. The play is, in essence, a response to that loss of substance in our culture which has been replaced by effect; it is not a manifesto of liberation, as may be expected. Crow's victory is not felt to be a triumph, but an indication that what has been lost is something essential to life and art. For Shepard, this newly ushered-in era is a hollow one; perception-altering innovation and originality is an important beginning but alone won't suffice.

And so it is with Shepard's own innovation and originality. They are instituted to accommodate central issues and concerns and are not simply aesthetic pyrotechnics designed to shock an idle public merely into awareness of self. Shepard wants the awareness (or consciousness) to be directed toward his central concern, which involves codes, the loss of them in modern American society. His works decry the loss of old codes as well as the fact that new codes can no longer be prescriptively substituted. Shepard senses that there *is* accessibility to a vital and substantial new "code"--in Shepard's case it seems to be a rekindling of an old code, actually--but that it can no longer be (perhaps never was able to be) formally, rationally conveyed or concretely documented. As Ron Mottram notes, Shepard doesn't "measure truth by simple, prosaic facts" (1-2), and so creating a prescriptive, rationally explicable code would be incomplete because it would lack subjectivity and therefore flexibility. It needs personal adaptability. What "codes" provide us is much too complex for such a reductive resolve. So Shepard does not provide "meaning" like an Arthur Miller. But equally unlike the seemingly liberating proclamations of various current 60s offsprings, Shepard's work still insists on something substantial and deep-rooted that binds human communities, something that goes beyond mere aesthetic endeavor, but of course that doesn't exclude it. Because for him social prescription alone is insufficient, if change is to occur at all, it must be deep-rooted and solidly, personally, based.

Geography of a Horse Dreamer (1974) is a case in point, a play that Ross Wetzsteon calls "an extended metaphor for the personal dilemma of the artist himself" (133). The action physically separates the central character, Cody (Buffalo Bill Cody?), from his source of strength, his source of "magic." Kidnapped and taken to England from his native American West--the source of his powers--his "seeing" powers diminish, though temporarily he is able to perform his role of a "horse dreamer," dreaming up winners of the next day's races. Thematically, the play has obvious psychological parallels. Without the revitalizing and substantive power of some non-rational source, a character's efforts become meaningless, hollow, insignificant, and finally fruitless. The selling out of talent to commercial interests is of course part of that theme, but so, too, is the dilemma of creating a product that has no substantive soul, whether for commercial reasons or not. In both *The Tooth of Crime* and *Geography of a Horse Dreamer*, the new forms created by the new ethic have not been able to reclaim or replace what is lost. And reclaiming what is lost--if possible--is Shepard's aim.

In many of Shepard's later works (since 1976) the above goal has become two-fold: to find what is lost in the individual consciousness and what has been lost in the national consciousness. To accomplish this end Shepard has turned increasingly to a realistic format, but has modified that realism to challenge the linear or causal expectations of the old naturalists. It is, as Shepard himself notes, "not the kind of realism where husbands and wives squabble and that kind of stuff" (Chubb 208). He claims to have moved from "ideas which speak only to the mind and leave out completely the body, the emotions and all the rest of it" ("Visualization" 55). What seem to be squabbles have taken on new dimensions, leaving only superficial parallels between any earlier incarnation of realism and Shepard's newer brand, which in turn has admittedly caused some confusion.

Take the first of Shepard's family plays, *Curse of the Starving Class* (1976), as an example of what confusion this new realism causes. Bigsby calls it "a realistic play, albeit charged with qualities which strain that realism in the direction of metaphor" (239-40). He further adds that it is a play

> about a lost lyricism, the collapse of dreams and hopes, and the decay of relationships. The family at the centre are the victims of gangsters and confidence tricksters . . . . They have allowed their farm to deteriorate, the father turning to drink, the mother to the false promises of a land agent. They are locked into a destructive cycle in which their dreams are finally the source of their destruction. (240)

The myth of America being the land of plenty and the guarantor of personal success for all has deteriorated, and Shepard is working to dramatize this fact. One metaphor presented in monologue is that of an eagle attacking a cat and carrying it into the sky, the bird unable to release the cat because the cat is unwilling to release the bird. The struggle ends as only it could, with both dying in an inevitable crash-- a fitting image of self-preservation leading to self-destruction.

Beyond this undramatized insert, the play as a whole is a similar metaphor of America's decay and self-destructive doom as well. The family is unable to support itself on the family ranch, instead reaching out for the unessential and ignoring the perhaps less tangible but nonetheless very real necessities for personal fulfillment. The members search for physical fulfillment in a materialist wasteland while being unaware that it is hunger for spiritual nourishment that is killing them. To dramatize this point in his play, Shepard presents it in extended metaphor. The family is starving, literally. The refrigerator is continually open and shut throughout the play in vain hope that it has been miraculously stocked. What they receive, to survive on, is a supply of artichokes, hardly sustaining nourishment and far from being considered a staple diet. Complementing this starving household is a cast of gangsters and con men, characters Shepard gleaned from late-night reruns. They are caricatures of romantic notions of a golden American past--that perhaps never was-- and they threaten the present with the misleading dreams and hopes they've instilled in this poverty-ridden setting. They enter without the least bit of realistic credibility--being stereotyped caricatures--but are nevertheless life-endangering realities to those family characters given more than two-dimensional form.

Such mixed application of the realistic and the unrealistic, needless to say, caused initial confusion among theatregoers and critics. Richard Eder, for example, makes the following remark:

Mr. Shepard has worked out the message in images of considerable power, and in a style that oscillates between realism and savage fantasy. A violent humor predominates, slipping into plain violence. Unfortunately, much of the force hangs in the air. It plays like a play that reads well, as if Mr. Shepard had failed to consider what would happen when his parable took physical form on the stage, and his images were played out by real actors performing in real time. (3)

Eder concludes by stating, "There is no reasonable relation between the message and the means employed to declare it; the metaphor and the metaphor's mechanics fight each other" (3). But the play asks that we avoid looking at it as Eder did. There are two levels, at least, working in the play, and Eder, expecting a consistent realism, is looking for only one level. At the other level, the controlling metaphor takes charge. Trying to thrive on the dreams haunted by the two-dimensional characters, the family has become spiritually malnourished in a manner parallel to the physical malnutrition. It seems, contrary to Eder's assertion, that the metaphor does work; perhaps the production he witnessed failed to actualize the play's potential.

So there are flesh-and-blood actions in the play, husband-and-wife squabbles, etc., that can be viewed with an expectation of linear consistency. Shepard's characters are eccentric, but there is at least some element of consistent characterization in them. An audience can judge this level from a perspective of "the old form." But at another level--metaphoric or mythic--consistency of overall image is the central concern, which involves a movement beneath or beyond characterization. Accepting the metaphorical as the higher level reveals a consistency that the former perspective will not. And where it had been difficult for Eder, with time and directorial sensibilities awakened to a need to clarify, it seems that *Curse of the Starving Class* has become more and more accessible. As Mel Gussow says in a 1985 review of a revival, "'Curse of the Starving Class' has deepened with every viewing" ("Starving Class" 3). It is perhaps thanks to productions of Shepard's next work that later productions of *Curse of the Starving Class* better realize *Curse*'s potential.

Shepard's next family play is *Buried Child* (1978; Pulitzer Prize 1979)). Don Shewey calls it "an eloquent depiction of inescapability of the family bond," and adds, "[I]n that respect it ranks right up there with *The Glass Menagerie* and *Long Day's Journey Into Night*" (*Sam Shepard* 127). In other respects, of course, it is quite different from these two plays. But despite this praise and despite the fact that it was awarded the Pulitzer Prize, the piece still failed to win Shepard universal approval or even full understanding. Finally, it is the difference between *Buried Child* and the two above-noted works that has caused the problem. Walter Kerr, for example, argues, "I am not certain there is a disciplined purpose, a mind dead set on making its inspiration clear. Evasiveness seems to me a weak form of theatrical life" ("Sam Shepard" 1). Kerr's criticism can be taken two ways: it may be an attack on craft or it may be an attack on intent. In an interview, Robert Woodruff, the collaborating director of *Buried Child*, provides information that actually addresses Kerr's concerns:

> A lot of the contradictions in the play own up to the fact that much of the third act was rewritten seven months after the first two acts and there were no major changes made in them. But it played. It played incredibly well, because the idea of contradictions was built into the play from the beginning . . . . It's not the mystery of who really did what. It's not Agatha Christy [sic]. (Coe "Interview" 157)

The play is admittedly constructed haphazardly, and the play seems destined to present contradictions as a result. On the former point, Shepard himself concedes the point: "I was real embarrassed by 'Buried Child'--lot of toe-scrunchers in there" (Coe "Saga" 122). But in this case contradictions are not necessarily flaws, given the fact that the more carefully crafted of Shepard's pieces consciously work toward contradiction. In fact, Shepard reports in 1979 that he believed "that if a play had faults, those faults were part and parcel of the original process, and that any attempt to correct them was cheating" ("Visualization" 57). At this stage in his development, at least, Shepard seemed more interested in sub-conscious concerns and wanted to leave the results of such a process intact. So on one point, Kerr's criticism stands: Shepard perhaps *should* take the time to polish his works to clear up areas of possible misinterpretation. On the point of interpretation, however, it is Kerr's own prejudices and shortcomings that need to be modified. As Woodruff admits, the play consciously avoids the rationalism of an Agatha Christie piece, an order and consistency that one would expect from naturalist drama but that Shepard is making a major point to confront. In fact, part of the answer to Kerr's question, "What's the message?" (the title of his essay) is exactly that--rational order and expectations have failed; let's look elsewhere.

Harold Clurman is one of many critics to admit that "several of his [Shepard's] plays baffled me and I may have misinterpreted some of them" ("Buried Child" 622). He adds, though, "I am convinced that he is not only a genuinely gifted but a meaningful writer" (622). What Clurman has discovered, at least in *Buried Child*, is that "meaning" has taken a different form than someone like Kerr--and perhaps the earlier Clurman--has come to expect. Clurman explains:

> Though the "story" of *Buried Child* is relatively clear, to make it intelligible one must take most of its details as metaphor or symbol, though these too are hardly exact. They do, however, convey a feeling-- like some Woody Guthrie type of chant--of Shepard's sense of America. (621-22)

As in *Curse of the Starving Class*, there is a need to recognize that consistent characterization takes a back seat to consistency of feeling or sense, as Clurman calls it. And questions about plot--whose child it was, whether incest actually occurred, if there ever really was a child, etc.--must also be accepted as secondary concerns, at best. Whether an event actually occurred or not is less important than the *sense* that it occurred (an act of pre-rational consciousness). The underlying rhythms, finally, are of central concern to Shepard; they are in essence reality. And to reveal that reality, one must strike through superficialities of outward appearances.

That *Buried Child* succeeds at striking through outward appearances perhaps more effectively than *Curse of the Starving Class* may be due to a tighter structure, somewhat of a surprise given the haphazard nature of the work's creation. Thomas Nash notes the play's structure:

> The first of the three acts of *Buried Child* establishes the naturalistic setting that Vince will invade in the second act . . . . When Vince, the grandson, finally arrives, the drama assumes a different character, a remoteness and communality . . . . Gradually, as Act III unfolds, the play reveals its ritual quality and its roots in folk drama. (488-89)

Though *Curse of the Starving Class* does evolve by the last act into a "ritual" drama--including the slaughter of a lamb--the play continually shifts from perceptions of straight realism into manipulation of realism as metaphor without much forewarning. *Buried Child*, however, prepares its audience by carefully slipping from one mode to the other, in essence announcing that it is slipping out of its seemingly naturalist format and revealing the mythic "explanations" of the earlier actions. Such revelation is the meaning Clurman speaks of and the message Kerr asks for but misses. But it obviously isn't "meaning" in any rational or scientific sense; it's meaning translated and conveyed through means similar to that of rituals. In many ways it *is* ritual on stage. Nash, in fact, makes a strong case that Shepard's play is a modern reworking of the European harvest ritual of the Corn Spirit or Corn King as found in Frazer's *The Golden Bough*, a tapping into a mythic pattern of death, fertility, and resurrection. Vince, the returning grandson, is the resurrection of the buried child. It is a return that coincides with a bountiful harvest and that opportunely provides for a replacement of the dying patriarch, Dodge.

This family is even more spiritually lost than the one in *Curse of the Starving Class*. Dark sins--incest and infanticide--threaten to destroy it. To regain a long-absent sense of harmony and order entails not appealing to social or rationalist concepts of justice, but somehow--inexplicably, in fact--attuning oneself once again to the rhythms of nature that was so long ago cast off by ignoring natural law and indulging unnatural urges.

Despite any perceived "toe-scrunchers," *Buried Child* goes far beyond *Curse of the Starving Class* in arguing Shepard's point that the

20th-century malaise in America is a spiritual one requiring treatment far beyond that which can be traditionally offered. The depth reaches down into essence itself, necessitating a sort of mythic reclamation of an American identity that had so long ago been blanched of any significance. *Curse of the Starving Class* attempts to reach the point that *Buried Child* reaches, but finally presents, as Kauffmann rather cynically sums it up, a rather naive "paean to agrarian values, to those who love Nature and Space and Simple Things and who are being forced off their land by exploitative commercial combines" (24). *Buried Child* succeeds because the play doesn't provide a list of goals; rather it provides an audience the opportunity to experience the need for a cleansing that perhaps triggers a longing for a new beginning. In many ways it does work like a Woody Guthrie chant, something that may very well be able to be analyzed but that offers much more than the analysis can explain. *Curse of the Starving Class* can work at this level, but because of unfortunate clutter, the play invites critiques such as Kauffmann provides above.

Shepard's third play of his family trilogy, *True West* (1980), focuses less on concern for the community and more on the effect that that community has on the individual. If consistent characterization had posed problems in his earlier plays, it has become the conscious focus of *True West*. Nash notes that Vince in *Buried Child* has "multifarious identities" (488). In *True West* Shepard dramatizes these "identities" by illustrating the disjunctive nature of human personalities subjected to a soul-less culture. Perhaps Shepard's most polished work, its New York debut, overseen by Joe Papp, suffered from the same lack of directorial vision that *Curse of the Starving Class* seemed to have experienced; it was a production so misdirected, in fact, that Shepard denounced it. The events of that controversial production are well documented, the consensus finally being that it was "not so much misdirected as undirected," as Brustein put it, adding, "It is heartbreaking in its failed opportunities" ("Crossed Purposes" 22). A series of external circumstances contributed to the production's failure, but the central issue certainly involved a misconception of the special demands of a Shepard product. Challenging convention by presenting it in ironic fashion is what the play strives to do, but Papp's production succeeded at presenting little more than "the look of a show [with Broadway and naturalist assumptions], the feel of a workshop [with its anti-naturalist experimentation]" (Brustein "Crossed Purposes" 22). The confusion could do little else but elicit condemning observations about the play itself:

> *True West* has the feeling of a first draft. Shepard rarely revises any of his works extensively, but at his best . . . the initial rush can carry him through. In *True West*, his impulse is not sustained; the play looks thin, even emaciated, like a healthy organism turning anorexic before your eyes. (Brustein "Crossed Purposes" 22)

Sam Shepard's *True West*. World premiere production (1980) at the Magic Theatre, San Francisco, directed by Robert Woodruff. Pictured are Austin (Peter Coyote) and Lee (Jim Haynie).

Photo: Ron Blanchette.

But by Shepard's own confession, this play is far from being unpolished copy: "I worked harder on this play than anything I've ever written. The play's down to the bone" (Coe "Saga" 122).

Subsequent productions of *True West* have managed to salvage the play's--and Shepard's--reputation, productions that proved the play could silence criticism such as the above and, perhaps more specifically, silence criticism like the following by Stephen Harvey:

> Local color notwithstanding, *True West* is no more than an uprooted transplant of the Ingmar Bergman *Persona* game, unless we can be persuaded that Austin and Lee [two brothers, central characters] recognize enough of themselves in each other to be tempted to trade psyches--or indeed that they exist dramatically in the first place. (123)

The above comment reaches into Shepard's actual intentions, though it notes the failure of the production to convey it. Shepard explains his aims:

> I wanted to write a play about double nature, one that wouldn't be symbolic or metaphorical or any of that stuff. I just wanted to give a taste of what it feels like to be two-sided. It's a real thing, double nature. I think we're split in a much more devastating way than psychology can ever reveal. It's not so cute. Not some little thing we can get over. It's something we've got to live with. (Coe "Saga" 122)

Working with double nature but foregoing overtly symbolic manipulation as practiced in *Buried Child*, Shepard ran the risk once again of having his work misinterpreted as a straight realistic/naturalistic work. In fact, Harvey notes the similarity between Shepard's work and Ibsen's *John Gabriel Borkman*, running simultaneously: "Both are basically naturalistic pieces that focus on the battle for dominance between a pair of adult siblings who have always loathed each other" (123). But as Shepard notes, the play is not Ibsenesque in that what appears to be a play about sibling rivalry is more accurately a play about a struggle between two halves of one self. The realist format invites such confusion, and it is the responsibility of a production--or reader--to be sensitive to the particular signals that indicate otherwise; there must be an awareness of symbolic and ironic manipulation of the realist format.

Commenting on a 1985 production, Leah Frank indicates that the production was a success, in that the following was actually suggested in performance: "There is a possibility that these two brothers are different aspects of one personality, or that they are not people but symbols of the American West. One is a degenerate cowboy, one is a civilized man" (14). In fact, when Shepard discounts symbolism in his own comments, he seems to ignore the very fact of the play's title, for it seems that the play is actually designed to include that level, simultaneous to working on a psychological plane. Perhaps Shepard more accurately meant that in this play he wanted attention to center on the psychologically "realistic" level than he had wanted in his earlier works. Given the title and various events in the play, then, *True West* returns to symbolically presenting the theme of the vanishing West and the consequences that loss has on individual identity, but from that point it addresses the nature of split identities, the focus Shepard wants us to note.

Concerning the former point, Shepard insists on a realistic set to illustrate his split-identity focus, as he states in a "Note on Set and Costume":

> The set should be constructed realistically with no attempt to distort its dimension, shapes, objects, or colors . . . . If a stylistic "concept" is grafted onto the 'set design it will only serve to confuse the evolution of the characters' situation, which is the most important focus of the play. (*True West* 3)

The "situation" that Shepard has forced upon his characters is a suburban Los Angeles home--their mother's--a seemingly idyllic set, the consummation of the American Dream. But in scene 2 the first hint of the intended impact of the set is made. Lee, the prodigal son, while talking to Austin, the other son house-sitting for their mother, observes that the country has been "wiped out" (11) by suburban encroachment. The hollow triumph of an acquisitive culture co-opting everything in its grasp is made increasingly more clear throughout the play until scene 9 finally reveals the set *"ravaged"* (50), and Austin, gone slightly berserk, illustrates the acquisitive urge for the absurdity it is by accumulating a whole kitchen of stolen toasters. Tucker Orbison concludes of the set that it is "superficially edenic; in reality it is a void" (508). Shepard has ironically used realism to comment on itself, the hollowness that such preoccupation provides. Orbison continues:

> The new, modern West, then, is a superficially civilized "collection of junk." This is the real West--the West of temporary living, full freeways, and empty hearts. It is the West . . . where because the present and future are everything, the past means nothing. But this new West is a false, demonic West: it has crushed imagination and feelings, and substituted material success. (508)

The suburban encroachment has wiped out significant life, spiritual or imaginative satisfaction. Austin himself realizes the changes, implies he agrees with Lee that something vital has been wiped out, when he makes a note in the following exchange:

AUSTIN: . . . Foothills are the same though, aren't they?
LEE: Pretty much. It's funny goin' up in there. The smells and everything. Used to catch snakes up there, remember?
AUSTIN: You caught snakes.
LEE: Yeah. And you'd pretend you were Geronimo or some damn thing.

> You used to go right out to lunch.
> AUSTIN: I enjoyed my imagination.
> LEE: That what you call it? Looks like yer still enjoyin' it. (11-12)

But Austin in fact no longer enjoys either the land or his imagination. He has sold out to the film industry, writing and selling scripts according to formula, marketable merchandise rather than genuine offspring of his imagination. The sterile, real West has deprived the imagination of any creativity it was once capable of generating.

Lee, on the other hand, has opted for the desert, physically a wasteland of little interest to the civilized West, but a spiritual source of energy that has acted as a reservoir of independence and freedom that epitomizes the ideal of the old West. But even Lee cannot avoid the corrupting influence of civilization. Like the wild coyotes of the deserts, Lee's freedom and instincts are compromised by the urge for "easy pickings," prowling the outskirts of civilization for easy burglaries, a human equivalent of coyotes raiding the garbage dumps. The old West is giving way to the new West, what despairingly must be labelled the "real" West.

But Shepard doesn't call his play *Real West*. It is *True West*, and finding that true West involves not looking for a geographical location, but a state of mind, one that may be conditioned by desert life but that doesn't absolutely necessitate it. True West ironically comes to life in the play in an imaginative enterprise using a form that has, to that point, been condemned as market trash--a film script. Lee manipulates himself into a contract to write a Western. The outline Lee makes of his film draws heavily from stereotypical plots of early, classic Westerns and runs the risk of being misinterpreted as trite amateurism. But the mythic dimensions underlying the plot are the essence, playing as Shepard does in *Curse of the Starving Class* with recognizable types in popular culture and inserting them in patterns of ritual and mythic import as he does in *Buried Child*. Two men, turned mortal enemies, engage in a chase across the wild Texas Panhandle; their trucks run out of gas, and they are forced to continue an endless chase on horseback. Lee summarizes:

> So they take off after each other straight into an endless black prairie. The sun is just comin' down and they can feel the night on their backs. What they don't know is that each of 'em is afraid, see. Each one separately thinks that he's the only one that's afraid. And they keep ridin' like that straight into the night. Not knowing. And the one who's chasin' doesn't know where the other one is taking him. And the one who's being chased doesn't know where he's going. (27)

Austin attacks Lee's idea because "It's not like real life . . . . Things don't happen like that" (21), but by play's end it is Austin and Lee who are caught up in exactly this kind of struggle. They find the essence of true West at that point, stripping themselves down to their essential selves and engaging in mortal combat on an uncharted and untamed psychological frontier.

Lee's script *is* unrealistic and may in fact appear trite, but its triteness is the result of its having been thoughtlessly overused and reduced by commercialism and has nothing to do with its intrinsic value, for it has metaphoric value that reveals an archetypal pattern of returning to the world of the primitive and openly engaging in an unrestricted struggle between two opposing forces that somehow--mystically--reveals "truth" and understanding itself. The Western once strove to capture that essential spirit, but the sterile imposition of Hollywood moguls has trivialized that essence, bleached it out of "contemporary" Westerns, as Austin calls them.

Having presented the film script outline, Shepard proceeds to actually dramatize it in the play in *true* contemporary fashion, casting Lee and Austin in the alternating roles of pursuer and pursued. As noted above, with the final scene set and the script previously outlined, Shepard considers this realistic "acting out" the focus of the play. The scene focuses on dramatizing the climax of a struggle between a renegade-spirited brother, Lee, and his spiritually depraved, "successful" brother, Austin, who oddly enough nearly kills the more aggressive Lee in the final scene. But if one moves beyond the realism and takes the action from a psychological point of view, one could see the play as illustrating not some facile urge toward total freedom, as was perhaps dramatized in *Curse of the Starving Class*, but a more sophisticated claim that the victory of one "urge" over the other leads to an intolerable imbalance. A purely renegade spirit would be too destructive and a purely civilized spirit would be too sterile. The struggle must continue interminably, as it does in the movie script, where the chase has no end.

On the literal level, Austin/civilization has the advantage at the play's close, but the struggle is guaranteed to continue, and that is what is important, not at a literal level, though, but at the mythic level. The realistic/literal surfaces have been lifted, and underneath it all is seen the raw energy that is true West, an energy stemming from the struggle that the real West effectively subdues rather than channels and that as a result is fast disappearing. In fact, without proper channeling, the force has become self-consuming and destructive, a fact in this play initially illustrated by relatively harmless burglaries but eventually vented in near fratricide. But fratricide is not the point in this play. Shepard has insisted that the play is one of double nature. Weales notes the following, commenting on a later, 1982, production of the play:

> Shepard is not interested here in conventional role reversal, but in the fact that the changes are an externalization of qualities implicit in the characters. Toward the end of the first act, both men indicate that each has envied the other for an imagined, a romanticized version of his life. This is not standard sibling rivalry, but a reflection of shared attitudes,

> ambitions, longings, inclinations behind a facade of apparent differences .
> . . . In this reading of the play, the brothers each discovering himself in
> the other, are actually aspects of a single character in which the destructive
> impulse and the need to escape share space with the urge to order and the
> longing for shelter. (50)

The play does not advocate victory of one side over the other, but
neither does it totally advocate a peaceful co-existence, sensing that
such an event is impossible. Rather, the true West is one that occupies
a psychological frontier within each self where the struggle should
exist continually and by existing guarantees life itself.

The effect of viewing (and presenting) the conflict as an essentially
internal one is that "Shepard steers clear of the facile Freudianism and
soap-opera sentimentality that floods most American family drama," as
Shewey puts it ("The True Story" 115). Without this perspective, the
result is what Harvey observed of the New York (Papp) premiere: "its
endless string of carefully matched dualities [are] reduced onstage to a
willful theatrical tic" (123). But the play takes on a complexity that
integrates the various seeming dualities, creating interchanges that
reveal complex interrelationships on several levels, not simply easy
dichotomies. It is not, for example, merely a symbolic drama pitting
what Frank calls "a degenerate cowboy" against a "civilized man"
(14). Instead, the play succeeds at more fully "integrat[ing]
contrasting images of masculinity: the idealized Western movie-hero
and the disappointingly average (or even lousy) all-American dad," as
Shewey notes ("The True Story" 115).

That one production failed to highlight the complexities and another
succeeded demonstrates the point that Shepard's work places demands
on realism that depart from typical realist or naturalist practices. The
key element is that, going beyond motives of individual
characterization, the play demands that two characters unite as the play
progresses. The play submerges into a realm of "consciousness" in a
manner that realism doesn't typically utilize. This distinction clarified
in production, the play reaches the level demanded by the play. And
Weales notes that the 1982 Steppenwolf production does achieve this
end, fusing the characters together by accepting the fact that the stage
is a physical manifestation of another realm:

> [The production] emphasizes the connection between the two brothers in
> terms of shared mannerisms that surface as the play progresses,
> particularly in Sinise's [the actor's] Austin, who uses and mocks Lee's
> grossness as he descends into drunken release. (50)

The characters' personalities have overlapped, confusing the easy
dichotomies that some have been unable to see beyond, and a
successful production requires the sensitivity to see the
transformation. At the same time, an audience must be able to see the
ironic use of the realistic set--its insubstantiality--and see that the

deeper level of understanding transcends first the play's surface and then even the reality of the characters themselves, they being part of a larger movement that takes on the psychological part of "self."

True West can be viewed, incompletely, as a competent naturalist drama, which is very likely the reason it has achieved recent popular success and has been called by many the most accessible of Shepard's plays. But on that count Shepard could respond that though they have seen a "real" play, they have missed the "true" play.

Shepard's next work, an addendum to the family trilogy, is *Fool for Love* (1982). Also essentially realistic, the play clearly works to set itself apart from such a misunderstanding as experienced above by inserting a ghost-like observer just beyond the proscenium who quietly comments on the play and occasionally interjects himself into the action. "Consciousness" is again the realm in which Shepard works. Brustein calls *Fool for Love* "the latest in that series of hyper-realistic lower middle-class family dramas that Shepard has been writing since *Curse of the Starving Class*" ("Love" 24). Brustein adds, this time speaking of all the family plays: "[T]he realism proves to be illusory, the fifth dimension of people from a different space-and-time zone, though they share the rivalries, enmities, passions, and recriminations of us all" ("Love" 25). At this stage in Shepard's career, his intentions seem to have become recognized. But still not all accept those designs.

Within the frame of the stage May and Eddie are pitted against each other, two lovers alternately violently repelled by and passionately attracted to each other in a classic love-hate relationship. The set is a seedy motel room along a lonely stretch of road somewhere in the American West. May and Eddie fill the stage with conflicting accounts of their relationship, which have led Kerr to conclude about the play: "I am afraid we must call them arbitrary and simply one more sampling of Mr. Shepard's fondness for disconnective, dislocating 'effect'" ("Where Has Sam Shepard Led His Audience?" 16). Judging the "effects" as rationally untenable, of course, is derived from an assumption, once again, that this "domestic drama" is hoping to conform to old presumptions about realism. But the disconnected quality is designed to tune the audience in to the true nature of the drama, and the old man beyond the frame of the stage should certainly help a critic avoid such an error of judgment as Kerr has committed. The text describes the "Old Man" as follows:

> He exists only in the minds of MAY and EDDIE, even though they might talk to him directly and acknowledge his physical presence. THE OLD MAN treats them as though they all existed in the same time and place. (*Fool for Love* 15)

It is irrelevant, finally, whether or not the action can indicate that the Old Man is May's and Eddie's imaginative creation, as the script suggests, or whether the play is the Old Man's memory fabrication.

Sam Shepard's *Fool for Love.* World premiere production (1983) at the Magic Theatre, San Francisco, directed by Sam Shepard. Pictured are May (Kathy Baker) and Eddie (Ed Harris).

Photo: R. Valentine Atkinson.

One of the two possibilities should be suggested, and with either suggestion, assumptions that logical or rationally motivated action will follow should come into question.

The play may have the appearance of a domestic drama, but the focus is more on the psychological and emotional underpinnings of that relationship, as perceived by three separate consciousnesses. As Frank Rich notes,

> In "Fool for Love," each story gives us a different "version" of who May, Eddie and the old man are, and the stories rarely mesh in terms of facts. Yet they do cohere as an expression of the author's consciousness: as Shepard's people race verbally through the debris of the West, they search for the identities and familial roots that have disappeared with the landscape of legend. ("Fool for Love" 3)

Each version is as laden with truth as it is with illusion, indistinguishable as they are, because the characters haven't found a satisfactory or mutually agreeable means to anchor themselves to reality. The following exchange reveals the confusion:

> (. . . . Stage lights drop to half their intensity as a spot rises softly on THE OLD MAN. He speaks directly to EDDIE.)
> THE OLD MAN: I thought you were supposed to be a fantasist, right? Isn't that basically the deal with you? You dream things up. Isn't that true?
> EDDIE: . . . . I don't know.
> THE OLD MAN: You don't know. Well, if you don't know I don't know who the hell else does. I wanna show you somethin'. Somethin' real, okay? Somethin' actual.
> EDDIE: Sure.
> THE OLD MAN: Take a look at that picture on the wall over there. (He points at the wall stage right. There is no picture but EDDIE stares at the wall.) Ya' see that? Take a good look at that. Ya' see it?
> EDDIE: (staring at wall) Yeah.
> THE OLD MAN: Ya' know what that is?
> EDDIE: I'm not sure.
> THE OLD MAN: Barbara Mandrell. That's who that is. Barbara Mandrell. You heard a' her?
> EDDIE: Sure.
> THE OLD MAN: Well, would you believe me if I told ya' I was married to her?
> EDDIE: (pause) No.
> THE OLD MAN: Well, see, now that's the difference right there. That's realism. I am actually married to Barbara Mandrell in my mind. Can you understand that?
> EDDIE: Sure.
> THE OLD MAN: Good. I'm glad we have an understanding. (26-27)

Reality has literally become internalized; consciousness of an event *is* the reality of the event, which argues that "reality" is as varied as individual perception is. There is no credibility whatsoever to the Old

Man's claim of being married to Barbara Mandrell. But the "fantasist's" insistence very nearly stamps it as real.

In this adversarial posture, the play seems almost an explanation of Shepard's earlier realist dramas, arguing that prior confidence in existence based on physical presence, void of understanding the roots of that existence, finally entails illusion or delusion and self-deceit.

If Eddie's dreams could be realized--those of recapturing the spirit of the Old West--then perhaps illusion and reality would once again separate and substantial physical reality could regain its position as reflecting truth, or the real itself. But reality has become filled with meaningless figures, a soul-less materialism that it is better off to replace with the figments of a fantasist than to allow to reign over us as "truth." Fragmented, personal reality is preferred to an empty communal reality, but life itself requires the communal bond in order to continue.

In the play, this debate over the preferred reality is manifest in the struggle dramatized by Eddie and May. At one level, jealousy is the cause of their arguments, a natural, much-discussed cause. But there's another level that actually "causes" this cause to exist, a reason why Eddie regularly runs away and spawns May's jealousy, and vice versa. Drawn together in deep love for one another since they first met, they are also naturally repelled by one another as a result of being siblings, born of the same father--the Old Man. Individual consciousness could certainly overcome the consequences of the communal taboo of incest and often runs dangerously close to effecting that end. But the repelling strength of the incest taboo--a communal universal that challenges a rebellious individual consciousness--mysteriously succeeds at keeping them apart (it is assumed) in a world that appears little concerned with enforcing the "law." The mythic dimensions of a communal or collective consciousness are still intact, but the battlefield itself has shifted from tangible outer forces (a communal law or code) versus individual inner forces (personal desire) to an entirely internalized struggle between the two forces within consciousness itself.

So the play moves on several levels. First there is the "confusing" level of the domestic squabble. Then there is the struggle between the memory of an old man who has indulged completely in individual fantasy against a son (and daughter) whose conscience won't allow him completely to forsake a sense of communal "right," even though communal right seems no longer to be of significance. And finally, there's the struggle that's been forced inward between individual and communal forces because there is no physical correlative to which communal sense can attach itself. Shepard's play has become a "memory" or "dream" play as a result, internalizing reality to "set the stage" for battles that formerly had physical forums in which to struggle.

With *Fool for Love*, the other plays come into even better focus. As Rich notes, Shepard "almost demands we see his plays as a continuum: they bleed together" ("Fool for Love" 3). The levels on which the plays function vary within the plays themselves, and unless one sees their highest level, they can easily be received with confusion or even complete misunderstanding. They are realistic, but they ask us to see realism from a perspective of skepticism. They question the very foundations of realism, ask us to consider the sources of our assumptions about the physical world--and hopefully to realize the emptiness of the forms we casually assume to be so "real."

Frank Rich may not have realized the significance of the following on a symbolic level when he rather literally observed of Shepard:

> His works often play more feverishly in the mind after they're over than they do while they're before us in the theater. But that's the way he is, and who would or could change him? Like the visionary pioneers who once ruled the open geography of the West, Mr. Shepard rules his vast imaginative frontier by making his own, ironclad laws. ("Fool for Love" 3)

But what Rich notes as literally occurring in the audience is designed to occur symbolically on stage, a sort of "all the mind's a stage" motif. Shepard is looking to capture the substance and vitality of the frontier spirit, knowing that the physical world we've created has lost the potential to reclaim that spirit for us. If we can see through the physical to the spiritual, then one level is reached. If that process can move from the stage into the audience, yet another level is reached. It has turned to the individual to recapture what is lost or, better, to rediscover a consciousness that our physical world no longer asks us to utilize but that is there--and necessary--nonetheless.

A recent product, *A Lie of the Mind* (1986), continues the family tradition of Shepard's works, and also continues to address the inner necessity to understand. Rich notes that the play "eventually bleeds its personal story into a larger cultural mythos" ("A Lie of the Mind" 3). And Gussow adds, "As is usual in the works of Shepard, there are transformations as various characters assume the identity of others" ("Sam Shepard Revisits the American Heartland" 7). In particular, Shepard presents a brain-damaged woman in this work, whose character, according to Felicia Londré, "is the most compelling" because she must "reinvent her own identity as the play progresses" (20). Shepard's creation of this role may be a response to various charges that he's ignored women or reduced them to stereotypes in his other works. She is indeed a strong character, and does extend Shepard's concern quite positively. In general, though, with *A Lie of the Mind*, the delusions of unsubstantiated belief reign over all the central characters--men and women--in the realm of consciousness. As Hart notes, the "point" of *A Lie of the Mind* is essentially a continuation of his earlier themes: "the curse of psychological disease passes from parents to children; the family's buried secrets eventually surface to demand confrontation; the truth of our experience collides

with the lies of our minds" (106).   Shepard's "quest," it appears,
continues.

   Though Shepard deals with family in these works and though he
utilizes realism, he has moved beyond both the family analysis and the
brand of realism that O'Neill used. Causes of disruption steer away
from the social level and even the analytically psychological level, and
they delve into the non-rational impulses of mythos--a level O'Neill
worked in but never fully extended to his realist works. That is the
critical point of departure; Shepard takes his family plays to levels that
essentially challenge the assumptions of realistic thought itself,
assumptions that O'Neill's works utilized rather than questioned. Of
necessity, the two forms, ostensibly the same on the surface, upon
closer scrutiny, reveal themselves as fundamentally different.
   As noted earlier, various critics have noted Shepard's "post-modern"
meta-theatricalism, some of whom have gone so far as to argue that
such techniques better align Shepard with European thought than
American. Rodney Simard, for example, argues that viewing Shepard
as an American "obscures his contribution to postmodern drama" (76).
It seems more accurate, however, to see Shepard as an American who
has adapted elements of a non-native methodology to his American
needs. His thematics involve, very specifically, the concerns of
Americans, though he has applied to those concerns a new
perspective. Perhaps it would be better to follow the leads of Ruby
Cohn and Ron Mottram, who argue that Shepard's vision has utilized
the post-modern perspective to extend the American vista (Cohn 185;
Mottram 159). Shewey agrees with Cohn and Mottram, noting:

> A true American artist, Sam Shepard is always searching for roots. And
> like Americans in the past, he looks west, to the frontier, the wilderness,
> the territories, hoping to find in the midst of the unknown something he
> can recognize as home, something he can recognize as himself. (*Sam
> Shepard* 13)

Shepard has put the tools of post-modernism to work to scour material
that American playwrights have mined for generations. There may be
differences between the generations' approaches, but there is much
that they still have in common.
   Seeing the differences between the various generations of American
realism and responding to them in the manner that each requires is a
sometimes difficult task, and occasional misinterpretation is still likely.
The risks involved seem to be to fall victim to outdated assumptions
about understanding as propounded by the old realism or to be thrust
into a post-modern meta-theatrical realm that fails fully to recognize
constructive efforts at comprehending and understanding the American
scene. Like Rabe and Mamet--though to an even greater degree--
Shepard seems to be walking a thin line between the two, both a
product of the 60s separated from past systems of thought as well as a

man aware of a heritage he is unwilling (and perhaps unable) to abandon. His realism cannot be like O'Neill's, but his attempts to fathom the depths can be--and are--prompted by the same ghosts.

Works Cited

Bigsby, C.W.E. *A Critical Introduction to Twentieth-Century American Drama*, Vol. 3: *Beyond Broadway*. London: Cambridge UP, 1985.

Brustein, Robert. "The Crack in the Chimney: Reflections on Contemporary American Playwriting." *Images and Ideas in American Culture*. Ed. Arthur Edelstein. Hanover, NH: Brandeis UP, 1979. 141-57.

--------. "Crossed Purposes." *New Republic* 31 Jan. 1981: 21-23.

--------. "Love from Two Sides of the Ocean." *New Republic* 27 June 1983: 24-25.

Chubb, Kenneth. "Metaphors, Mad Dogs and Old Time Cowboys: Interview with Sam Shepard." *Theatre Quarterly* 4 (Aug./Oct. 1974): 3-16.

Clurman, Harold. "Buried Child." *Nation* 2 Dec. 1978: 621-22.

--------. "The Tooth of Crime." *Nation* 26 Mar. 1973: 410-12.

Coe, Robert. "Interview with Robert Woodruff." *American Dreams: The Imagination of Sam Shepard*. Ed. Bonnie Marranca. New York: Performing Arts Journal Publications, 1981. 151-58.

--------. "Saga of Sam Shepard." *New York Times Magazine* 23 Nov. 1980: 56+.

Cohn, Ruby. *New American Dramatists: 1960-1980*. New York: Grove Press, 1982.

Eder, Richard. "The Starving Class." *New York Times* 3 Mar. 1978, sec. 3: 3.

Frank, Leah D. "Shepard's 'West': A Tale Well Told." *New York Times* 28 Apr. 1985, sec. 21: 14.

Gussow, Mel. "Sam Shepard Revisits the American Heartland." *New York Times* 15 Dec. 1985, sec 2: 3+.

--------. "'Starving Class' By Shepard Is Back." *New York Times* 24 May 1985, sec. 3: 3.

Hart, Lynda. *Sam Shepard's Metaphorical Stages*. Westport, CT: Greenwood Press, 1987.

Harvey, Stephen. "True West. " *Nation* 31 Jan. 1981: 123-24.

Herman, William. *Understanding Contemporary American Drama*. Columbia: U of South Carolina Press, 1987.

Kauffmann, Stanley. "What Price Freedom?" *New Republic* 8 Apr. 1978: 24-25.

Kerr, Walter. "Sam Shepard--What's the Message?" *New York Times* 10 Dec. 1978, sec. 2: 1.

--------. "Where Has Sam Shepard Led His Audience?" *New York Times* 5 June 1983, sec. 2: 3+.

Londré, Felicia, "Sam Shepard Works Out: The Masculinization of America." *Studies in American Drama, 1945-Present* 2 (1987): 19-27.

Mottram, Ron. *Inner Landscapes: The Theater of Sam Shepard*. Columbia: U. of Missouri Press, 1984.

Nash, Thomas. "Sam Shepard's *Buried Child*: The Ironic Use of Folklore." *Modern Drama* 26 (1983): 486-91.

Orbison, Tucker. "Mythic Levels in Shepard's *True West*." *Modern Drama* 27 (1984): 505-19.

Putzel, Steven. "Expectation, Confutation, Revelation: Audience Complicity in the Plays of Sam Shepard." *Modern Drama* 30 (1987): 147-60.

Rabillard, Sheila. "Sam Shepard: Theatrical Power and American Dreams." *Modern Drama* 30 (1987): 58-71.

Rich, Frank. "'Fool for Love,' Sam Shepard Western." *New York Times* 27 May 1983, sec. 3: 3.

--------. "'A Lie of the Mind,' by Sam Shepard." *New York Times* 6 Dec. 1985, sec. 3: 3.

Sauvage, Leo. "Acts of Insanity." *New Leader* 10 Mar. 1986: 21-22.

Shepard, Sam. "American Experimental Theatre: Then and Now." *American Dreams: The Imagination of Sam Shepard*. Ed. Bonnie Marranca. New York: Performing Arts Journal Publications, 1981. 212-13.

--------. *Fool for Love*. San Francisco: City Lights, 1983.

--------. *True West*. In *Seven Plays*. New York: Bantam, 1981, 1-59.

--------. "Visualization, Language and the Inner Library." *The Drama Review* 21, iv (Dec. 1977): 49-58.

Shewey, Don. *Sam Shepard: The Life, The Loves, Behind The Legend Of A True American Original*. New York: Dell, 1985.

--------. "The True Story of 'True West.'"*Village Voice* 30 Nov. 1982: 115.

Simard, Rodney. *Postmodern Drama: Contemporary Playwrights in America and Britain*. Lanham, MD: UP of America, 1984.

Smith, Michael. "Theatre: *Cowboys* and *The Rock Garden*." *Village Voice* 22 Oct. 1964: 13,

--------. "Theatre Journal." *Village Voice* 27 Jan. 1966: 19-20.

Weales, Gerald. "Shepard Rides Again: The Device is a Simple One." *Commonweal* 28 Jan. 1983: 49-50.

Wetzsteon, Ross. "Looking a Gift Horse Dreamer in the Mouth." *American Dreams: The Imagination of Sam Shepard*. Ed. Bonnie Marranca. New York: Performing Arts Journal Publications, 1981. 133-35.

Wilson, Ann. "Fool of Desire: The Spectator to the Plays of Sam Shepard." *Modern Drama* 30 (1987): 46-57.

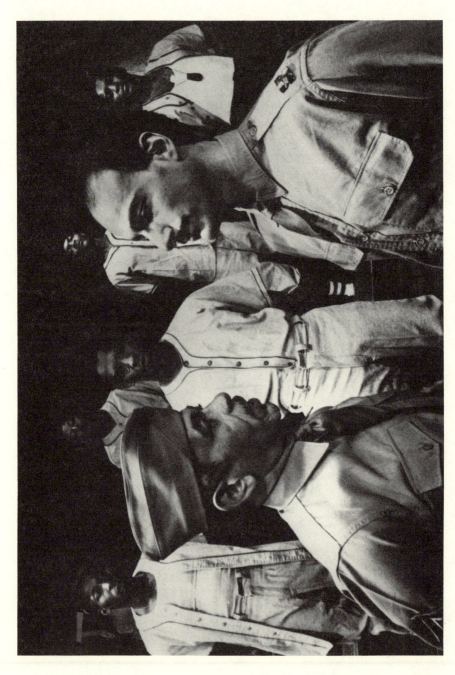

Charles Fuller's *A Soldier's Play*. New York cast of N.E.C. production. Pictured in foreground are Sgt. Waters (Adolph Caesar) and Capt. Taylor (Peter Friedman); background center is P.F.C. Peterson (Denzel Washington). Courtesy of Goodman Theatre, Chicago.

Photo: Bert Andrews.

Chapter Five

New Voices Using New Realism: Fuller, Henley, and Norman

Rabe, Mamet, and Shepard may be relatively young playwrights, but behind them is already what must be regarded as a second generation of new realists. Though there isn't much difference in age between the two groups, the recognition and exposure of this new group warrants labelling them a new wave when compared to the more established writers. Three such playwrights are Charles Fuller, Beth Henley, and Marsha Norman, writers who, though relative newcomers, have already had their quality evaluated and rewarded with Pulitzer Prizes. But much as with their more established colleagues, these writers have not been received completely with open arms. For example, in a January 1982 review of Beth Henley's *Crimes of the Heart*, Stanley Kauffmann made the guardedly laudatory statement, "The Pulitzer Prize for drama is looking up a little, anyway" ("Two Cheers" 54). This is of course not a glowing commendation, except possibly when compared to a 1983 article, where Kauffmann returned to his former impression of Pulitzer decisions, attacking Marsha Norman's *'night, Mother*:

> If the hoopla about Marsha Norman's new play were credible, the current state of American drama would be better than it is . . . . Because the play has only two characters, is in one long act, and ends with a death, some commentators have called it classical and have invoked Aristotle. I envy their rapture; the play itself keeps me from sharing it . . . . I think it has been misconstrued by most who have written about it, and apparently by the author herself. ("More Trick" 47)

Fuller's *A Soldier's Play* (Pulitzer 1982) has likewise been received as a work that is less than impressive. The reasons for such lukewarm receptions, it seems, is that the works look like little more than reworked versions of old realism and so are often ignored as a result.

The efforts of Fuller, Henley, and Norman, however, have actually taken on the look of Rabe, Mamet, and Shepard, and the result would, expectedly, be mixed, given the latter group's own reception. As with Rabe, Mamet, and Shepard, the realism of these second generation playwrights is not rationalistic in design, but in fact plays against the rationalism of the old school, and so a tendency to confuse the old and the new is once again likely. Because their works have been confused as belonging to the old school of realism, they deserve closer attention and scrutiny, closer than that already given them. Another reason to turn a closer eye toward them is that their use of the new realist mode of presentation means that certain minority elements of society under-represented in our drama now have voices, since these playwrights offer us black, Southern, and feminist points of views. Their success is important, given the fact that few blacks or women have been accorded such recognition. But what is even more important here is that their works have utilized a means of dramatic presentation that is currently being used by today's most capable, established writers, and with that form these new voices have dramatized issues and concerns which simultaneously speak to a minority and which have been accorded mainstream attention at least partly because of their choice of form. This new realism is expanding the reach of traditional theatre, which is being revitalized by new voices and fresh perspectives as a result.

Charles Fuller and *A Soldier's Play*

Charles Fuller's realism in *A Soldier's Play* (1981; Pulitzer Prize 1982) plays against naturalist prejudices and assumptions of the theatre itself in an effort to awaken audiences to epistemologically related racial prejudices and presumptions. In other words, the mental process leading to the two types of prejudice are essentially the same. So Fuller's work has become a sort of deconstructive technique of unearthing flaws in naturalist-motivated assumptions in general which is in turn used to reveal closely related thematic elements involving race and race relations. It is a process that has subtly succeeded in translating Fuller's black thematic concerns into a theatrical idiom that can more readily be identified as an "American" experience.

Fuller is closely connected to the Negro Ensemble Company, a group that was founded in the late 60s (first play produced in December 1967) because, as Gilman puts it, "the established American theater didn't seem to have any place for the black experience" (90). Gilman continues:

> So the group proceeded to carve such a place for itself, with determination
> if not always a clear notion of what it was doing. Its stance was either

aggressive, that of an adversary, or defensive, which meant insular and self-validating. (90)

Charles Fuller is one of the playwrights responsible for bringing the N.E.C. into mainstream theatre. *A Soldier's Play* has capped that struggle to present something more than a work that "self-validates" the Black perspective. Gilman writes of *A Soldier's Play*: "[I]t's about the black experience but is supple enough in its thematic range and social perspectives to treat that experience as a part of a complex whole, as part of American reality in its widest sense" (90). Fuller is very conscious of the value of theatre as a tool for social reform, but though he does use his plays to make his case for reform, his dialectic is neither directly confrontational nor in any real sense "agit-prop." As is the case with Rabe, Mamet, and Shepard, Fuller speaks less for social change than for a more subtle, yet profound, change in consciousness. And because he is less than confrontational in his art, Fuller has met with occasional, though vocal, criticism from black contemporaries. One very outspoken critic of Fuller is 60s dramatist/activist LeRoi Jones/Amiri Baraka. To him, Fuller's plays cater to the desires of the white power structure rather than to the needs of the oppressed blacks, as Baraka himself argues in the following observations of both Fuller and the N.E.C.:

An oppressed people demand that all their resources be put to the service of liberating them, no matter what these resources are. Certainly art and culture must be seen in such a light. Either we are trying to fashion an art of liberation, whatever its forms, or we are creating an art that helps maintain our chains and slave status . . . . The Negro Ensemble has been, in the main, a skin theater, offering only colored complexion but not a sustained thrust in concert with the whole of the BLM [Black Liberation Movement] to liberate ourselves. It has been fundamentally a house slave's theater, eschewing struggle for the same reason that the house niggers did--because they didn't have it so bad! (53)

But this adversarial posturing (blacks against whites) is clearly a phenomenon of the social protest period of the 60s (though it occurs in some writers, like Baraka, to this day), and though Fuller isn't the activist Baraka wishes he were, Fuller has benefited from Baraka's (and the 60s') breakthroughs, despite being a disappointment to Baraka. What Fuller has learned is that blacks have a right to a place in society, on their own terms, and are now confident enough to demand that right. Fuller, finally, is not a social activist, choosing rather to follow a more intimate agenda. He observes: "If attitudes change then fewer people are involved in racism. I don't believe that writers can change the world by themselves. But we can change the climate. You must get to the point where certain ideas can be perceived" (Savran 76). So though Fuller isn't a 60s-style political activist, his work is informed by a 60s tradition that has given him a sort of independence to write as he does, neither maintaining a strictly "self-validating" posture nor taking a "humble" stand on issues as a pre-60s black writer may have felt inclined to take. And changing the climate requires a sophisticated and subtle approach.

Through his sophisticated portrayal of the whole spectrum of character types, Fuller reveals subtleties and complexities that black characterization has rarely received, which in turn successfully argues that for Fuller the black experience is ready to be assimilated fully into mainstream American culture. Frank White III suggests the same point when he discusses *A Soldier's Play*:

> Some Blacks have bemoaned *A Soldier's Play*'s ending, which focuses on the detriment of Blacks' hatred of other Blacks. Fuller shakes his head when reminded of this. "I don't spend a lot of time trying to make Black people unreal," he says. "Violence in the Black community is a fact of life. Not that I think it ought to be glorified, but I think we need to be responsible for what goes on in our community." (117)

Willing to take the risk of presenting blacks even in a negative way, Fuller's portrayals help to break a long tradition of stereotyping blacks in literature, cinema, drama, and television, which portray them as

> [i]neffectual types who just can't get themselves together, the kind Hattie McDaniels used to chase out of the kitchen . . . . We speak [in traditional portrayals] one abominable language--hip; we have one interest--women. Our lives have no beginning, no ending. We're highly emotional in terms of reactive violence, and we do not use our minds in any way. (White 117)

Fuller's plays do include such characterizations as well, but also many others that awaken the audience to a more rounded understanding of blacks as individuals who perhaps have been brought up in different cultural circumstances rather than of blacks as some group different than others and therefore easily "ghetto-ized." The result is that breaking from a defensive stance, as Fuller does, the experiences of his characters are no longer racially limited and assume a more "universal" quality. Fuller argues, "I can't see how any growing people would want to be continually portrayed as sweet and innocent" (White 117), a portrayal that would possibly be the natural reaction to the former stereotyping of blacks. Breaking one stereotype to establish another is not the answer. Stereotypes of any sort isolate people from true understanding, and finally, according to White, Fuller contends that it is blacks who "have more to lose by staying remote from the white community" (116). Fuller completes the thought: "[Y]ou change or they change or, if nobody changes, somebody loses in this equation. And I'm thinking it's us" (White 116). Fuller's approach leads to an equation that asks both sides to see and change.

His arrival at this conclusion in *A Soldier's Play* is the result of an evolution that can be seen in the thematic progress of his three most successful works, *The Brownsville Raid* (1976), *Zooman and the Sign* (1980), and finally *A Soldier's Play* (1982).

The Brownsville Raid portrays blacks as a minority oppressed by the hatred and misunderstanding of the white majority. Fuller takes an historical event (1906) in which a predominantly white town, Brownsville, Texas, is attacked by a band of marauders shortly after an all-Negro infantry battalion is bivouacked on its outskirts. The ensuing action, historically and in the play, fails to prove that the blacks were involved in the raid, but without due process the battalion is disbanded in disgrace. Within this clash of blacks and whites lies a trademark of Fuller's. Amid the public accusations and denials Fuller has inserted a reasonable cause for private suspicion among the blacks that in their midst may be a guilty party. The richness of ambiguity leaves serious doubt as to who is to blame, and the result in the play is not some reductive "finger pointing" but a more general and subtle condemnation of the suspicion itself, the result of mistrust and lack of communication existing between blacks and whites.

In *Zooman and the Sign* the confrontation becomes more focused, virtually eliminating any black-white opposition in favor of studying oppositions among blacks themselves. Again an actual event is the germ of the play, a report of a senseless, violent killing of a small black girl in the streets of Philadelphia. Frank Rich summarizes the play:

> His play is an indictment of black Americans who capitulate to tyrannical punks within their midst. Yet it is much to the play's credit that his compassion is not merely reserved for the heroic Reuben Tate [the girl's father] . . . . In "Zooman and the Sign," there are no real villains, only victims. Every character is locked into the same cycle of terror, and it's a nightmare only courage can end. ("New Fuller Drama" 13)

Though he focuses on blacks in *Zooman and the Sign* , Fuller produces a subtly tempered treatment of his black characters, guilty as well as innocent, the result of Fuller recognizing the larger issue that blacks, forced in their current situations, are victims of the machinations of white culture. But Fuller's play argues not that, since blacks are trapped by white institutions, it is the whites' responsibility to enact change or even that it is the blacks' responsibility to force them to enact change. The superficial changes created by social activism are not what Fuller is working toward. Rather, Fuller's work assumes the trap and argues that blacks should show initiative to change conditions themselves, being the direct beneficiaries. However, it's not necessarily change in any material sense but in a more important psychological and spiritual sense. That is Fuller's formula for change: internal growth and development.

With *A Soldier's Play*, Fuller pursues the issue of internal change, this time striking a balance that he seems to have been striving for throughout his early works. In very clear terms we see the hatred and prejudices of whites, while more specifically we see the interactions of blacks within that circle. The play studies the broad social structure portrayed in *The Brownsville Raid* and achieves a similar depth of study of both blacks and whites that was limited to blacks in *Zooman and the Sign*. At one level the play condemns white oppression, but at the more specific, focused level, it attacks the flaws in the black response to that oppression.

A Soldier's Play has no historical source, but Fuller does return to a military setting, for it offers him the opportunity, as he says, to have "men confront men" more honestly, since "you can't call a man a fool whose principal function is to defend his country" (White 118). In these rarefied conditions, black-white relations are more pointed and perhaps more consequential, since one's survival may eventually depend on the support of a racially different companion. And black interrelations themselves take on the same weight for the same life-or-death reasons.

In this camp, set in Louisiana during World War II, an investigation is being conducted into what seems to be a racially motivated murder of a black sergeant. A black investigator, initially convinced of a white conspiracy, eventually discovers the murderer to be a black soldier under the sergeant's charge.

The right "equation" seems to have been established in this play. *The Brownsville Raid* presents conditions resulting in a hopeless stalemate between the races, and *Zooman and the Sign* avoids a stalemate by focusing on one of the factions--the black community. But *A Soldier's Play* places fault directly on both blacks and whites, though it does focus on blacks, both accusing them but also significantly having them resolve the conflict.

Thematically, then, Fuller's plays argue for blacks to engage actively in personal change and, in doing so, to accept their own failings as well as strengths rather than to adopt the stance of being oppressed innocents. Change is similarly requested of whites. To present his case, Fuller utilizes a very conventional type of drama, the murder mystery, but uses its conventions in a manner that transcends the typical form. As Weales notes, "Fuller is clearly not interested in the genre [mystery] in the classic (i.e., dessicated) sense; he uses it for his own purposes" ("American Theater Watch" 519).

The play is designed to cause its audience to investigate and evaluate racial tensions. For this the mystery form is appropriate, being a form that encourages "investigation" among its audiences. One "formula," for example, would be to look for extremes: radical blacks confronted by KKK whites. *A Soldier's Play*, however, overturns the standard, comfortable assumptions that tension exists only between such radical elements of both races. For Fuller that is too reductive an approach. Instead the play works to challenge cool foundations of reasoned abstraction in the audience itself, and for Fuller, the way to challenge the audience best is to feed it with clues, allow classic assumptions to develop within that audience, and then reveal the previously unperceived complexity of the situation, which in turn shows how complacent, comfortable solutions/approaches are insufficient. Fuller manipulates the mystery plot to accomplish this unexpected end, revealing the insufficient nature of current racial assumptions in a manner that actually moves beyond "demonstrating" its point on stage and engages the audience into an actual "experience" of the point. The form of the play engages the audience and leads it to think it is solving the mystery, but in fact the audience is revealing its own prejudiced assumptions in the process of trying to solve a mystery. Thomas Adler notes, "In its overall physical conception of the setting and its fluid, cinematic shifting between present and past, Fuller's work recalls Peter Shaffer's *Equus*, also an investigation of sorts" (81). But where *Equus* works to unfold events to show the psychiatrist Dysart's private "guilt," *A Soldier's Play* works quite differently. It is less concerned with unfolding facts identifying a guilty party than it is concerned with revealing subtle undercurrents of the events under scrutiny. And that concern is in fact only a means to a more central end. Audiences invariably jump to the wrong conclusions, which force them into conceding having taken a superficial approach to the issue, assisted by prejudice and stereotypical assumptions. Guilt lies in the murderer, but there is a certain guilt that the audience will feel as well. Though the game of mystery-solving is essentially the same as in conventional mysteries, the stakes are much higher. The process is one where at one level Fuller challenges our expectations about dramatic conventions of such a formula. But this level merely prepares the audience for the more significant parallel challenge designed to overturn stereotypical racial expectations.

To begin the challenge, Fuller manipulates the mystery convention in order to analyze the central character, the murdered Tech/Sergeant Waters, a manipulation that actually draws attention away from solving the mystery and toward analyzing a complex and troubling character who is working to improve the image of "his people" but in the end does more to hurt that image.

Waters is a character who has taken upon himself the job of refashioning the black image, assuming a missionary zeal and adopting what he considers a self-justifying posture almost similar to an "amoral" stance of declaring war, where anything goes. In fact, in World War I, he distinguished himself in actual combat, as did many blacks, but as he says, "The First War, it didn't change much for us" (72), and he justifiably feels the time has come to develop an alternate strategy for change. The intention of bringing about change is a noble one, but the strategy becomes obsessive to the point of near megalomania. Waters recounts one event that occurred during the "First War":

> Do you know the damage one ignorant *Negro* can do? . . . We were in France during the First War, . . . We had won decorations, but the white boys had told all the French gals we had tails. And they found this

> ignorant colored soldier. Paid him to tie a tail to his ass and parade around
> naked making monkey sounds . . . . And when we slit his throat, you
> know that fool asked us what he had done wrong? (90)

Fuller inserts this formative incident into the play and follows it up
with descriptions of similar actions that lead to Waters's own radical
actions in the play itself, which in turn lead to his murder.

It is Waters's assault on the easy-going C.J. that is the crucial action
in the play. That assault outlines for the audience Waters's current as
well as former *modus operandi*. He frames C.J. and has him
stockaded, thereby singly succeeding in eliminating one more "geech"
from the public eye. Waters triumphantly comments:

> I waited a long time for you, boy, but I gotcha! And I try to get rid of you
> wherever I go. I put two geechies in jail at Fort Campbell, Kentucky--
> three at Fort Huachuca. Now I got you--one less fool for the race to be
> ashamed of! (73)

The audience clearly sees this scheme of purifying his race and the
methods used as being unethical at best, especially when presented
with World War II and Nazi Germany in the background, complete
with the connotations of its own system of purification. But Waters is
made to be more complex than this initial response might suggest.
When discussing his family, for example, we see more precisely the
motives behind his actions: to improve the world for future black
generations, not necessarily for himself: "When this war's over
[World War II], things are going to change . . . . and I want him
[Waters's son] to be ready for it--my daughter, too! I'm sendin' bot'
of 'em to some big white college" (28). So though he appears "evil"
in executing his plan, Fuller refuses to offer Waters as a pure source
of evil, instead allowing him to be human and even eventually to
express keen remorse upon the ultimate realization of the inhumanity
of his plan. Unable to tolerate a strangling incarceration, C.J.
commits suicide, and Waters is driven to drink because he realizes he
is to blame for the man's death. Following C.J.'s suicide, Waters
seemingly accepts blame and in turn challenges the source that has so
twisted him into his obsession: the white establishment. He confronts
and attacks two white officers in his drunken stupor: "Followin'
behind y'all? Look what it's done to me!--I hate myself! . . . I've
killed for you! . . . And nothin' changed! (52-53). Waters's goals
were noble, but he finally realizes his ends have failed to justify the
means. He has been misdirected all along by a blind admiration of his
white superiors. That Waters is murdered/executed in the play is a
sort of justice, retribution for all his past crimes, and finally something
he himself likely welcomed.

Uncovering the personality of Waters is an intriguing process in
itself. Fuller has created a complex "villain" whose rich character can
actually explore a variety of complex emotions. This very complexity

of character, paralleling the growing complexity of Fuller's mystery, sheds light on the complexities of trying to "solve" the race problem in general.

At another level, the use of the murder mystery allows Fuller to present a variety of responses to Waters's character, introducing a variety of characters as suspects and leading his audience to consider each, which should uncover a variety of stereotypical and prejudiced responses. As Kerr notes, "[F]igure out who the dead man is, or who he thought he was, and you're gonna nail the culprit" (3). Any of a number of suspects could have committed the crime, we realize, and the effect is that uncovering the actual criminal is less important than uncovering the various violent responses to Waters's life and what he represents. Presented are views of white bigots, stereotypically malleable blacks, radically sophisticated blacks, etc. That Fuller chooses to select a "sophisticated" black, P.F.C. Peterson, as the actual culprit is less a dramatic trick than a thematic necessity, one in which Fuller can maintain that a more dangerous "enemy" lies within black ranks rather than without, one that is at least as dangerous as Waters himself.

A murder of such a nature leads to instant assumptions that it was racially motivated. (At one ironic level it in fact is so motivated, since the death of C.J. was racially motivated and since Waters's murder was the result of C.J.'s death.) Working from that assumption, the investigation dully takes the predictable turn of assuming white complicity. Two white officers are interrogated, one of whom presents the standard white bigot's view, first insisting that Waters broke with military protocol and then revealing formerly hidden feelings: "He wouldn't salute! Wouldn't come to attention! And where I come from, colored don't talk the way he spoke to us--not to white people they don't" (80). But the simple solution of accusing a white, though seriously posed and considered, is not the actual solution. The effect of vindicating the whites late in the play is that the audience's stereotyped racial prejudices (the result of engaging dramatically induced speculation) are allowed to develop so that Fuller can eventually challenge and overturn them.

The next logical suspect is Private Wilkie, a black G.I. busted by Waters from the rank of sergeant, which took Wilkie ten years to earn. The revenge motive is there, but Wilkie is finally too weak and innocuous to commit such a crime, too weak, in fact, to seek any type of revenge. Instead he actually subordinates himself to the will of Waters. Wilkie, we eventually realize, is destined to be a subordinate his entire life, a kind of black to whom the white power structure is pleased to grant a few privileges without the fear of blind ambition ruining his benign disposition. (This realization, too, leads Waters to take advantage of Wilkie in the same manner as the whites would.) So here, too, audience expectations and racial prejudices are challenged. It is not a black, uncontrollably overwhelmed by emotion and rage,

who is guilty. Wilkie is innocent of Waters's murder, though guilty
of complicity in framing C.J.

P.F.C. Peterson, the man who finally confesses, places an ironic
sense of closure on the mystery. He is strong and opinionated, in
many ways the kind of man Waters is trying to make out of all his
men. Unlike Waters, though, Peterson maintains his attachment to his
black heritage. He's a man from "Hollywood, California--by way of
Alabama" (32).   But unlike C.J., the suicide from Mississippi,
Peterson is a Southerner who has been introduced to the sophisticated
world and has developed the tools to defend himself, to stand up for
himself. The self-reliance is what Waters admires; the black pride and
sense of separatism is what Waters wants to beat out of him. The
conflicting perspectives lead first to a fistfight and finally to Peterson
murdering Waters for destroying C.J. C.J. represents a kind of
innocence that Waters was ashamed of and that Peterson seemed
anxious to stand up for and wanted to help preserve, at least in part.
The hatred stemming from the confrontation eventually leads to mutual
elimination, perhaps an argument against Baraka's form of militancy
in favor of diversity, self-development, and acceptance among the
races.

Yet another level in the play involves the investigators of the murder,
the white Captain Taylor and the chief investigator, Captain
Davenport, a black.   In a way, their work is the on-stage
representation of the type of investigations going on in the audience.
They are the audience's leads. And their rational attempts to determine
the guilty party are constantly clouded by overt prejudices that
neutralize their formal efforts to uncover the truth. Taylor considers
himself to be a fairly liberal white, concerned about blacks as human
beings, though they are still his social inferiors. His attempts, though,
at honesty and sincerity are comical: "Forgive me for occasionally
staring, Davenport, you're the first colored officer I've ever met" (17).
And his observations are stereotypically naive. Referring to Waters,
Taylor observes, "[C]olored soldiers aren't devious like that" (78).
Blinded by a consequent overzealousness to do right, Taylor falls into
a sort of "liberal" trap and over-reacts to the facts presented him. In
the second interview with the two suspected white officers, Taylor is
the one to charge the officers with murder, going only on an unsound
suspicion that the men, obvious bigots, are lying. The charge comes
despite Taylor's own earlier insistence that the men had sound alibis.
Davenport, however, at this point releases them.

But though reasonable during this interrogation, Davenport is not
much different from Taylor at other times. Feeling like a crusader for
his race, he first considers the KKK until common-sense evidence
eliminates it as a possible force. The KKK would have cut off
Waters's insignia. Then, even before Taylor does, Davenport attacks
the white officers with a conspiracy charge. He blindly argues against
fact, claiming that their alibis are "nothing more than officers lying to
protect two of their own" (54). When the conspiracy theory extends

to implicating the camp commander, Davenport still rages, "They're all lying!" (54). He does eventually settle into looking at the facts and eventually coming upon the truth. The mystery is finally solved, more by perseverance and pressure than by rational means. Peterson and an accomplice are caught deserting and confess the crime.

Once the investigation is solved, Davenport offers a fitting eulogy to those men destroyed by the event and a fitting condemnation of those blinded by color, himself ironically included, observing, "[N]othing anyone *said* or *did*, would have been worth a life to men with larger hearts--men less split by the madness of race in America" (99). The madness has captured all in the play, not just the four victims, and presumably not just those *in* the play.

Finally what happens on stage, the formal "lesson" Davenport provides, is not nearly as profound as what occurs in the audience. And it is this level that the play as a whole has been building up to. The murder-mystery plot first forces upon the audience a dramatically leading interest in solving the crime. Stereotypical assumptions naturally develop. The ensuing curiosity to know the victim and to understand the complexities of a conscientious but misguided man in his search for a racial identity leads to a realization that the assumptions developed by the audience *are* stereotyped and inadequate. Each of the audience's members has naturally strung together information along a line of individually preconceived notions, which are overturned by play's end, leaving the audience invariably troubled at the various prejudices surfaced by the play.

That the play is designed to exact such a response is further suggested by the events Davenport reports at the end of the play. Waters's death is mistakenly filed as heroic. The troops involved are shipped out and soon wiped out in an operation in Germany. Davenport alone survives to benefit from the affair. That is, Davenport is the only stage character carrying the lesson. Beyond the footlights sits an enlightened audience to disseminate the lessons.

Manipulating what the audience considers a "form of entertainment" has turned into an alarmingly disarming and finally effective technique. The play has taken the conventional assumptions of a naturalistically molded murder plot to engage the audience, but goes the significant step further, challenging the audience's naturalistically predisposed values and judgment processes concerning race in America. Fuller has taken a form, overturned it, and by overturning it, has managed to make it turn outward and challenge the audience at another level. The play insists that we self-evaluate our responses to the events of the play rather than merely "objectively" analyze the characters' responses to the play's events. The form and the content have fused to accomplish this end, as Kerr suggests when he says that Fuller doesn't mean to settle for the mere cat-and-mouse pleasures of turning suspense-story conventions back to front . . . . I don't think there's an assumption made or posture adopted--noble or otherwise--that isn't instantly, and properly, stood on its ear. We learn in a hurry to take nothing for granted. (3)

It is through the manipulation of a conventional methodology of realistic techniques, finally, that Fuller succeeds in achieving his ends: the need for personal awareness not preached but experienced.

Beth Henley and *Crimes of the Heart*

Winning the 1981 Pulitzer Prize for *Crimes of the Heart* at age 29, Beth Henley was the first woman to win the award in twenty three years. As a successful female dramatist, her voice is a valuable addition to an under-represented element in the field. Her works do focus on women and even on their struggle for independence from a male-dominated hierarchy, but perhaps the unique contribution Henley makes to American theatre has its roots in her Southern heritage; through her, Southern drama returns to mainstream theatre. Concerning her Southern background, Brendan Gill offers the following generalization: "Northern writers have inherited a Puritan disinclination to tell whoppers; Southern writers do little else" ("Crimes" 182). In Henley's case, being raised in Mississippi has certainly cultivated in her a penchant for "whoppers." But more important is her keen Southern sense of the grotesque and absurd experienced in daily existence, a sense that has often triggered loose comparisons between her and other Southern writers like Eudora Welty and Flannery O'Connor. The reason for the comparison, as one critic notes, is that "she writes with wit and compassion about good country people gone wrong or whacko" (Haller 40).

The comparisons are valid if for no other reason than the fact that Henley has mastered the art of the grotesquely comic by co-mingling serious, life-threatening concerns with mundane daily activities. In her work what seem to be serious issues are reduced to trivialities, and the mundane is raised to seemingly unwarranted but nonetheless believable levels of importance. The result is she overturns whatever system of moralizing an audience may have, and then refuses to return us to any sense of order. The extreme subjectivity illustrated in the various characters' value systems leaves us in a state of uncertainty, but this uncertainty doesn't lead to despair; it is simply a state of being to be accepted. We shouldn't struggle to objectify the events, attributing to them some god-given meaning, nor should we fully expect to understand the events even under our own systems of order.

Edith Oliver summarizes *Crimes of the Heart* as being "a comedy of private disasters among three sisters in Hazlehurst, Mississippi" ("Crimes" 81). She explains:

Beth Henley's *Crimes of the Heart*. Original 1979 Human Festival production at the Actors Theatre of Louisville, Kentucky. Pictured are Babe (Lee Anne Fahey), Lenny (Kathy Bates), and Meg (Susan Kingsley).

Photo: David S. Talbot.

> The sisters . . . are Lenny . . , the oldest of them, whose thirtieth birthday
> is being insufficiently celebrated on the day the action takes place, and
> who is fading into spinsterhood; Meg . . , the middle one, who has been
> away from home unsuccessfully pursuing a career as a popular singer (she
> has spent the past year as a clerk in a dog-food store); and Babe . . , who
> has just shot her husband, Zachary, the best lawyer in town, because, she
> explains, she didn't like the way he looked, although she later reveals to
> Meg that she has been having delightful sexual episodes with a young
> black boy of fifteen, whom she is shielding. (81)

In addition, it is variously revealed that Lenny's old horse had recently
been struck and killed by lightning, that the mother had committed
suicide several years earlier, hanging herself and her cat, that Lenny is
sterile and that their guardian/grandfather is currently in the hospital
following a stroke. And as a sort of climax, we witness a comically
failed suicide attempt on stage by Babe.

This unlikely string of events, though, "marches," as Gill notes, "at
a pace that keeps us from ever questioning the degree of clever
manipulation that we are being made subject to" (182). The separate
incidents are added to the list in such an un-self-conscious way that
they are looked at and weighted separately, given individual credibility
and acceptance almost before we consider the "absurdity" of the entire
menagerie. The success of this on-stage diffuseness establishes a
singularly important element of realistic credibility--the play slips into
the realm of realistic possibility--and because we don't pause to
reflect, her "whopper" is allowed to stand. We simply turn to
laughing at the "succession of misfortunes inflicted upon people who
lack the capacity to avoid them" (Gill "Crimes" 182). The yarn is
spun, we accept it, and can move on to the business of the play.

But as is typical with such Southern tales, *Crimes of the Heart* is not
just an entertaining situation or laughing comedy. Her play goes well
beyond such empty conventionality, as Haller observes:

> Although *Crimes of the Heart* is structured as a six-character, three-act,
> one-set comedy, Henley's accomplishment is not the resurrection of the
> traditional well-made play, but rather the ransacking of it. She has chosen
> the family drama as her framework--the play takes place entirely in the
> MaGrath kitchen--but she has populated the household with bizarre
> characters. In effect, she has mated the conventions of the naturalistic
> play with the unconventional protagonists of absurdist comedy. (42)

Despite its wealth of comic material, it is a palatable presentation of
material previously reserved for more esoteric forms of theatre--theatre
of the absurd--and that is Henley's triumph, the triumph in fact that is
a product of her Southern heritage. Henley's play presents, as
Kauffmann argues, "the tension between the fierce lurking lunacy
underlying the small-town life she knows so well and the sunny
surface that tries to accommodate it" ("Two Cheers" 55). As such, her
work escapes the intellectual detachment of the French absurdists and

existentialists, and because it takes the horrors of life out of the lecture halls and puts them in a kitchen, it argues that the absurd has an immediacy and relevance to daily existence that other works can't claim to argue. "In short," says Kauffmann, "what begins as more wistfulness under the wisteria eventually becomes a compound of giggle and decay on the edge of an abyss" ("Two Cheers" 54). Henley has taken domestic comedy and infused it with an absurdist perspective.

The fusion of these two components is primarily effected by Henley's use of a disconnected, fragmented style of dialogue, a style comically reminiscent of another playwright, David Mamet, who works in another dialect from another region of the country but whose approach to that dialect is similar. Because her play focuses on dialogue, she has also met with criticism similar to that which Mamet received. For example, Kauffmann notes, "Too much of the action occurs offstage and is reported" ("Two Cheers" 54). But the actions, finally, aren't what bring on the humor; it's the *recounting* of the actions. The opening lines set the pattern. The sisters' first cousin, Chick, introduces Babe's crime to the play with the following: "It's just too awful! It's just way too awful! How I'm gonna continue holding my head up high in this community, I do not know. Did you remember to pick up those pantyhose for me?" (4). The incident of the shooting shifts to egocentric concerns of Chick's own reputation and finally to concern about a pantyhose purchase. The psychological consistency is evident--we learn of Chick's character very efficiently in this passage--but the weighting of events does not coincide with any logical consistency other than Chick's own extremely subjective logic.

Within the first minutes of the play, confusion completely asserts itself. The news of the shooting is replaced by concern for the death of an old horse--apparently "struck by lightning" (11)--followed by news that "Old Granddaddy's gotten worse" (12), and concluded with anxiety over a child's "first time at the dentist" (13). Additionally, the important decision of determining who should defend Babe is settled by hiring a son of a friend (Annie) because they would "be doing Annie a favor by hiring him up" (18).

Discrepancies between feelings and expression of those feelings add to the confusion. Babe reports that she shot Zachary because she "just didn't like his stinking looks" (27). Other disclosures inform against this claim, but nothing actually reported and confirmed justifies the attempted murder, at least from an objective/rational point of view. Babe also recounts making lemonade and offering some to Zachary, lying wounded on the floor. Dramatizing the event as Kauffmann seems to wish (and as the movie version did), would draw out the horror of the event, but the choice of simply having Babe describe the events comically reveals the discrepancy between Babe's feelings and a perhaps more "proper," though unfelt, expression of feelings. Added to the unfolding of central events is a string of similar interchanges. And though overall events in the play are perhaps painful to the sisters, the reports they give are far from despairing and often make for pure comedy. Lenny, for example, reminds Meg of an unanswered letter explaining Granddaddy's stroke: "I wrote you about all those blood vessels popping in his brain?" (20). And Meg mumbles about the shooting: "So, Babe shot Zachary Bottrell . . . slap in the gut" (21).

In many ways, the dialogue is a refreshing break from the coldly clinical analyses often given of such events. But the dialogue goes a step further and suggests a certain solipsism among the characters, the result of an inevitable self-interest and resulting miscommunication. The above line of Meg's is followed by a typical example of miscommunication. Meg continues, saying, "It's hard to believe" (21), to which Lenny replies, "It certainly is. Little Babe--shooting off a gun" (21). Whether or not Meg is thinking in the same way as Lenny, one point is likely: the audience has been led to assume that it is "hard to believe" that Babe shooting her husband would happen. Lenny--and perhaps Meg--is thinking of the unlikelihood of "little" Babe shooting a gun under any circumstances; she isn't even thinking of a circumstance where Babe's husband would be in front of it. Lenny has lost focus on Zach's involvement altogether, shifting her thoughts to how Babe has grown up, a musing having started by first considering current events. In fact, the play continues with Lenny: "She was always the prettiest and most perfect of the three of us" (21). As with the opening scene with Chick, no one can seem to keep on the subject at hand, continually shifting from subject matter of seemingly vastly varying significance. The varied layers produce a completely interwoven product that confuses any rational, ordered, "objective" hierarchy that an audience may have come to expect in more conventional works of art.

The method Henley uses is a simple one of inserting horrifyingly significant events into a world of the mundane. The result is two-fold. First, the facts of death, suicide, and assault take on a certain intimacy. They are no longer only distantly experienced, and neither are they either abstractly or exotically/sensationally experienced as in much literature, drama, and the media in general. The potential for Henley is that such presentation of events, set in a household that could be our neighbor's, could lead to the terrifying surmise that assault and death lurk at every corner, even in the most normal of neighborhoods. Forwarding this thesis alone, however, is not the play's purpose. If it were, it would be a work, like many others, striving to alert its audience to painful visions of apocalyptic doom, and its effect would be to have its audience look at the world with some fearfully heightened sense of tragic potentialities.

But not only does Henley succeed in giving these threatening facts of life a certain intimacy, she also moves to a level where this fusion of the significant with the mundane succeeds in convincing us that death, suicide, and assault are realities that we face every day to some extent. And the comic touch suggests that we do not need any heightened, redirected awareness about such things because such responses are little more than misguided over-reactions. People are currently equipped to handle tragedy and handle it successfully, especially when they are aware that such events are not the result of some mystical curse handed down only to those chosen to suffer, but rather are random, inexplicable events that we are all subject to but that we can overcome, or at least endure. In a way, the Southern "superstition" of Christian mystery has been updated to embrace a modernist posture of the absurd.

Doc Porter is an example of a character in the play who has endured without bitterness, a man whose life was ruined by a crippling accident caused by Hurricane Camille several years earlier. Though he never fulfills his (and the community's) dream of becoming a doctor, he does settle down and raise a family. He even confronts the ghost of his past catastrophe, in the person of Meg. Meg is partially responsible for Doc's accident, and though the two presumably were in love, she abandons him shortly after the storm. New hopes seem to rekindle when Meg returns home during the action of the play, but rather than running away with Meg and beginning a new life, Doc seemingly accepts his "fate" and opts for the life he has already made. Meg reports their meeting together:

> I was out there thinking, What will I say when he begs me to run away with him? . . . . But . . . he didn't ask me. He didn't even want to ask me. I could tell by this certain look in his eyes that he didn't even want to ask me. (98)

For Doc, the confrontation has demystified the past and the despair (if there was any) over lost opportunity. The events weren't the result of some curse handed down by a conscious god who required confrontation and defiance, but were random accidents requiring acceptance. So Doc's acceptance of his current life is less an expression of defeat than an acknowledgment of his having accepted the "mystery."

The confrontation defuses some sense of loss for Meg, too. She asks herself: "Will I have pity on his wife and those two half-Yankee children? I mean, can I sacrifice their happiness for mine? Yes! Oh, yes! Yes, I can!" (98). He never asks her, of course, and her response is, "Why aren't I miserable! Why aren't I morbid! . . . I don't know. But for now it was . . . just such fun. I'm happy" (98). The hoped-for escape doesn't come, the easy, romanticized solution isn't offered, but a sobering relief from the depression of an unfulfilled existence is the result.

Relief of another sort is found by the sisters as a group, in the form of an attack of hysterical laughter when it is announced that "Old Granddaddy" is about to die. Tension, at the very least, is released. And when the mystery of their mother's suicide is "solved," another burden is lifted. Babe discovers through her own suicide attempt why their mother hung the cat with her in the suicide: "She needed him with her because she felt so alone" (119). The discovery leads to the conclusion that the family's string of bad luck is not the result of some curse of insanity. It's not a curse of any sort. It has been the result of a series of "bad days," as it is simply but finally and authoritatively put. Says Babe of her day of shooting her husband, of having her affair with a black youth revealed, of being threatened with blackmail and commitment to an asylum: "I'm having a bad day. It's been a real bad day" (119).

The general answer that Henley offers is that survival requires a concerted effort of love and community support. Babe, we feel, will survive. She says, "I'm not like Mama. I'm not so all alone" (121). And Meg learns the same lesson. After her night with Doc, she says, "I realized I could care about someone. I could want someone" (98). Lenny's revelation is similar, only her problems are given instant relief through the traditional and somewhat overworked entrance of a lost suitor. For the two other central characters, Meg and Babe, the lesson is learned but less euphorically resolved. Their lessons in the play lead to the fair conclusion that "we've just got to learn to get through these real bad days" (120), and that one cannot do so alone. No "prince charming" is offered; rather, the learning process has taken on the realistic dimension of just beginning for them, and the play ends without resolution, only a set determination to face the next, inevitable crisis together and endure it as well.

In a way, Henley's argument is similar to Mamet's. Her characters have demonstrated an at times extreme sense of solipsistic subjectivity that logic and language can't fully overcome and in fact seem to encourage. As such, "community" seems impossible. But if they move beyond the efforts to rationally objectify life and find an alternative unifying bond, then survival is tolerable. In the play, this alternative is found. Very simply put, in the face of other failed answers, love in general and the comforts of family in particular are what Henley offers as "solutions."

The answer Henley offers is by no means profound. It is a common-sense abstraction that is far from a set, soundly articulated philosophy. But solid answers aren't what the play is designed to offer. As Kauffmann says:

> *Crimes* moves to no real resolution, but this is part of its power. It presents a condition that, in minuscule, implies much about the state of the world . . . and about human chaos; it says, "Resolution is not my business. Ludicrously horrifying honesty is." ("Two Cheers" 55)

Exactly how these characters resolve their current dilemmas is irrelevant, finally. Even the events themselves are irrelevant. Henley's play is one that presents a common condition of isolation, posits a general means to handle the isolation, but promises no particular prescriptive solutions to the dilemma. As with Mamet, Henley senses first a need to re-establish the basic bonds of human existence before more artificial social bonds can be sufficiently established.

And it is up to humanity itself to exact the necessary changes because there is, finally, no perceivable grand design giving meaning to events and actions in our lives. Henley's technique of binding the significant and the mundane into a confusion that clouds the relative importance of each event fairly illustrates that point. Our efforts to see an importance in various events assume that the events have "meaning." We must realize, however, that such meaning is purely subjective and finally arbitrary. It is this revelation that uncovers Henley's vision of the essentially absurd nature of the human condition. And that condition infiltrates what could very well be our own homes.

That her work has been taken perhaps too lightly by critics and audiences is possibly the result of the fact that it is a laughing comedy, which downplays the seriousness of its design, and the fact that its simplistic--incidental--"solution" bears too much of the critical weight of the play: critics, looking for results, see little and so look less deeply at the rest of the play. But closer scrutiny reveals a serious design behind that laughter and prior to the resolution. Henley has taken the conventional realistic format and has infused it with the esoteric reflections of absurdist thinkers and writers.

Martin Esslin, in *Theatre of the Absurd*, points out that the end of absurdist drama is to challenge "the possibility of knowing the laws of conduct and ultimate values, as deducible from a firm foundation of revealed certainty about the purpose of man in the universe" (290). Absurdist theatre strives "to re-establish an awareness of man's situation when confronted with the ultimate reality of his condition" (291). It is these tenets that are seen in Henley, but they are presented in a context--a middle-class kitchen--familiar to its audience rather than being presented in an abstracted setting of intentionally unfamiliar conditions. The material has become accessible to a broader audience as a result. For Henley, Southern Christian mysticism has been replaced by and updated with a perhaps equally mystifying absurdist perception of existence, but updated nonetheless.

Though Henley has dispensed with the classical Southern outlook on existence, she has transferred to that new perception a key ingredient of the old: a sense of inevitable triumph over despair (though sufficiently guarded from easy, romanticized answers), something the absurdists themselves, arguably, never ventured to do, or at best, only ambiguously hinted at.

Two Beth Henley plays closely followed *Crimes of the Heart*: *The Wake of Jamie Foster* (1982) and *The Miss Firecracker Contest* (1984). Unfortunately, *Wake of Jamie Foster* is, as Gill notes, "a coarse and clumsy reworking, in all too recognizable terms, of Miss Henley's excellent earlier play" ("Wake" 161). But *The Miss Firecracker Contest* proves that though her voice may be "limited," as

Kauffmann noted ("Two Cheers" 54), Henley is not a one-play playwright. Rich sums up this recent success:

> This time, we hear about midgets, orphans and deformed kittens--and they're the fortunate ones. Other characters, whether on stage or off, are afflicted by cancer, tuberculosis, venereal disease and, most of all, heartbreak. Even so, the evening's torrential downpour of humor-- alternately Southern-Gothic absurdist, melancholy and broad--almost never subsides. ("Firecracker" 11)

The broadly comic and touchingly poignant are mixed in the play, in a manner similar to that process used in *Crimes of the Heart*. For example, one character, Popeye, tells a comic tale that elicits laughter but ends with a bite:

> I once knew these two midgets by the names of Sweet Pea and Willas. I went to their wedding and they was the only midgets there. Rest a their family was regular-size people. But they was so happy together they moved into a little midget house where everything was mite size like this little ole desk they had and this ole stool. Then Sweet Pea got pregnant and later on she had what they called this Caesarian birth where they slice open your stomach and pull the baby out from the slice. Well, come to find out, the baby's a regular-size child and soon that baby is too large for Sweet Pea to carry around and too large for all a that mite-size furniture. So Sweet Pea has to give up her own baby for her mama to raise. I thought she'd die to lose that child. It about crushed her heart. (43)

The passage incites laughter until the condition of suffering is pointed out, revealing that suffering is inescapable and often comes upon us unawares, even in the guise of a humorous anecdote.

Much like Faulkner himself, with his Yoknapatawpha County creation, Henley has been able to--and perhaps will continue to be able to--draw from and build upon her small-town world of Mississippi and use her uniquely trained eyes to perceive in that microcosm the modern absurdities of existence. For example, Oliver observes of Henley's latest play, *The Lucky Spot* (1987):

> The action of "The Lucky Spot" . . . takes place in a dance hall in Pigeon, Louisiana in 1934--the depths of the Depression. More precisely it takes place in the world of the dramatist Beth Henley--erratic, eruptive, and always surprising. ("The Lucky Spot" 80-81)

The insights of that world will in turn inform us of the world at large.

Marsha Norman and *'night, Mother*

With Marsha Norman's play *'night, Mother* (1982; Pulitzer Prize 1983), the Pulitzer Prize was awarded to a play with designs more

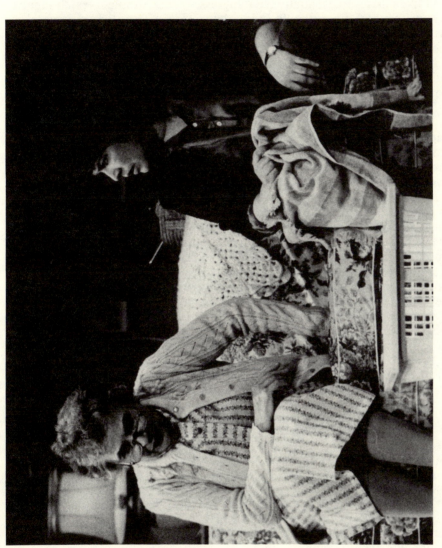

Marsha Norman's 'night, Mother. American Repertory Theatre's 1982 premiere. Pictured are Thelma (Anne Pitoniak) and Jessie (Kathy Bates).

Photo: Richard Feldman.

closely related to feminist concerns than Beth Henley's more Southern pieces. Norman's focus is on women, and her plays present worlds filled with commonplace events and common people, those not in privileged positions in society. Their portrayals in turn reveal worlds and lives that are essentially meaningless. These simple lives, though, extend beyond those people living them. The effect is more general, as Jack Kroll in a review of Norman's *Traveler in the Dark* (1984) observes: "Marsha Norman is one of those writers who are natural lightning rods for the shattering assaults on faith and hope that come to all of us" (76). But even when dealing with suicide, Norman refuses to despair over the condition of humanity.

To present her perspective on the human condition, Norman utilizes a simple realist format. As Rich notes, *'night, Mother* "looks like simplicity itself . . . . [It is] a totally realistic play, set in a real time, counted by onstage clocks" ("Suicide Talk" 3). In fact, with the exception of "doubling" her central character in *Getting Out*, all of her works are simple and realistic on the surface. But Norman's work-- *'night, Mother* in particular--goes beyond merely documenting mundane existence. Norman admits in an interview that "I listen better than any other thing" (Stone 56), but, as her interviewer adds, "In part what Norman listens for is the chance utterance that carries so much more meaning than it seems to, but does say, with miraculous compactness, exactly what it means" (56). Norman uses this faculty for capturing meaning in a new voice to present characters as under-represented as Fuller and Henley's characters. With the exception of *Traveler in the Dark*, they are women. They are the common characters of life that one often passes unnoticed on the streets. Says Norman of her intentions:

> I grieve so for people who do not have the power of language, and what I want to be able to do in my work is to make my language skills available to them. In a sense, Arlene [in *Getting Out*] agrees, Jessie [in *'night, Mother*] agrees, to trust me to present them fairly, and I in turn agree to grant them a voice. (Stone 57-58)

Such a choice of character types has posed a problem for Norman. Given the realistic design of her works, some critics have perceived an inconsistency between the type of characters she presents and the level of thought they often rise to in their speeches. Kauffmann's attack of *'night, Mother* is in fact based on just this criticism. He notes the simple-minded mother of the play who has just been informed of her daughter's plan to commit suicide:

> Instead of the hysteria we might expect from this dodo, instead of the screaming or fainting or struggle or even a transparent ruse to get the gun, she casts herself as a partner in a "clever" cat-and-mouse duet, as if she were accustomed to such crises and were competent to handle them. ("More Trick" 48)

This critique of the play attacks the very premise that Norman is asking the audience to accept, namely that the common characters she presents are inwardly complex but finally unable to express themselves as fully as desired. Consequently, she asks that the audience tolerate any possibly perceived inconsistency in strict verisimilitude; otherwise the plights of these characters could never be uncovered and portrayed.

Kauffmann refuses to accept this explanation. In fact, Kauffmann's criticism is one that parallels a similar, more general criticism of realism itself, by such critics as Ronald Hayman (see 4-29). Hayman's criticism of modern drama, one founded on use of language on stage, is that to make its common characters real, the playwright is forced to subvert his or her language skills to accommodate the code of realism which dictates that such characters are likely to be inarticulate and should be depicted as such. Consequently, these critics would argue that Norman's attempts to make her language skills available to her less skilled protagonists is destined to failure unless she moves outside the realm of realist dictates.   Given these stipulations, Norman's dialogue does in fact appear to break from realistic credibility since she presents her characters' feelings more as she translates them than as they would perhaps articulate those feelings themselves. It seems that Norman fails from both critical points of view: she is neither poetic nor realistic.

But at another level, Norman's use of language *is* realistic, for she has worked to patch the holes made by such an attack as the above by fusing the realistic jargon, phraseology, and rhythms of common speech with the heightened thought that she wishes to introduce. Though perhaps not strictly "realistic" from an old-school frame of reference, the result should be acceptable to all but perhaps the most discriminatingly determined advocates of naturalist doctrine. The rhythms, etc., are a common factor for Norman and for stylists in general, but Norman has a design that perhaps less completely marries form to content than, say, Mamet does, which is perhaps why she is less often recognized as a stylist than Mamet is. But since she wants to assist her characters in communicating when in actuality they haven't the tools, her style, of necessity, must differ. Wanting to show dignity when perhaps there is no logical reason to expect it, Norman both reveals the sentiments and stylistically cloaks the articulations of her characters. Strict verisimilitude is less necessary, finally, than the illusion of common speech, a fact noted by Lewes himself in the 1800s.

More cerebral than Henley and working on a different plane than Fuller does, Norman uniquely presents the world's absurdity and a need to re-evaluate that condition in a way that argues such dilemmas aren't restricted to an intellectual, elitist clique. Rather they engage the thoughts of a much broader strata of people, which would be better recognized if those people were given the needed tools of expression. Accepting this claim, then her lower- and middle-class characters become sorts of democratic representatives of the age, characters not articulating new or visionary thoughts, but expressing concerns that have saturated the entire the social hierarchy.

Norman's first play, *Getting Out*, premiered in 1977 at the Actors Theatre in her hometown of Louisville, Kentucky. Concerning the play, Kate Stout observes:

> In it are Marsha Norman's trademarks: powerful language that draws on not only dialect (of Eastern Kentucky in this case) but the lyricism of the commonplace; a fearless commitment to honesty, even if the truth reaches to the unpleasant; and dry, always perfectly timed humor . . . . And it champions the underdog. (32)

The play addresses the issue of an individual's need to confront the past, in particular the past of a woman currently paroled for the murder of a cab driver eight years earlier. On stage is the central character, divided into two roles and portrayed by two actresses, one being Arlene, the character in the present, the other, Arlie, placed at various points earlier in life. Such a technique of presentation is, to date, Norman's only significant deviation from realist methods, but it is a successful technique, studying the psychological dimensions of this woman.

The next work, *Third and Oak* (1978), consists of two one-act plays: *The Laundromat* and *The Pool Room*. Though the work is little more than an experiment in realistic characterization, it is full of the detail that marks Norman's use of language. For example, in *The Laundromat*, Alberta, a widow still clinging to the spirit of her lost husband, refuses to part with anything that was his. She declares that when she finds a beach ball in her basement, "I can't let the air out of it. It's his breath in there" (24). The fragile nature of relationships in general is presented in these lines as is the urge to "possess" that which we know can't be possessed but which is coveted nonetheless. And, of course, it is a passage that is susceptible to the criticism that such a character would be incapable of so succinctly articulating such a point. Regardless of such criticism, the passage does make its point, quite clearly, that feelings of this sort exist in classes other than an articulate upper class.

Two plays followed *Third and Oak*; they are *Circus Valentine* (1979), about a small-time circus troupe, and *The Holdup* (1980), about "new" West adventures recounted by Norman's grandfather. Neither work was a success. These efforts, though, were eventually followed by *'night, Mother* in 1982 and *Traveler in the Dark* in 1984.

Traveler in the Dark documents the crisis experienced by a successful surgeon who fails in his efforts to save a close friend. As Kroll notes, "Like everything Norman writes, the play has moments of insight, poetry and humor" (76). But it does not compare well to *'night, Mother*, her best play to date. Kroll explains why:

> In "'Night, Mother," the play's shattering resonance developed inexorably from the piling on of one piercingly observed detail after another. In "Traveler in the Dark," the action seems whipped up under the lash of Norman's urgent need to dramatize a crisis of faith. (76)

Kroll concludes his review with a warning that Norman's noble intentions may lead to her artistic decline: confronting that which leads us to crises is courageous in Norman, but "[t]he danger is that her moral urgency will drive her into the too-conscious role of crisis laureate" (76).

With *'night, Mother*, Norman's work escapes the charge of being self-conscious. Like Henley, Norman escapes mere social commentary and presents common representatives of humanity confronting a growing sense of the absurdity of their worlds. But where Henley presents an essentially comic vision, Norman utilizes tragic rhythms to address the dilemma. Rather than argue that we have to learn to deal with those "real bad days," as Henley does, Norman's confrontations and solutions are more extreme and approach a level of despair that Henley's never do. But to despair is not Norman's message, even when suicide is the result. Says Norman of the general nature of her work: "Kierkegaard says there are two primary forms of illusion--recollection and hope. My work, I think, reflects a sense that you hope in spite of what you know" (Stone 58). Both of her better plays (*Getting Out* and *'night, Mother*) present these "illusions" as necessary tools for survival and that when illusions fail, so does life. Elizabeth Stone suggests that

> Arlene survives because she won't altogether relinquish the "killer kid" she once was, and perhaps Jessie does not survive because too much of her past--her early epileptic seizures, or whom her ex-husband betrayed her with--has been kept secret from her by her mother. (58)

A sense of continuity of existence helps to extenuate the feeling of fragmentation that humanity almost always experiences. And if recollection is important to accomplish that end, it also serves as a catalyst that creates the other illusion--hope. The presence of hope, it seems, is in fact more central to survival than anything recollection alone can offer. Says Norman, "If Arlene survives, it is because she hopes for something better. Jessie does not survive because she no longer hopes" (Stone 58).

Two approaches to hope are posited in *'night, Mother*: waiting for and expecting change to occur, and taking control to enact change. Jessie has tried the formal "Beckettian" approach of waiting. Abiding by tenets often endorsed for women in this culture, Jessie has invested all hope in her marriage, trusting to some hope in a future with her husband and child. Her husband, however, leaves her, and all hopes invested in her child are dashed by the realization that her son is a lost delinquent. Waiting has failed to satisfy hope or to justify relying on the process in the future. The activity of waiting now produces only mundane, predictable rewards of no real value, and these are finally no longer worth waiting for. Unbeknownst to Jessie, she is about to move beyond the world Beckett portrays; she plans to act.

Jessie's conceptualization of waiting is apparently one handed down to her by her mother, and it is one which the mother dully accepts, but which Jessie has implicitly come to reject. Combining abstraction with common daily conversation, Norman creates the following exchange, discussing "how the washer works":

> MAMA: I know how the washer works. You put the clothes in. You
>   put the soap in. You turn it on. You wait.
> JESSIE: You do something else. You don't just wait.
> MAMA: Whatever else you find to do, you're still mainly waiting. The
>   waiting's the worst part of it . . . .
> JESSIE: (Nodding): O.K. Where do we keep the soap? (21-22)

At this point Jessie refuses to challenge her mother's fatalistic tenet, preferring to continue within the conversational confines of the actual topic at hand: washing. But Mama has introduced the approach to life that she has taught Jessie, and Jessie's distaste for it is clear. Waiting for the particulars of marriage and parenthood has produced negative results. Waiting for herself to develop has also resulted in disappointment. Evaluating her 30-year-old self, she cruelly but fairly concludes, "I'm what was worth waiting for and I didn't make it" (76).

Action is the alternative, an action that at least proves control if it doesn't necessarily guarantee some justifiable hope. But Jessie hasn't been given any opportunity to develop skills necessary to take control of her life. She can't even hold down a simple job in a hospital gift shop. However, Norman goes further than merely to list Jessie's personal limitations; she sums them up by making Jessie an epileptic, a physical condition that takes on metaphorical significance. Weales, in fact, sees Jessie's epilepsy as a symbol of her overall entrapment by the world at large:

> The restrictions implicit in her epilepsy, in the response to it rather than
> the disease itself, reflect a society of limited possibilities, mandatory roles
> . . . . [It] is another example of the way in which these women are
> creatures of not-so-great expectations, caught in a social and psychological
> web that gives them very little room to maneuver. ("Really 'Going On'"
> 370)

Norman, however, makes it clear that the actual epilepsy is under control so that Jessie's final action does not appear to be a response to her physical illness. Rather, Jessie argues that her suicide is a response not merely to despair or anger, but is finally an act of control.

Despair or anger may be partly involved, as Jessie notes in a passage again showing Norman's trademark. Mama asks Jessie what's so wrong that she should want to commit suicide. Jessie responds, "Oh, everything from you and me to Red China" (30). It seems almost a throw-away line with Red China casually enough presented, but it is inserted again later in the play (see 75). Though "Red China" seems logically absurd in relation to the more personal complaints that surround it (and as a result draws a laugh from the audience), it shows Jessie's awareness that in international affairs, as in all things, she has no control. And it is additionally significant in helping to expand the context of the play beyond the confines of the mother's house and daughter's life, as Weales notes in reference to the passage:

> The sense of helplessness that most of us feel in face of events in the world at large provides a macrocosmic malaise for the smaller space of the play in which Jessie and her mother have few choices about what to make of their lives. ("Really 'Going On'" 370)

The phrase "Red China" is compact but fraught with meaning, a perfect example of the approach to language that Norman takes in her playwriting.

But though perhaps partly an act of despair, the suicide is finally less an act of surrender or even of violent rebellion than it is a considered act of control on Jessie's part, taken by a composed, thinking human being. As Gill notes, "[T]here is only the fact that a woman of intelligence, energy, and good will is going to end her life, and with reason" ("'Night, Mother" 110). And her reason is simple: "I can't do anything . . . about my life, to change it, make it better, make me feel better about it. Like it beter [sic], make it work. But I can stop it" (36). Jessie's decision to act lies in direct contrast to her mother's decision merely to survive. Says Weales:

> Her mother, who admits at one point that she has an intense fear of death, has mastered the limitations of her life by embracing the small activities and inactivities that fill a day with busy work which has no meaning beyond itself. That is not enough for Jessie. ("Really 'Going On'" 371)

Limited as Jessie is in her choices, she chooses to act in a way that authoritatively says "no" to her world and that finally does put her in control of her life. She refuses to wait and has no other means to take control than literally to take her life.

The physical loss of life involved in Jessie's suicide has perhaps been overemphasized by too many critics. Taking Weales's lead in his analysis of Jessie's epilepsy, one should look more abstractly at the suicide being an act of a woman choosing, in one final gesture, to take control of her destiny, especially in light of the fact that she has already spiritually lost her life. Hope has died, but, says Stone, death "does not negate the fact that she exercises her will to the last--by deciding what will become of her life. Not she chooses to *die*, but she *chooses* to die" (58). Stone further generalizes the observation: "If there's advocacy [in the play], it's not in favor of suicide, but in favor of autonomy" (57).

Norman uses her skills to help communicate the despair experienced by those who have fallen through the social safety net. But those she shares her skills with are less misfits of a culture than they are outcasts never given a real chance to assimilate. Jenny Spencer notes of `night, Mother* that "because the way in which the text foregrounds issues of female identity and female autonomy . . . the relatively detached position available (however tentatively) to male viewers simply cannot (without great risk) be taken up by women" (365). This separatist perspective is relevant to a great degree. But though Norman does very consciously focus on women in her works, the message goes beyond gender to embrace all members of our culture who sense despair over personal impotency in the face of overwhelming odds against happiness. Norman has adopted a style to relay that sense. And if her plays can be called "problem plays," they certainly don't rifle the rationalist debris for logical answers to the problems or search for a strict causality to determine the sources of the despair. The lives she dramatizes are not simple lives; they are infinitely more complex than any naturalist dogma can portray. And her form has been molded to fit the message.

A recent work, *Sara and Abraham* (1988), was given an unreviewed workshop production at the 1988 Festival of New Plays by the Actors Theatre of Louisville. It juxtaposes the biblical tale with a modern-day equivalent. The implication is that the condition Norman describes is one that has been thoroughly culturally ingrained and that change is by no means assured. Nevertheless, Norman fully intends to carry on the struggle.

A Final Word

The right to choose to confront the world head on and not merely to resign oneself to quiet desperation is a right reserved for no particular stratum of society, but is one that extends to all. In an interview, Norman draws from the Gospel of Matthew: "Inasmuch as you have done it to the least of these, my brethren, you have done it unto me" (Stout 32). She explains herself: "That's what I'm doing. I'm saying, 'Let's take the least of these, our brethren. Let's look at them'" (32).

Norman's self-assessment easily applies to Fuller and Henley as well. The playwrights each address concerns of and give voices to under-represented elements of our society. But not only do they write of the struggles of the "least of our brethren," showing that these brethren experience the same complex emotions as others; they also use a technique of presenting that material--a modified realism--so that even these "least of our brethren" could go to the theatre and better comprehend the dramatic material produced about them and *for* them. In this regard, the new realism is used as an "equalizer," making material more accessible to parts of the public that may often be confused by alienating techniques regularly utilized in more experimental formats. This use of new realism is still prone to misunderstanding or incomplete understanding, and all three playwrights have experienced both. But the format is at least identifiable and does provide opportunity for exposure of these writers' views as a result, and with that comes the hope for greater understanding, acceptance, and assimilation.

On another level, these writers have proven that the realism of the 80s can in fact be regarded as "new" realism rather than a reworking of old realist products. Fuller has succeeded at overturning assumptions that were founded on decades of realist dependency on naturalist tenets, actively challenging those assumptions. *A Soldier's Play* is realist in form but ironically manipulates the outdated assumptions implicit in realist drama, as thrust upon realism by naturalist dogma. And where Fuller illustrates the folly of maintaining those assumptions and holding to old doctrines, Henley and Norman have succeeded in showing that new doctrines can in fact replace the old and still be supported by a realist form.

In these three playwrights the Pulitzer committee has recognized valuable qualities that are very likely necessary to cultivate if popular theatre hopes to remain a vital medium of expression, working to include more than a privileged coterie audience under its influence.

Works Cited

Adler, Thomas P. *Mirror on the Stage: The Pulitzer Plays as an Approach to American Drama*. West Lafayette: Purdue UP, 1987.

Baraka, Amiri. "The Descent of Charlie Fuller into Pulitzerland and the Need ror African-American Institutions." *Black American Literature Forum* 17 (1983): 51-54.

Esslin, Martin. *The Theatre of the Absurd*. London: Eyre and Spottiswoode, 1961.

Fuller, Charles. *A Soldier's Play*. New York: Hill and Wang, 1981.

Gill, Brendan. "Crimes of the Heart." *New Yorker* 16 Nov. 1981: 182-83.

--------. "'Night, Mother." *New Yorker* 11 Apr. 1983: 109+.

--------. "Wake of Jamie Foster." *New Yorker* 25 Oct. 1982: 161.

Gilman, Richard. "A Soldier's Play." *Nation* 23 Jan. 1982: 90-91.

Haller, Scot. "Her First Play, Her First Pulitzer Prize." *Saturday Review* Nov. 1981: 40+.

Hayman, Ronald. *British Theatre since 1955: A Reassessment*. London: Oxford UP, 1979.

Henley, Beth. *Crimes of the Heart*. New York: Viking Press, 1981.

--------. *The Miss Firecracker Contest*. Garden City, NY: Doubleday, 1985.

Kauffmann, Stanley. "More Trick than Tragedy." *Saturday Review* Sept./Oct. 1983: 47-48.

--------. "Two Cheers for Two Plays." *Saturday Review* Jan. 1982: 54-55.

Kerr, Walter. "A Fine New Work From A Forceful Playwright." *New York Times* 6 Dec. 1981, sec. 2: 3.

Kroll, Jack. "A Modern Crisis of Faith." *Newsweek* 27 Feb. 1984: 76.

Norman, Marsha. *'night, Mother.* New York: Hill and Wang, 1983.

--------. *Third and Oak: The Laundromat* and *The Pool Room.* New York: Dramatists Play Service, 1977.

Oliver, Edith. "Crimes of the Heart." *New Yorker* 12 Jan. 1981: 81-82.

--------. "The Lucky Spot." *New Yorker* 11 May 1987: 80-81.

Rich, Frank. "Beth Henley's 'Crimes of the Heart.'" *New York Times* 5 Nov. 1981, sec. 3: 21.

--------. "'Firecracker,' A Beth Henley Comedy." *New York Times* 28 May 1984: 11.

--------. "New Fuller Drama, 'Zooman and the Sign'." *New York Times* 8 Dec. 1980, sec. 3: 13.

--------. "Suicide Talk in ̄night, Mother.'" *New York Times* 1 Apr. 1983, sec. 3: 3.

Savran, David. *In Their Own Words: Contemporary American Playwrights.* New York: Theatre Communications Group, 1988.

Spencer, Jenny S. "Norman's *'night, Mother*: Psycho-drama of Female Identity." *Modern Drama* 30 (1987): 364-75.

Stone, Elizabeth. "Playwright Marsha Norman: An Optimist Writes About Suicide, Confinement and Despair." *Ms.* July 1983: 56-59.

Stout, Kate. "Marsha Norman: Writing for the 'Least of Our Brethren.'" *Saturday Review* Sept./Oct. 1983: 29-33.

Weales, Gerald. "American Theater Watch, 1981-1982." *Georgia Review* 36 (1982): 517-26.

--------. "Really 'Going On': Marsha Norman's Pulitzer Winner." *Commonweal* 17 June 1983: 370-71.

White, Frank, III. "Pushing Beyond the Pulitzer." *Ebony* Mar. 1983: 116-18.

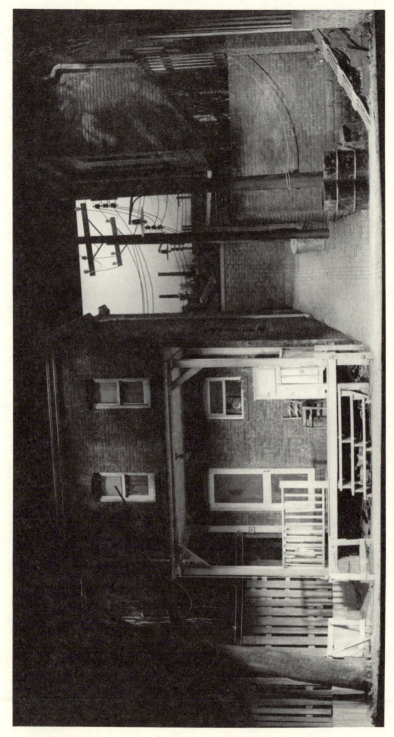

Broadway set of August Wilson's *Fences* (1987). Designed by James D. Sandefur. *Photo: Ron Scherl.*

Toward Re-establishing a Popular Theatre

With American new realism, contemporary theatre has slipped into a vital new phase in its growth. It is at times despairing, but it is based on mature experiences that in turn encourage an engaging ironic perspective. In *Hurlyburly*, Rabe has turned realism/ naturalism on itself, allowing it to consume its own presumptions, leaving the form free to start from a new beginning. Within this emptied form, Mamet has turned language itself loose so that it can reveal its own presumptive stance. And Shepard has moved to reveal postures and assumptions that, when allowed to develop, likewise reveal their cracks. Playwrights like Fuller, Henley, and Norman have also taken the form and argued against audience assumptions in order to reveal their own unique perspectives on current conditions. But despite the noteworthy accomplishments of these writers, one senses that the potential of this newly awakened form has yet fully to be realized. Whether that potential will be realized is left for the future to reveal.

The above studied playwrights are each crucial in re-molding realism into a viable modern form of expression, but they are by no means the only American playwrights to do so. Among minorities, August Wilson is a new black playwright (though long active in writing poetry and in theatre production) who has recently won the Pulitzer Prize for his play *Fences* (1985). And his 1987 work, *Joe Turner's Come and Gone*, deserves praise as well. Many attack his frankly naturalistic approach, using a well-made frame, but none deny his vital new strength of characterization (reminiscent of Fuller) and his experimentation with jazz rhythms within that structure. Documenting these rhythms is what ultimately qualifies Wilson as a new realist. And his ambitions assure Wilson of a place in American theatre for some time to come. Richard Bernstein observes of Wilson:

> His ambition is to write a play for every decade since the Civil War,
> depicting an aspect of the black experience. With four in the series
> already complete . . . it is not too much to say that Mr. Wilson's oeuvre
> is turning into something more significant than mere personal success.
> The plays mark a new stage in American theater--the flourishing of drama
> about the black identity, a transformation onto the stage of what, Mr.
> Wilson says, has for decades been preserved largely in oral tradition and
> blues music. (34)

One playwright on the scene since the 60s, Lanford Wilson, has also
moved into the realm of new realism, adapting his style to fit the new
mode. Though Wilson has utilized realism throughout his career,
most of his products have been more reminiscent of William Inge of
the old school than of Rabe, Mamet, or Shepard. Julius Novick, for
example, observes:

> There is something cozy about most of Lanford Wilson's plays. Unlike
> so much of modern drama, they are not nightmares: they are not
> frightening, and they are not bewildering. They raise the possibility that
> the world is both benign and comprehensible, two notions without much
> currency in the serious theater nowadays. (87)

But first came a 1986 revival of *The Mound Builders* (1975) that
revealed a subtle shift in Wilson's perspective. Novick reports: "The
mode is still psychological realism. But problems are not solved,
wounds are not healed, victories are not won" (88). And in 1987,
with *Burn This*, Wilson seems fully to have shifted away from
comforting old frames of thought and moved toward a vision of
contemporary realities as revealed beneath various facades. Mel
Gussow observes of the play:

> In the sense that it deals with lonely and displaced characters, "Burn This"
> is in the Wilson tradition. Where it breaks dramatic ground for the author
> is in its passion. The playwright has specialized in characters with a
> certain reserve and in situations not generally marked by their
> explosiveness . . . . In "Burn This," however, Mr. Wilson exposes deep,
> uncauterized emotional wounds--and offers no salves. (5)

And 1988 saw the production of David Hwang's *M. Butterfly*, a
play that David Savran reports "focuses on the interrelationship
between sexist, racist and imperialist adventure . . . expressing it in a
fluid passage between the styles of Western realism and of opera, both
Chinese and Italian" (118). It isn't purely realist in form, but it uses
realism in a manner similar to the more pure realists. Frank Rich
reports that "[t]he play's form . . . is wedded to its content" in that
such "cultural icons" as opera and realism "bequeath the sexist and
racist roles that burden Western men" ("M. Butterfly" 13).
   In general, as Rich notes in a 1988 article, "there has been a recent
resurgence of playwriting, most of it American, on and off Broadway"

("A Season" 1), and most of it has directed itself towards this new realist mode. Such revitalized interest in realism among playwrights suggests two important points. The break and/or deviation from naturalism has uncovered the flexibility of realism and has proven to each of these writers that "new realism" is a form that can be used efficiently in presenting any number of new perspectives and that can effectively handle a variety of contemporary concerns on a variety of intellectual levels. And the relative success of these creators of realist drama indicates that there is a substantial (and perhaps growing) audience interested in having its own skills of understanding realistic material utilized by these writers in their efforts to communicate to the public. Realism can indeed be the form that can both introduce modern concerns and perspectives while at the same time hold the interests of something more than an elitist, coterie audience.

Carol Gelderman, in an article entitled "Hyperrealism in Contemporary Drama: Retrogressive or Avant-Garde" (1983), addresses many of the issues raised in this study concerning the perception of the realist movement in drama, concentrating, however, on British and Continental drama in her essay. She notes that the term she uses, hyperrealism, has several synonyms, terms the art world coined to identify a new brand of realism in that field--"New Realism, Realism Now, Sharp-Focus Realism, Photographic Realism, Hyperrealism, the Realist Revival, Radical Realism" (357). Her essay notes that the interest in realism in the theatre world is similar to that which has evolved in the more avant-garde circles of painting and sculpture. In answering the question in her essay's title--concluding that "new realism" (or whatever term is preferred) in the theatre is avant-garde--she fails to include any of the American playwrights included in this study.

In fact, oftentimes these writers are completely excluded from such discussion, with the occasional exception of Sam Shepard (see Zinman's "Sam Shepard and Super-Realism"). Such exclusion is very likely a result of the fact that these American playwrights have yet fully to establish themselves beyond American borders. And a possible reason for this failed recognition may be that critics have yet to fully recognize American new realism's break from its dated ancesters and movement toward more updated perceptions of existence. In essence, the overall effect of new realism in America and the resulting conclusions of that effect have been overlooked. The consequences of such an oversight is actually implied in the title of Gelderman's article. Without the benefit of these writers' examples, it is understandable that one could assume that "retrogressive drama" and "avant-garde drama" are perhaps comprehensive and inclusive categories. Playwrights like Shepard and those Gelderman discusses--Edward Bond and Franz Xaver Kroetz, among others--could easily be categorized avant-garde writers, and so new realism could be considered an avant-garde form if they alone were discussed. But if we include Fuller, Henley, Norman, Rabe, Mamet, Shepard (as realist), and the others, then it becomes less clear that Gelderman's categories are in fact sufficiently inclusive. Using only her categories, these writers would have to be labelled "avant-garde" in that they are confronting modern issues using modern points of view, points that disqualify them from being categorized "retrogressive." But if they're using a form that is accessible to mainstream theatre, can they really be "avant-garde" in the pure sense of the phrase? After all, can mainstream drama be labelled "avant-garde"?

It seems more appropriate to look at these playwrights as writers who have absorbed and utilized avant-garde concepts, approaches, or ideologies, but who are by no means "avant-garde" playwrights. This, to me, is an important distinction because it makes their accomplishments that much more pronounced. They have managed to break a barrier that has been assumed to exist between a select audience capable of absorbing elitist art and a larger, unprivileged audience generally excluded from such enterprises. With America's "new realism," this larger audience is no longer excluded.

That these playwrights are, perhaps unwittingly, part of the movement Gelderman identifies is undeniable. They present surfaces, as Gelderman argues of her own paradigms, only to reveal that beneath them lies nothing of value. The practical wisdom that the protagonists of each play may spout is eventually revealed to be hollow, empty. And while each writer may present variations on the theme, some adhering more closely to Gelderman's classifications than others, the fact remains that they utilize realism to overturn the assumptions that realism was formerly recruited to uphold. Language is used to reveal the barriers it creates rather than breaks down; reason uncovers irrationality. And surfaces are presented to reveal their essential unreality.

Gelderman's main thesis is certainly accurate: this new form of realism has succeeded in expressing the modern condition of despairing over lost securities and in making that expression "concrete in an aggressive and provocative manner" (366). She adds, though, that "because hyperrealistic plays achieve both of these ends, they merit the name avant-garde" (366). If she is merely arguing that such realism is doing what the avant-garde formerly did, then her claim is acceptable. But she could surely go much further with the point, namely to argue that this new realism has brought avant-garde thought to popular theatre, an accomplishment indeed.

If America's new realist dramatists are allowed to take their rightful positions with the realists of other nations, then perhaps the mainstream potential of new realism as well as America's general contribution to this developing form will be fully appreciated.

Works Cited

Bernstein, Richard. "August Wilson's Voices From the Past." *New York Times* 27 Mar. 1988, sec. 2: 1+.

Gelderman, Carol. "Hyperrealism in Contemporary Drama: Retrogressive or Avant-Garde?" *Modern Drama* 26 (1983): 357-67.

Gussow, Mel. "Lanford Wilson's Lonely World of Displaced Persons." *New York Times* 25 Oct. 1987, sec. 2: 5.

Novick, Julius. "Digging for Meaning." *Village Voice* 11 Feb. 1986: 87-88.

Rich, Frank. "'M. Butterfly,' a Story Of a Strange Love, Conflict and Betrayal." *New York Times* 21 Mar. 1988, sec. 3: 13.

--------. "A Season for Eastern Sissy Playwrights." *New York Times* 5 June 1988, sec. 2: 1+.

Savran, David. *In Their Own Words: Contemporary American Playwrights.* New York: Theatre Communications Group, 1988.

Zinman, Toby Silverman. "Sam Shepard and Super-Realism." *Modern Drama* 29 (1986): 423-30.

Bibliography

Adler, Thomas P. *Mirror on the Stage: The Pulitzer Plays as an Approach to American Drama.* West Lafayette: Purdue UP, 1987.

Baraka, Amiri. "The Descent of Charlie Fuller into Pulitzerland and the Need for African-American Institutions." *Black American Literature Forum* 17 (1983): 51-54.

Barnes, Clive. "'Boom Boom Room' by Rabe at Lincoln Center." *New York Times* 9 Nov. 1973: 31.

--------. "David Rabe's 'Streamers' in New Haven." *New York Times* 8 Feb. 1976, sec. 2: 45.

--------. "Skilled 'American Buffalo.'" *New York Times* 17 Feb. 1977: 50.

--------. "Streamers." *New York Times* 22 April 1976: 38.

Bede, Jean-Albert. *Emile Zola.* New York: Columbia UP, 1974.

Bennetts, Leslie. "Rabe's New Play Due Next Month on Upper West Side." *New York Times* 11 May 1984, sec. 2: 2.

Bentley, Eric. *The Playwright as Thinker.* 1946. New York: Harcourt, Brace, and World, 1967.

Berkvist, Robert. "If You Kill Somebody. . ." *New York Times* 12 Dec. 1971, sec. 2: 3+.

Bernstein, Richard. "August Wilson's Voices From the Past." *New York Times* 27 Mar. 1988, sec 2: 1+.

Bernstein, Samuel J. *The Strands Entwined.* Boston: Northeastern UP, 1980.

Bigsby, C.W.E. *A Critical Introduction to Twentieth-Century American Drama,* Vol. 3: *Beyond Broadway.* London: Cambridge UP, 1985.

--------. *David Mamet.* London: Methuen, 1985.

Bogard, Travis. *Contour in Time: The Plays of Eugene O'Neill.* New York: Oxford UP, 1972.

Brustein, Robert. "The Crack in the Chimney: Reflections on Contemporary American Playwriting." *Images and Ideas in American Culture*. Ed. Arthur Edelstein. Hanover, NH: Brandeis UP, 1979. 141-57.

--------. "Crossed Purposes." *New Republic* 31 Jan. 1981: 21-23.

--------. "Love from Two Sides of the Ocean." *New Republic* 27 June 1983: 24-25.

--------. "Painless Dentistry." *New Republic* 6 Aug. 1984: 27-29.

--------. *The Theatre of Revolt*. Boston: Little, Brown, 1964.

Carlson, Marvin. *Theories of the Theatre: A Historical and Critical Survey, from the Greeks to the Present*. Ithaca, N.Y.: Cornell UP, 1984.

Carroll, Dennis. *David Mamet*. London: Macmillan, 1987.

Chubb, Kenneth. "Metaphors, Mad Dogs and Old Time Cowboys: Interview with Sam Shepard." *Theatre Quarterly* 4 (Aug./Oct. 1974): 3-16.

Clurman, Harold. "American Buffalo." *Nation* 12 Mar. 1977: 313.

--------. "The Basic Training of Pavlo Hummel." *Nation* 7 June 1971: 733.

--------. "Boom Boom Room." *Nation* 28 Dec. 1974: 701.

--------. "Buried Child." *Nation* 2 Dec. 1978: 621-22.

--------. Introduction. *Six Plays of Clifford Odets*. New York: Grove Press, 1979. ix-xiv.

--------. "A Life in the Theatre." *Nation* 12 Nov. 1977: 504-505.

--------. "The Tooth of Crime." *Nation* 26 Mar. 1973: 410-12.

--------. "The Water Engine." *Nation* 28 Jan. 1978: 92.

Coe, Robert. "Interview with Robert Woodruff." *American Dreams: The Imagination of Sam Shepard*. Ed. Bonnie Marranca. New York: Performing Arts Journal Publications, 1981. 151-58.

--------. "Saga of Sam Shepard." *New York Times Magazine* 23 Nov. 1980: 56+.

Cohn, Ruby. *New American Dramatist: 1960-1980*. New York: Grove Press, 1982.

Corrigan, Robert W. "The Search for New Endings: The Theatre in Search of a Fix, Part III." *Theatre Journal* 36 (1984): 153-63.

Denby, David. "Stranger in a Strange Land: A Moviegoer at the Theater." *The Atlantic* Jan. 1985: 37-50.

Donohue, Joseph, Jr. *Dramatic Character in the English Romantic Age*. Princeton: Princeton UP, 1970.

Dukes, Ashley. *Modern Dramatists*. London: Frank Palmer, 1911.

Dukore, Bernard. "Off-Broadway and the New Realism." *Modern American Drama*. Ed. William E. Taylor. DeLand, FL: Everett/Edwards, 1968. 163-74.

Eder, Richard. "David Mamet's New Realism." *New York Times Magazine* 12 Mar. 1978: 40 +.

--------. "Mamet's 'Perversity,' Mosaic on Modern Mores, Moves." *New York Times* 17 June 1976: 29.

--------. "Mamet's 'The Woods' Redone at Public." *New York Times* 26 Apr. 1979, sec. 3: 15.

--------. "The Starving Class." *New York Times* 3 Mar. 1978, sec. 3: 3.

Esslin, Martin. "Naturalism in Context." *The Drama Review* 13, ii (Winter 1968): 67-76.

--------. "The Stage: Reality, Symbol, Metaphor." *Themes in Drama,* Vol. IV. Ed. James Redmond. London: Cambridge UP, 1982. 1-12.

--------. *The Theatre of the Absurd.* London: Eyre and Spottiswoode, 1961.

Feingold, Michael. "Moving Experiences." *Village Voice* 9 Oct. 1984: 96.

Frank, Leah D. "Shepard's 'West': A Tale Well Told." *New York Times* 28 Apr. 1985, sec 21: 14.

Freedman, Samuel G. "Rabe and the War at Home." New York Times 28 June 1984, sec. 3: 13.

Freedman, Samuel G., and Michaela Williams. "The Craft of the Playwright: A Conversation Between Neil Simon and David Rabe." *New York Times Magazine* 26 May 1985: 37+.

Fuller, Charles. *A Soldier's Play.* New York: Hill and Wang, 1981.

Gale, Steven H. "David Mamet: The Plays, 1972-1980." *Essays on Contemporary Drama.* Eds. Hedvig Bock and Albert Wertheim. Munich: Max Hueber Verlag, 1981. 207-24.

Gassner, John. *Form and Idea in Modern Theatre.* New York: Dryden Press, 1956.

Gelderman, Carol. "Hyperrealism in Contemporary Drama: Retrogressive or Avant-Garde?" *Modern Drama* 26 (1983): 357-67.

Gill, Brendan. "Crimes of the Heart." *New Yorker* 16 Nov. 1981: 182-83.

--------. "The Lower Depths, Glengarry Glen Ross." *New Yorker* 2 Apr. 1984: 114.

--------. "'Night, Mother." *New Yorker* 11 Apr. 1983: 109+.

--------. "Trilogy's End." *New Yorker* 3 May 1976: 76-77.

--------. "Wake of Jamie Foster." *New Yorker* 25 Oct. 1982: 161.

Gilman, Richard. "A Soldier's Play." *Nation* 23 Jan. 1982: 90-91.

Gosse, Edmund. "Introduction to *Lovell's Series of Foreign Literature: The Prose Drama of Henrik Ibsen.*" 1890. *Ibsen: The Critical Heritage.* Ed. Michael Egan. Boston: Routledge and Kegan Paul, 1972. 94.

Gottlieb, Richard. "The 'Engine' That Drives Playwright David Mamet." *New York Times* 15 Jan. 1978, sec. 2: 1+.

Gussow, Mel. "The Daring Visions of Four New Young Playwrights." *New York Times* 13 Feb. 1977, sec. 2: 1+.

--------. "'Goose and Tomtom' Opens." *New York Times* 8 May 1982: 17.

--------. "Illusion Within an Illusion." *New York Times* 21 Oct. 1977, sec. 3: 3.

--------. "Lanford Wilson's Lonely World of Displaced Persons." *New York Times* 25 Oct. 1987, sec. 2: 5.

--------. "Mamet's 'American Buffalo.'" *New York Times* 28 Jan. 1976: 30.

--------. "Real Estate World a Model for Mamet: His New Play Draws on Life." *New York Times* 28 Mar. 1984, sec. 3: 19.

--------. "'Reunion,' 3 Mamet Plays." *New York Times* 19 Oct. 1979, sec. 3: 3.

--------. "Sam Shepard Revisits the American Heartland." *New York Times* 15 Dec. 1985, sec. 2: 3+.

--------. "'Starving Class' By Shepard Is Back." *New York Times* 24 May 1985, sec. 3: 3.

--------. "Two Pungent Comedies by New Playwright." *New York Times* 1 Nov. 1975: 15.

Haller, Scot. "Her First Play, Her First Pulitzer Prize." *Saturday Review* Nov. 1981: 40+.

Hart, Lynda. *Sam Shepard's Metaphorical Stages*. Westport, CT.: Greenwood Press, 1987.

Harvey, Stephen. "True West." *Nation* 31 Jan. 1981: 123-24.

Hayman, Ronald. *British Theatre since 1955: A Reassessment*. London: Oxford UP, 1979.

Henley, Beth. *Crimes of the Heart*. New York: Viking Press, 1981.

--------. *The Miss Firecracker Contest*. Garden City, NY: Doubleday, 1985.

Herman, William. *Understanding Contemporary American Drama*. Columbia: U of South Carolina Press, 1987.

Hertzbach, Janet S. "The Plays of David Rabe: A World of Streamers." *Essays on Contemporary American Drama*. Eds. Hedwig Bock and Albert Wertheim. Munich: Max Hueber Verlag, 1981. 173-85.

Hunt, Leigh. "The Jew of Malta." *Dramatic Criticism, 1808-1831*. Eds. L.H. Houtchens and Carolyn Washburn. New York: Columbia UP, 1949. 195-98.

Innes, C.D. *Modern German Drama*. London: Cambridge UP, 1979.

James, Henry. "Letter: 29 Jan., 1889." *Ibsen: The Critical Heritage*. Ed. Michael Egan. Boston: Routledge and Kegan Paul, 1972. 94.

Kauffmann, Stanley. "More Trick than Tragedy." *Saturday Review* Sept./Oct. 1983: 47-48.

--------. "Two Cheers for Two Plays." *Saturday Review* Jan. 1982: 54-55.

--------. "What Price Freedom?" *New Republic* 8 Apr. 1978: 24-25.

Kernodle, George and Portia. *Invitation to the Theatre*. New York: Harcourt, Brace, Jovanovich, 1971.

Kerr, Walter. "David Has Never Been Alive." *New York Times* 12 Mar. 1972, sec. 2: 3.

--------. "David Rabe's 'House is Not a Home.'" *New York Times* 2 May 1976, sec. 2: 5.

--------. "Easy Does It Playwrighting Comes of Age." *New York Times* 15 Aug. 1976, sec. 2: 5+.

--------. "A Fine New Work from A Forceful Playwright." *New York Times* 6 Dec. 1981, sec. 2: 3.

--------. "He Wonders Who He Is--So Do We." *New York Times* 30 May 1971, sec. 2: 3.

--------. "Language Alone Isn't Drama." *New York Times* 6 Mar. 1977, sec. 2: 3+.

--------. "Sam Shepard--What's the Message?" *New York Times* 10 Dec. 1978, sec. 2: 1.

--------. "Unmistakably a Writer--Why, Then, Does His Play Stand Still?" *New York Times* 14 Nov. 1971, sec. 2: 1+.

--------. "We Leave the Girl Where We Found Her." *New York Times* 18 Nov. 1973, sec. 2: 3.

--------. "When Does Gore Get Gratuitous?" *New York Times* 22 Feb. 1976, sec. 2: 1+.

--------. "Where Has Sam Shepard Led His Audience?" *New York Times* 5 June 1983, sec. 2: 3+.

Kirby, Michael. "On Literary Theatre." *The Drama Review* 18, ii (June 1974): 103-13.

Kolin, Philip C. "Staging *Hurlyburly*: David Rabe's Parable for the 1980s." *Theatre Annual* 1987: 63-78.

Kroll, Jack. "A Modern Crisis of Faith." *Newsweek* 27 Feb. 1984: 76.

Lamb, Charles. "On the Artificial Comedy of the Last Century." *Elia*. 1823. Menston, Eng.: Scolar Press, 1969. 323-37.

Lawson, John Howard. Preface. *Processional*. New York: T. Seltzer, 1925. i-xii.

Lewes, George Henry. *On Actors and the Art of Acting*. 1875. New York: Grove Press, 1957.

--------. "The Old and Modern Dramatists." *Dramatic Essays*. London: Walter Scott, 1896. 101-104.

--------. "Recent Novels: French and English." *Fraser's Magazine* 36 (Dec. 1847): 686-95.

Londré, Felicia. "Sam Shepard Works Out: The Masculinization of America." *Studies in American Drama, 1945-Present* 2 (1987): 19-27.

Mamet, David. *American Buffalo*. New York: Grove Press, 1976.

--------. *Edmond*. New York: Grove Press, 1983.

--------. *Glengarry Glen Ross*. New York: Grove Press, 1984.

--------. *A Life in the Theatre*. New York: Grove Press, 1977.

--------. *Sexual Perversity in Chicago* and *The Duck Variations*. New York: Grove Press, 1978.

--------. *Writing in Restaurants*. New York: Viking Penguin, 1986.

Marranca, Bonnie, ed. *Theatre of Images*. New York: Drama Book Specialists, 1977.

McCarthy, Mary. "The American Realist Playwrights." *Discussions of Modern American Drama*. Ed. Walter Meserve. Boston: D.C. Heath, 1965. 114-27.

Moore, Sonia. *The Stanislawski System*. Harmonsworth, Eng.: Penguin, 1965.

Moses, Montrose J. *The American Dramatist*. 1925. New York: Benjamin Blom, 1964.

Mottram, Ron. *Inner Landscapes: The Theater of Sam Shepard*. Columbia: U of Missouri Press, 1984.

Murphy, Brenda. *American Realism and American Drama, 1880-1940*. London: Cambridge UP, 1987.

Nash, Thomas. "Sam Shepard's *Buried Child*: The Ironic Use of Folklore." *Modern Drama* 26 (1983): 486-91.

Nathan, George Jean. "Our Premiere Dramatist." *O'Neill and His Plays*. Eds. Oscar Cargill, N. Bryllion Fagin, and William J. Fisher. New York: New York UP, 1961. 283-91.

Nightingale, Benedict. "David Rabe Explores a Different Kind of Jungle." *New York Times* 1 July 1984, sec. 2: 3+.

--------. "Is Mamet the Bard of Modern Immorality?" *New York Times* 1 Apr. 1984, sec. 2: 5+.

Norman, Marsha. *'night, Mother*. New York: Hill and Wang, 1983.

--------. *Third and Oak: The Laundromat* and *The Pool Room* . New York: Dramatists Play Service, 1977.

Novick, Julius. "Digging for Meaning." *Village Voice* 11 Feb. 1986: 87-88.

Nuwer, Hank. "Two Gentlemen of Chicago: David Mamet and Stuart Gordon." *South Carolina Review* 17 (Spring 1985): 9-20.

Oliver, Edith. "Crimes of the Heart." *New Yorker* 12 Jan. 1981: 81-82.

--------. "David Mamet of Illinois." *New Yorker* 10 Nov. 1975: 135-36.

--------. "The Lucky Spot." *New Yorker* 11 May 1987: 80-81.

--------. "Twice Hail." *New Yorker* 20 Nov. 1971: 114+.

Orbison, Tucker. "Mythic Levels in Shepard's *True West*." *Modern Drama* 27 (1984): 505-19.

Putzel, Steven. "Expectation, Confutation, Revelation: Audience Complicity in the Plays of Sam Shepard." *Modern Drama* 30 (1987): 147-60.

Rabillard, Sheila. "Sam Shepard: Theatrical Power and American Dreams." *Modern Drama* 30 (1987): 58-71.

Rabe, David. "Each Night You Spit in My Face." *New York Times* 18 Mar. 1973, sec. 2: 3+.

--------. *Goose and Tomtom*. New York: Grove Press, 1986.

--------. *Hurlyburly*. New York: Grove Press, 1985.

Rich, Alan. "Streamers." *New York* 10 May 1976: 78.

Rich, Frank. "Al Pacino in 'American Buffalo.'" *New York Times* 5 June, 1981, sec. 3: 3.

--------. "Beth Henley's 'Crimes of the Heart.'" *New York Times* 5 Nov. 1981, sec. 3: 21.

--------. "'Firecracker,' A Beth Henley Comedy." *New York Times* 28 May 1984: 11.

--------. "'Fool for Love,' Sam Shepard Western." *New York Times* 27 May 1983, sec. 3: 3.

--------. "'Hurlyburly.'" *New York Times* 22 June 1984, sec. 3: 3.

--------. "'A Lie of the Mind,' by Sam Shepard." *New York Times* 6 Dec. 1985, sec, 3: 3.

--------. "'M. Butterfly,' a Story Of a Strange Love, Conflict and Betrayal." *New York Times* 21 Mar. 1988, sec. 3: 13.

--------. "A Mamet Play, 'Glengarry Glen Ross.'" *New York Times* 26 Mar. 1984, sec. 3: 17.

--------. "Mamet's Dark View of Hollywood As a Heaven for the Virtueless." *New York Times* 4 May 1988, sec. 3: 17.

--------. "New Fuller Drama, 'Zooman and the Sign.'" *New York Times* 8 Dec. 1980, sec. 3: 13.

--------. "A Season for Eastern Sissy Playwrights." *New York Times* 5 June 1988, sec. 2: 1+.

--------. "Suicide Talk in 'night, Mother.'" *New York Times* 1 Apr. 1983, sec. 3: 3.

Roudane, Matthew C. "An Interview with David Mamet." *Studies in American Drama, 1945-Present* 1 (1986): 73-82.

Sauvage, Leo. "Acts of Insanity." *New Leader* 10 Mar. 1986: 21-22.

Savran, David. *In Their Own Words: Contemporary American Playwrights*. New York: Theatre Communications Group, 1988.

Schjeldahl, Peter. "Pursuing a Bogus 'Manhood.'" *New York Times* 11 July 1971, sec. 3: 1+.

Schlueter, June, and Elizabeth Forsyth. "America as Junkshop: The Business Ethic in David Mamet's *American Buffalo.*" *Modern Drama* 26 (1983): 492-500.

Scott, Clement. "A Doll's House." *Ibsen: The Critical Heritage.* Ed. Michael Egan. Boston: Routledge and Kegan Paul, 1972. 114.

Shepard, Sam. "American Experimental Theatre: Then and Now." *American Dreams: The Imagination of Sam Shepard.* Ed. Bonnie Marranca. New York: Performing Arts Journal Publications, 1981. 212-13.

--------. *Fool for Love.* San Francisco: City Lights, 1983.

--------. *True West.* In *Seven Plays.* New York: Bantam, 1981. 1-59.

--------. "Visualization, Language and the Inner Library." *The Drama Review* 21, iv (Dec. 1977): 49-58.

Shewey, Don. *Sam Shepard: The Life, The Loves, Behind The Legend Of A True American Original.* New York: Dell, 1985.

--------. "The True Story of 'True West.'" *Village Voice* 30 Nov. 1982: 115.

Simard, Rodney. *Postmodern Drama: Contemporary Playwrights in America and Britain.* Lanham, MD: UP of America, 1984.

Simon, John. "Three Fizzles, A Sparkler, and a Slow Burn." *New York* 23 Dec. 1974: 62.

Smith, Michael. "Theatre: *Cowboys* and *The Rock Garden.*" *Village Voice* 22 Oct. 1964: 13.

--------. "Theatre Journal." *Village Voice* 27 Jan. 1966: 19-20.

Spencer, Jenny S. "Norman's `night, Mother*: Psycho-drama of Female Identity." *Modern Drama* 30 (1987): 364-75.

Stanislavski, Constantin. *An Actor Prepares.* 1936. Trans. Elizabeth R. Hapgood. New York: Theatre Arts Books, 1984.

Stone, Elizabeth. "Playwright Marsha Norman: An Optimist Writes About Suicide, Confinement and Despair." *Ms.* July 1983: 56-59.

Stout, Kate. "Marsha Norman: Writing for the 'Least of Our Brethren.'" *Saturday Review* Sept./Oct. 1983: 29-33.

Styan, J.L. *Modern Drama in Theory and Practice,* Vol. 1: *Realism and Naturalism.* London: Cambridge UP, 1981.

Weales, Gerald. "American Theater Watch, 1981-1982." *Georgia Review* 36 (1982): 517-26.

--------. "Clifford's Children: or, It's a Wise Playwright Who Knows His Own Father." *Studies in American Drama, 1945-Present* 2 (1987): 3-18.

--------. "Pleasant Dreams: Diagnostic, Not Curative." *Commonweal* 19 Oct. 1985: 558-60.

--------. "Streamers." *Commonweal* 21 May 1976: 334-35.

--------. "Really 'Going On': Marsha Norman's Pulitzer Winner." *Commonweal* 17 June 1983: 370-71.

--------. "Rewarding Salesmen: New from Mamet, Old from Miller." *Commonweal* 4 May 1984: 278-79.

--------. "Shepard Rides Again: The Device is a Simple One." *Commonweal* 28 Jan. 1983: 49-50.

--------. "Stronger Than Water." *Commonweal* 14 Apr. 1978: 244+.

Wetzsteon, Ross. "David Mamet: Remember that Name." *Village Voice* 5 July 1976: 101+.

--------. "Looking a Gift Horse Dreamer in the Mouth." *American Dreams: The Imagination of Sam Shepard.* Ed. Bonnie Marranca. New York: Performing Arts Journal Publications, 1981. 133-35.

White, Frank, III. "Pushing Beyond the Pulitzer." *Ebony* Mar. 1983: 116-18.

Wilson, Ann. "Fool of Desire: The Spectator to the Plays of Sam Shepard." *Modern Drama* 30 (1987): 46-57.

Zinman, Toby Silverman. "Sam Shepard and Super-Realism." *Modern Drama* 29 (1986): 423-30.

Zola, Emile. "The Critical Formula Applied to the Novel." 1893. Trans. Belle M. Sherman. *The Naturalist Novel.* Ed. Maxwell Geismar. Montreal: Harvest House, 1964. 81-84.

--------. "The Experimental Novel." 1893. Trans. Belle M. Sherman. *The Naturalist Novel.* Ed. Maxwell Geismar. Montreal: Harvest House, 1964. 1-32.

Index

About the Author

WILLIAM W. DEMASTES teaches American literature and drama at the University of Tennessee-Knoxville. He has published articles on modern American playwrights in such journals as *Comparative Drama* and *Studies in American Drama, 1945-Present,* and is a contributor to *American Playwrights Since 1945* (Greenwood Press, forthcoming 1989).